Son of
Guilty Pleasures of the Horror Film

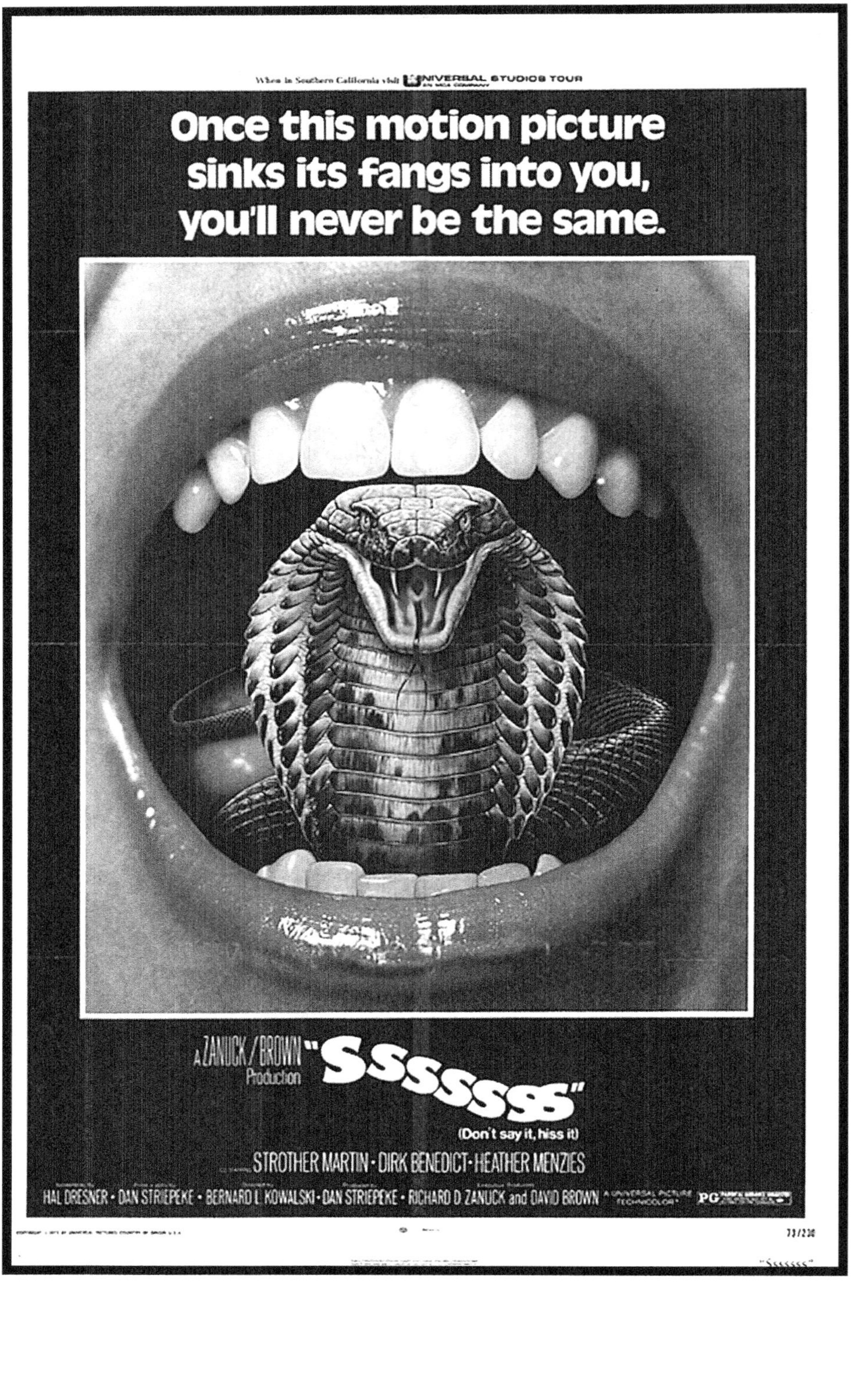

When in Southern California visit UNIVERSAL STUDIOS TOUR
Once this motion picture sinks its fangs into you, you'll never be the same.
A ZANUCK/BROWN Production
"SSSSSSS"
(Don't say it, hiss it)
STROTHER MARTIN · DIRK BENEDICT · HEATHER MENZIES
HAL DRESNER · DAN STRIEPEKE · BERNARD L. KOWALSKI · DAN STRIEPEKE · RICHARD D. ZANUCK and DAVID BROWN
A UNIVERSAL PICTURE TECHNICOLOR
PG
73/230

Son of Guilty Pleasures of the Horror Film

Edited by Gary J. and Susan Svehla

MIDNIGHT MARQUEE PRESS, INC.
Baltimore, Maryland

Copyright © 1998 Gary J. Svehla and Susan Svehla
Cover and Layout Design by Susan Svehla

Without limiting the rights under copyright reserved above, no part of this publication may be reproduced, stored in or introduced into a retrieval system, or transmitted, in any form, or by any means (electronic, mechanical, photocopying, recording, or otherwise), without the prior written permission of the copyright owners or the publishers of the book.

ISBN 1-887664-04-1
Library of Congress Catalog Card Number 97-76034
Manufactured in the United States of America
Printed by Odyssey Press, Inc., Gonic, New Hampshire
First Printing by Midnight Marquee Press, Inc., February 1998
Second Printing by Luminary Press, September 2005

Acknowledgments: John E. Parnun, Photofest, Larry Springer, Linda J. Walter

To Diann Smith—
my friend, cousin and partner in youthful adventures
that changed both our lives for the better
—Susan Svehla

Table of Contents

9	Introduction: What's There to Feel Guilt About? by Gary J. Svehla
11	The Brain That Wouldn't Die by Bryan Senn
28	Creature with the Atom Brain by David J. Hogan
41	Frankenstein Conquers the World by David H. Smith
57	Frankenstein's Daughter by Steve Kronenberg
65	The Giant Gila Monster by Jim Doherty
77	Horror Island by John "J.J." Johnson
91	The Hunchback of Notre Dame by Don G. Smith
101	Invasion U.S.A. by Bruce Dettman
111	Juggernaut by Nathalie Yafet

125	The Omega Man by Jeff Hillegass
137	Private Parts by Gary J. Svehla
147	Robot Monster by Dennis Fischer
160	Sssssss by John E. Parnum
173	The She-Creature by Randy Palmer
189	The Strange Door by Nathalie Yafet
199	The Two Faces of Dr. Jekyll by Tom Johnson
213	The Unholy Night by John Soister
227	The Vampire's Ghost by John Soister
240	Credits
247	Index
251	Authors

SHOCK-FULL OF THRILLS!
Terror true to science, based on laboratory experiments described in national magazines!
A dead man stalks his prey! Here is horror that can happen NOW... TO YOU!
CREATURE WITH THE ATOM BRAIN
YOU WON'T BELIEVE YOUR EYES!
Starring
RICHARD DENNING
with ANGELA STEVENS
Story and Screen Play by CURT SIODMAK
Directed by EDWARD L. CAHN
A CLOVER PRODUCTION
A COLUMBIA PICTURE

INTRODUCTION

In this second volume of cinematic guilty pleasures, our writers again eloquently explain why movies which the majority of viewers consider subpar are so very special as movie experiences to them personally. These movies are not extraordinary in any way, and most of them contain fundamental flaws in craft, yet as filtered through the psyches of the writers involved, these guilty pleasures ultimately become something very special. And thus the reason why this book exists... to demonstrate the fact that the pleasures movies give far outweigh any guilt factor involved.
—Gary J. Svehla

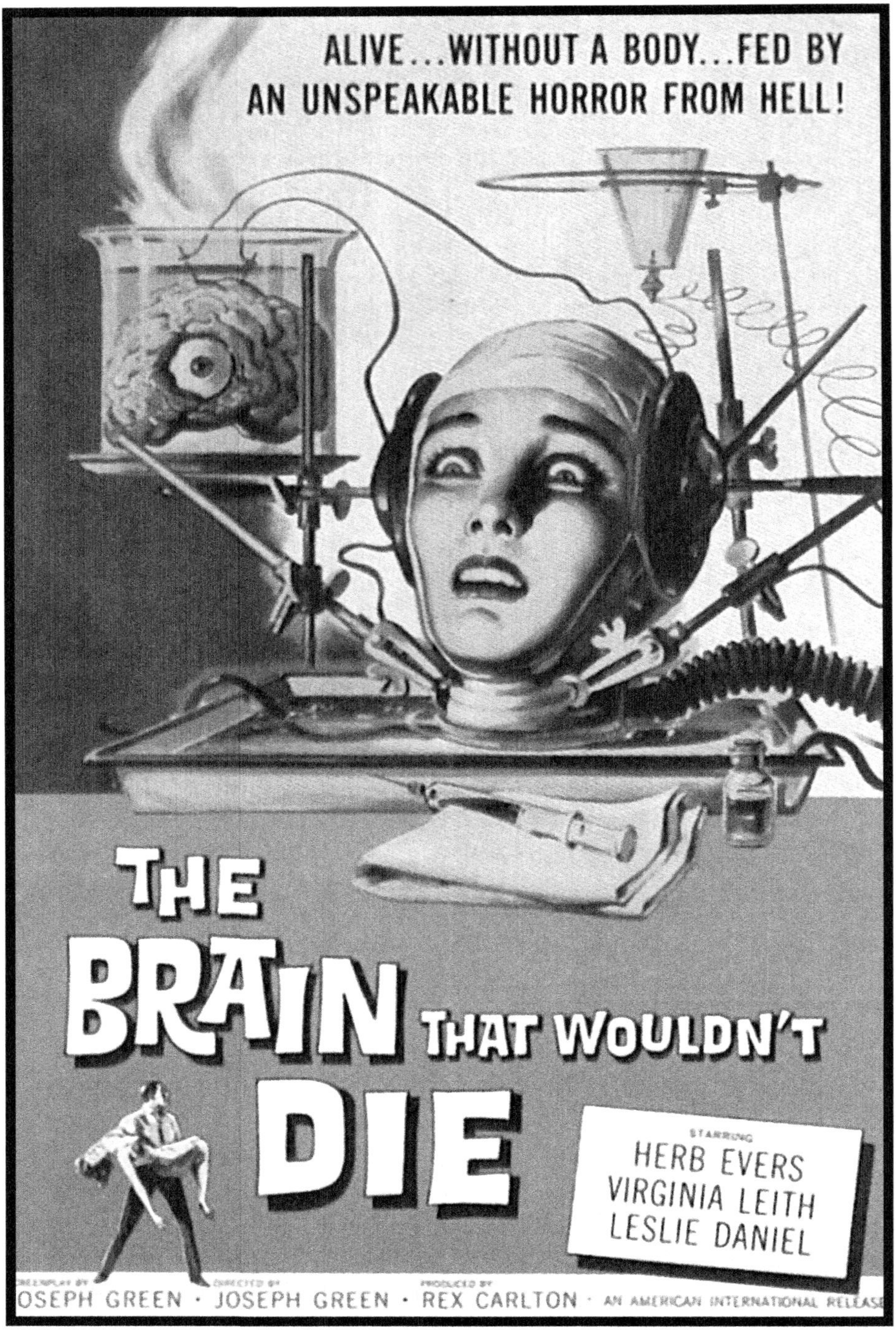
ALIVE...WITHOUT A BODY...FED BY
AN UNSPEAKABLE HORROR FROM HELL!
THE
BRAIN THAT WOULDN'T
DIE
HERB EVERS
VIRGINIA LEITH
LESLIE DANIEL
OSEPH GREEN · JOSEPH GREEN · REX CARLTON · AN AMERICAN INTERNATIONAL RELEASE

THE BRAIN THAT WOULDN'T DIE
by Bryan Senn

While not the first Disembodied Head movie, and not the best (1985's *Re-Animator* wins that dubious distinction), *The Brain That Wouldn't Die* is undoubtedly the most offbeat and entertaining of its ilk. Filmed in thirteen days in 1959 (but not released until 1962 by American International Pictures), the New York lensed *Brain* remains a treasured guilty pleasure for many a horror/science fiction aficionado.

AIP's publicity department called the picture "an adventure into a terror-filled world of science gone mad where anything and everything can—and does—happen." For once, the PR crew was guilty of understatement. Arms ripped from sockets, flesh bitten from necks, decapitation, reanimation, mysogination... *The Brain That Wouldn't Die* is indeed a film in which anything can—and does—happen.

"I met the late Rex Carlton," recalled director Joseph Green about the film's genesis, "through a mutual friend, Broadway producer Harry Blancy. Rex had already produced about seven medium-budget films by then. So, one day he was sitting in my office and he says we ought to make a movie together. I agreed, but what kind of a movie? 'Well,' said Rex, 'let's make a picture called—' and he pauses, obviously grasping for an effective title, 'let's make a picture called *I Was a Teenage Brain Surgeon*!'... Rex and I threw a few ideas back and forth until I had a story in mind, and two or three days later I had completed the screenplay for what was initially titled *The Head That Wouldn't Die*." [All quotations are from either a late 1980s *Filmfax* interview by Rudolph Grey or from a 1995 interview conducted by the author.] Written in only three days, Green called his hurried script "sufficient for what we wanted to do, which was capitalize on a title that we thought would bring in the audience."

While chock full of all sorts of disturbing (and appealing) issues, *The Brain That Wouldn't Die* clips along at such a rapid pace and becomes so engulfed in the wave of sleaze it creates for itself that the viewer scarcely realizes the various implications riding the undercurrents of this exploitative eddy. With its unwholesome themes of guilt, loss of control, manipulation, and visceral gruesomeness, the film would be downright unsettling if it weren't so outlandish. What's more, the picture also represents the ultimate male sexual/control fantasy—to create the perfect body for the woman you love. And all this from a picture about a head on a table!

In racing up to his country house laboratory, experimental surgeon Dr. Bill Cortner (Herb Evers) runs his car off the road, resulting in the gruesome decapitation of his loving fiancée, Jan (Virginia Leith). Bill grabs up Jan's head and runs cross country to his lab where, amazingly, he tells his assistant Kurt (Leslie Daniel), "I've got to save

A gruesome car accident forces Dr. Cortner to try to save his girlfriend.

Bill (Herb Evers) grabs up Jan's head and runs cross country to his lab where, amazingly, he tells his assistant Kurt (Leslie Daniel), "I've got to save her!"

her!" Using his new experimental "adreno-serum," Bill keeps Jan's disembodied head alive in a tray. "She'll live and I'll get her another body," exclaims Bill. "I can make her *complete* again." His subject doesn't share his enthusiasm, however, and moans, "Let me die."

Undeterred, Bill begins cruising strip joints and "Body Beautiful" contests seeking the perfect physique to graft to Jan's head. Back at the lab, however, Jan has been secretly communing with the unseen thing in the closet ("a mass of transplanted tissue" brought to life by Bill's serum). "I hate him for what he's done to me," the embittered Jan tells the mute monster, "together we will wreak our revenge."

With time running out (he can only keep Jan alive without a body for about 48 hours), Bill seeks out an old school friend, Doris (Adele Lamont), who works as a photographer's model. (In one scene she poses in a bikini for a group of leering shutterbugs, one of which is played by an unbilled Sammy

Doris (Adele Lamont) is the unlucky winner of the find Jan a body contest.

Son of Guilty Pleasures

Petrillo, the Jerry Lewis impersonator of *Bela Lugosi Meets a Brooklyn Gorilla* fame). Luring Doris to his lab with the promise of a plastic surgery consultation (though her body is stunning, her face sports a terrible scar), Bill drugs her drink.

Meanwhile, Jan's exhortations have resulted in the closet creature grabbing Kurt through the door's small view panel and tearing the assistant's one good arm from its socket. Kurt staggers about, leaving bloody trails on the walls before expiring in a heap on the floor.

Bill takes the unconscious Doris to his basement lab to prep her for the operation and discovers Kurt's bloody body. Undaunted, he simply drags it out of the way and continues with his preparations. "I told you I'd bring you a body," Bill proudly proclaims to Jan, "a *beautiful* one." When Jan's protestations grow too loud, Bill tapes her mouth shut(!).

Suddenly, the closet creature begins banging on its cell door. Bill's concentration broken, he goes over to the closet and (for no other reason than it was in the script) turns his back on the door to stand there, apparently "thinking." Behind him, the small panel silently opens and a gigantic hand suddenly closes over Bill's face. As the panicked surgeon struggles to free himself from the pinioning paw, the door's hinges give way and the creature emerges. In the melee, the mutant knocks over some chemicals which promptly burst into flame. The monster then bites a chunk of flesh out of his creator's neck and tosses Bill's writhing body to the floor. As the flames rise higher, the creature scoops up Doris' unconscious body and carries her out.

Working the tape free while the flames billow up around her, Jan declares, "I told you to let me die!" As the screen goes black, her cold laughter wells up and we see it is "THE END" of "THE HEAD THAT WOULDN'T DIE."

"*The Brain That Wouldn't Die* is a bleak, black story," observed the director/screenwriter. "The characters are all down, for one reason or another, and are trying to get out of their dilemma." Indeed, you can't get much more "down" than a guilt-ridden and obsessively desperate doctor, a hideous patchwork monster, a crippled and bitter assistant, and an unhappy head that's missing its body!

The characters continually bicker and needle each other, setting up scene after scene of verbal friction which effectively distracts the viewer from the occasional spells of inactivity. Talk is cheap, and Green fills his low-budget picture with plenty of it. Fortunately, the frequently over-the-top conversations make for some fascinating moments of intense absurdity, with the disembodied head blathering away to the unseen monster in the closet ("I've *got* to see your hideousness; you've got to see *mine*... Can your horror match mine?") or the high-strung lab assistant petulantly sniping back at the insulting cranium ("Listen you, I warn you. You better stop pestering me, you hear?! I'm getting fed up with you and your *insidious talk*! He should have cut out your tongue while he was at it!").

Green makes sure he gets his money's worth out of his actors by filling their mouths with plenty of odd, unwieldy dialogue. Pretentious lines such as "there are many things left for tomorrow" and "you're nothing but a freak of life, and a freak of death" proliferate, adding a so-serious-it-becomes-funny tone to the various exchanges. For example:

> Jan: What's locked behind that door?
> Kurt: *Horror* no normal mind could imagine—something even more *terrible* than you.
> Jan: No, my deformed friend. Like all quantities, horror has its ultimate—and I am *that*.
> Kurt: No, there is a horror beyond yours, and it's in there, locked behind that door! Paths of experimentation twist and turn through mountains of miscalculation and often lose themselves in error and darkness.

Whew! Would disembodied heads and deranged, one-armed lab assistants *really* talk like that? Though far from natural, the dialogue certainly is *entertaining*. And since nothing else is "natural" in this deviate little film, why should the dialogue be any different?

First-time director Joseph Green does wonders with a tight budget and little time. (In an earlier interview Green put the cost at $62,000, though he later maintained that the final budget was "about $125,000 to $150,000" with the $62,000 figure being "for certain preliminary work." From what appears onscreen, the original lower figure seems the most likely.) Green begins dramatically enough with the camera focused on a tight shot of a contoured cloth. As an ominous string vibrato plays on the soundtrack, the camera tracks back to reveal that the material is actually a surgical sheet covering a body in an operating room. Four gowned and masked medicos surround the prostrate form. "I tried for a bleak mood right from the first scene," explained Green.

With inventive camerawork and careful shot selections, Green, along with cinematographer Stephen Hajnal, makes the hurried car ride a harrowing event. Warning road signs flash by, tires squeal on the soundtrack, and shots of Bill's foot determinedly

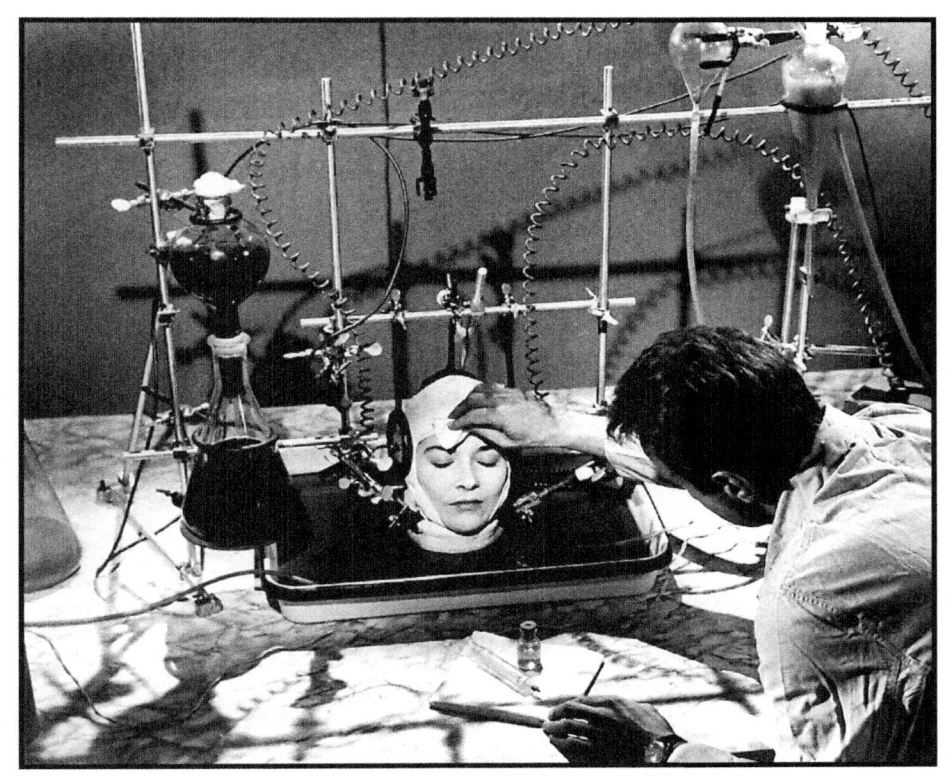

Using his new experimental "adreno-serum," Bill keeps Jan's (Virginia Leith) disembodied head alive in a tray.

pressing the accelerator all add a sense of urgency. Green places the camera on the side of the car so that we ride along with the speeding vehicle, watching the road go whizzing by and the dangerous curves accelerate toward us. (He even takes it a step further and shoots out of the back of the car as well in order to generate even more visual variety in the sequence.) Many a harried director on a shoestring production would simply shoot a few master shots and let it go at that. Green, however, takes the time and effort to really put his viewers in the driver's seat.

The crash itself shows just how inventive a low-budget filmmaker can (and must) become. The fateful moment begins with a shot of the car racing over the word STOP painted on the roadway. After a quick cut to a road sign warning CURVE, the jostling camera shows the guardrail rapidly approaching. In close-up, Bill shouts in alarm and we see his foot frantically stamp on the brake before the camera runs directly into the guardrail and seemingly flips up into the air in a sudden, violent motion. Next we see Bill rolling over and over down a hill. He sits up and a pained look of horror crosses his face while he clutches at his stomach. Struggling to his feet, he staggers forward. The camera cuts to a close-up of the car's shattered side window, viewed from inside the automobile. Flames burn in the left foreground while a hand seemingly reaches upwards for help from the right. Bill staggers forward and reaches over the jagged glass toward the hand, but it collapses and falls out of the shot. Bill

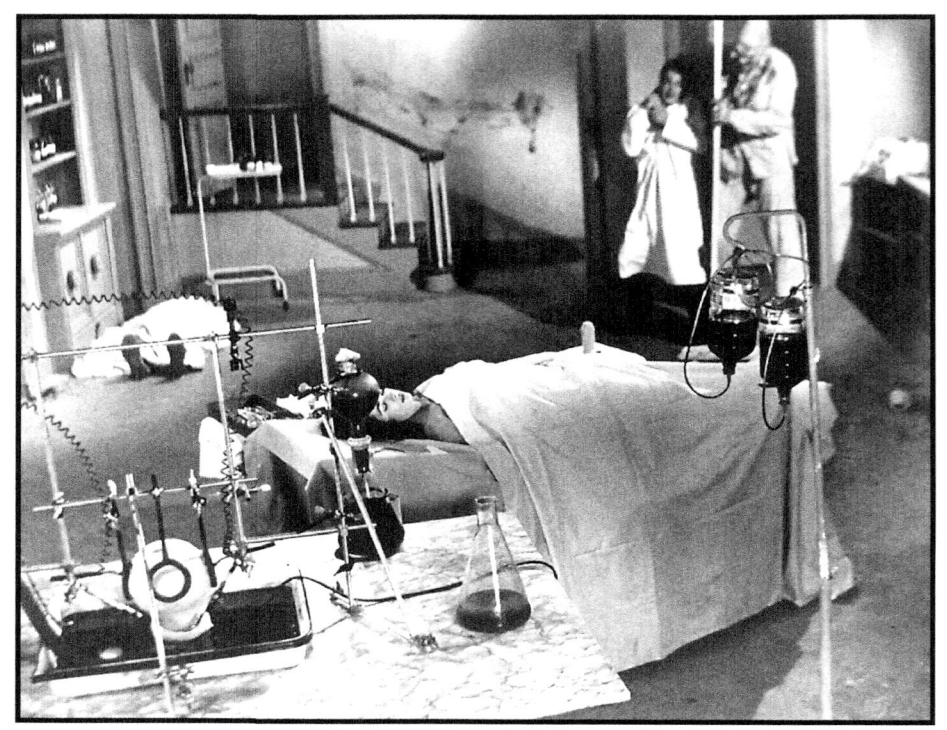

The bare bones sets do little to hide the film's (literal) bargain-basement roots.

takes off his jacket and lowers it into the car out of camera range. When he draws it back again, there's something wrapped up inside.

Green shows some real inventiveness here, using camera angles and p.o.v. shots to give the feel of a fatal car crash without the expense (none of those overpriced stuntmen and pyrotechnicians with specialty vehicles here—just a junkyard car door, a hand-held camera, and some lighter fluid). Amazingly, it does the job by allowing our imagination (rather than money) to do the work. "It was all suggestion," recalled Green. "The picture was not a big-budget picture so I had to pick out ways to *suggest* a violent automobile crash and her head being severed from her body." Sometimes a suggestion is worth a thousand greenbacks.

Of course, the next sequence turns almost comically absurd as Bill dashes with his gruesome package through the landscaped woods (the manicured grounds of the Detmer Estate) like an NFL running back. For a full minute and a half, the camera jogs alongside and in front like some macabre blocker intent on seeing his teammate carry the pigskin across the goal line. It is strange juxtapositions like these (inventive sequences alternating with moments of amusing preposterousness) which create much of the film's bizarre charm and make it so enjoyable.

Even the music in *The Brain That Wouldn't Die* is peculiar and twisted. In one scene a shrill piccolo maniacally trills up and down the scale to generate some audio suspense, while in another sequence a saxophone blows long and sleazy notes as Bill cases the neighborhood for female flesh. "I think the music was quite good in this movie," remarked Green. "It was all done by Ed Craig, who had been in the business for many years and had a large library of stock music. He was a real technical pro, an old-timer. The only original piece of music in the picture was 'The Web' (written by Abe Baker and Tony Restaino). Whenever the surgeon went out looking for a female victim, we brought that 'Web' music in, with its wonderful sleazy saxophone."

The bare bones sets do little to hide the film's (literal) bargain-basement roots. "The interior scenes were shot in the Lance Studio," stated Green, "which was in the basement of the Henry Hudson Hotel. It was a small compact studio, 75 feet by 75 feet. I had three sets standing simultaneously for *The Brain That Wouldn't Die*, each in a corner. Set construction went on even after we started filming, but, of course, the carpenters would stop when I did a sound take."

While such compact quarters may have been convenient, the economy shows. Following an exterior shot of the truly impressive palatial mansion (the Detmer house) which serves as Bill's "country place," all we ever see of its interior is one threadbare entry room and the shabby basement lab. The entire hospital consists of half an operating room with an open window in one of the two walls which the docs can stand behind to speak their dialogue as they ostensibly wash up at an unseen sink. The "Moulin Rouge" strip club looks like nothing more than a cramped greasy spoon cafe (complete with vinyl bar stools at the counter and a checkerboard tile floor) where the feather-wearing female dancer simply stands in the middle of the floor to bump and shimmy (obviously, a real stage was simply not within the budget). And Bill's "cutting edge" medical lab looks no more sophisticated than a Junior High biology classroom. Furnished with nothing more exotic than a few beakers and tubes held by a couple of support rods and clamps (there's even a cheap voltage meter and a pair of ordinary *batteries*), one expects to see a formaldehyde-soaked frog sitting on the table awaiting dissection.

Art director Paul Fanning, who worked at Walt Disney Productions and MGM as well as for television, does little to brighten the dismal surroundings, often leaving the gray walls bare and perfunctorily dressing his spaces with cheap, minimalist furnishings. On the plus side, however, these sparse sets actually add to the claustrophobic ambiance of sleazy dives and half-baked horrors.

While the film slows considerably during the various body-search sequences, there are still a few laughs to be found. Though much of the movie's amusement is unintentional (with most of the supporting cast straining their thespian muscles as if they were playing *Othello*), Green still shows that he didn't check his sense of humor at the door. When Bill offers to help Doris with plastic surgery, she shoots back, "Why should you want to do this for me; what's in it for you?" Bill blithely quips, "I'm gonna make your face beautiful again, cut it off and give your body away." Thinking he's kidding, of course, Doris apologizes for being so suspicious. At the close of the fight sequence between the two strippers, Green cuts to a shot of two cat plaques hung on the wall while a loud "meooow" hits the soundtrack—crude but funny.

Green admittedly often overuses the medium shot, relying on the master too heavily at times or holding on the same scene too long. But he usually manages to shoot enough close-ups and inserts to at least partially offset the visual monotony—again showing enough care to get some varied shots on a beleaguered schedule.

Green is not afraid to move the camera, either. For instance, the titular head's introduction (after one heck of a long buildup in which Bill fiddles with various clamps and test tubes) begins with a tight shot of the clock on the wall above the table. The camera pans right and down to follow a bubbling liquid as it passes from beakers into tubes and then abruptly swings left to reveal the head held upright in clamps as the life-giving fluid runs into its supportive tray. Working with cinematographer Stephen Hajnal, Green at least makes the *effort* to generate some visual interest (and often succeeds).

Joseph Green studied drama and speech at the University of Maryland. After a stretch in the service, Green began writing and directing commercials. "And," remarked Green, "like everybody else, I was looking for my first shot as a director of a feature film." The shot came in the form of producer Rex Carlton and *The Brain That Wouldn't Die*. After this cerebral debut, however, Green's directing career did not take off as he'd hoped. "I was supposed to make another film for Rex," declared Green, "a Caribbean adventure story from a script that we had found. But after a while, Rex decided to return to California and I had begun to make commercials again." Green's next involvement with a feature film was on a movie called *Daydream*. "It was a Japanese picture [released in the U.S. in 1969]," Green explained, "and I directed the fantasy scenes—the dream sequences—but I did not direct the entire movie. That was my second directorial assignment." Green then became involved in the distribution end of the business. "I've been distributing pictures since 1970. So that's kept me very very busy. That's why my directing work was pushed slightly to the side." Green directed one additional film, Sammy Davis, Jr.'s last feature called *The Perils of P.K.*, shot in the mid-1980s. "It's been held up by the producer," he explained. Green (who still runs a company aptly named Joseph Green Pictures) is back at it again. He has a film in production now called *Psychedelic Generation*. "It's about 80 percent completed," announced Green, who hopes to finish it soon.

On any rushed low-budget production, there's bound to be a few continuity problems here and there, and *The Brain That Wouldn't Die* is no exception. For example, it's bright daylight when Bill makes his mad dash to the country house with his bleeding bundle. When Kurt opens the door to his employer's frantic knocking, however, it's pitch black outside—the result of shooting on a cramped basement soundstage. Also, wouldn't somebody notice Bill's burned automobile with its headless occupant? "I don't think anyone will trace us here because her body was burned in the wreckage," Bill absurdly asserts. But he's right; no police show up to even fill out so much as an accident report. Apparently, a burned-out car and charred, decapitated corpse simply aren't worth the trouble of investigating in this neck of the woods. But in a picture as outré as this, minor gaffes like these only add to the bizarre fun.

Though Herschell Gordon Lewis is credited as "The Godfather of Gore" for his early string of splatter-fests like *Blood Feast* (1963) and *Two Thousand Maniacs* (1964), Joseph Green should receive at least partial credit, for he filmed his simple-but-effective visceral gruesomeness a full four years before Lewis forced an actor to rip a bloody sheep's tongue from a victim's mouth. The first bit of grue comes at the very beginning, with a wonderfully realistic shot of a patient's exposed brain—which Bill promptly sticks with sharp prongs! But this is nothing compared to Kurt's lingering, blood-smearing death scene in which he ends up wiping his bloody stump all over the lab walls. Kurt's mutilated shoulder is a gruesome sight, a mass of dark blood and shredded lab coat which dangles like strips of tattered flesh and clotted gore. The *piè*ce de

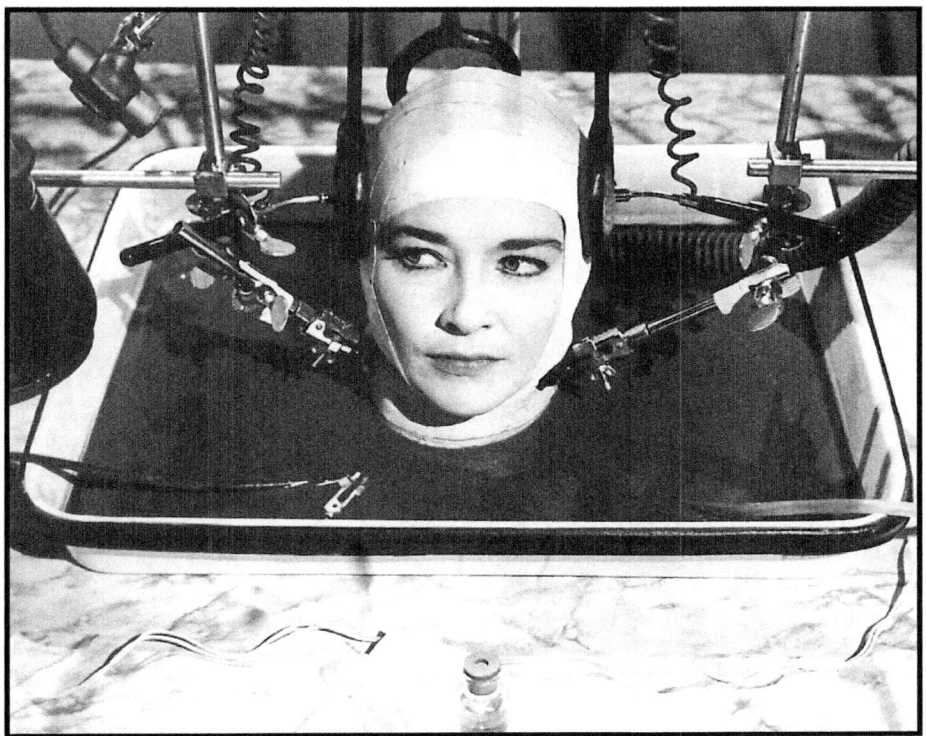

"Heading" up the cast was actress Virginia Leith, a dark-haired beauty born and raised in Cleveland, Ohio.

résistance, however, comes in the form of a well-chewed piece of liver. When the closet creature crashes out of its cell, it grabs its creator by the hair, forces his head to the side, and lowers its misshapen face to the doctor's neck. After a quick cutaway to the watching Jan, we hear an agonized cry, and the camera cuts back to the monster raising its head from Bill's neck with something moist dangling from its mouth. Bill drops to the floor, where he writhes in pain, his neck and half his face awash in blood. The creature then pulls a hunk of ragged flesh out of its mouth, holds it up to get a good look, then throws it to the floor for an in-your-face close-up of the gory mass of tissue. "Well, maybe that was a bit overdone," conceded Green, "but I *was* trying to instill a real element of horror into the scene. After all, the monster was biting into the flesh of the very person who put him together. I felt there was an irony to it. That hunk of neck flesh was actually a piece of liver, but in black and white it was rather convincing." Indeed.

"Heading" up the cast was actress Virginia Leith, a dark-haired beauty born and raised in Cleveland, Ohio. After her parents moved the family to Los Angeles, she met director Stanley Kubrick, who cast her in *Fear and Desire* (1953). Following a stint as a fashion model, Leith signed a contract with Twentieth Century-Fox, for whom she did several pictures. Publicity articles claimed that *The Brain That Wouldn't Die* was Virginia's "bid for renewed stardom." Sadly, the cerebral role didn't exactly take the actress to the head of her profession; she only appeared in one more film, *First Love* (1977), and

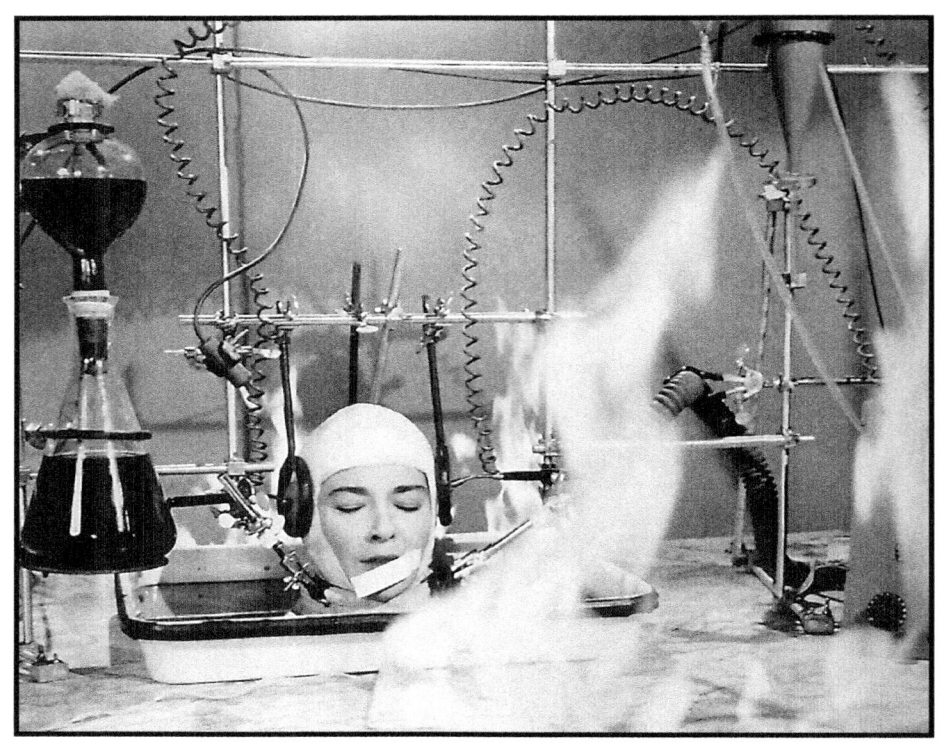

Leith does extremely well in her rather limited role (especially considering she spends all but a few moments up to her neck in lab equipment and developer's trays).

a few sporadic television shows (including *Great Ghost Tales* in 1961 and *Next Step Beyond* in 1978).

One wonders what she thought about playing a disembodied head in a no-budget independent only a few scant years after starring in such prestige pictures as *Toward the Unknown* (1956, with William Holden) and *A Kiss Before Dying* (1956, with Robert Wagner and Joanne Woodward). While Leith's *thoughts* may have been one thing, her actions were never less than professional according to director Joseph Green. "She was a professional in every sense of the word." Even thorough professionals, however, have their limit. "During the last two days of shooting," admitted Green, "she was getting a little restless because she was in this very complicated contraption that made it look like her head was severed from her body—and it was very uncomfortable. So I can appreciate how she felt and we got her scenes done as quickly as possible."

Leith does extremely well in her rather limited role (especially considering she spends all but a few moments up to her neck in lab equipment and developer's trays). "You should remember," reminds Green, "that we are not talking about a script which required some real deep method or 'technical' acting. The parts were written in, not stereotyped *per se*, but we are talking about monsters in closets and a woman's head brought back to life. I mean, the emotions are pretty basic and very much to the point." Before losing her head, Ms. Leith fairly exudes a pleasant sultriness, coming off as a rather sweet sex kitten. She speaks lines like, "Oooh, every time you touch me

I go out of my mind," and "Bill, I want to get married; I can't stand not having you" with a subtle but potent sensuality. If sex really does begin in the mind, then it's no wonder Bill goes to such lengths to preserve this woman's head!

Leith launches herself into her part gamely. When she intones (as she does so frequently) "Let me die," her small whimperings and pleading voice sound as if she really means it. (Of course, the less-than-pleasant physical circumstances under which the confined actress was forced to work may have added some realistic conviction to the line.) When a disembodied, mummy-wrapped head speaks dialogue like, "If he only knew what it's like being like this," one has to crack a smile, but Leith manages to make it sound sincere. Even more impressively, the actress uses her voice and face to create some real *frisson* in what *should be* a strictly risible situation. In particular, her laugh—an unhealthy, bitter sound devoid of any actual mirth—is downright chilling. Leith also appropriately alters her voice, coarsening it to add a hoarse quality (as if her larynx had been damaged). Leith (thankfully) keeps her facial expressions subtle (anything broad or theatrical from a disembodied head on a 20-foot-high movie screen would push a situation already teetering on the brink of ludicrousness over the edge into burlesque). An almost subliminal flash of her eyes and a hard line to her mouth effectively conveys her hate, while a slight downturn at the lips and dropping of eyelids reflect her bouts of self-pity. Thanks to Leith's sincerity and naturalistic expressions, her living head seems more real than many of the full-bodied characters around her.

Director Joseph Green does well to encase his "head" actress in a white bandage/dressing which completely covers her cranium and neck—giving the unbelievable sight of a disembodied head a more clinical—and alien—look than if Ms. Leith's luxuriant, curly locks had continued to cascade around her. But then, like so many incongruities in this amusing/amazing feature, Green sees to it that Leith's eyeliner and lipstick remain perfectly in place!

Making his big-screen debut—and supporting the main body of the film (since Leith doesn't even *have* one after the first few minutes)—is Herb (later "Jason") Evers. (Immediately after this picture he changed his professional name to *Jason* Evers.) Coincidence? In any case, a good actor by any other name emotes just as sweetly, and Herb/Jason holds up his end nicely. Evers mixes in quiet smirks and subtle leers with his more studied appraisals as he seeks the perfect body for his lady love, thereby letting his unhealthy obsession peek through the ostensible facade of "working for science." Evers also possesses a smooth manner and comfortable charm. "Oh come on now Doris, do I look like a maniac who goes around killing girls?" he jokes affably. "You've got to learn to trust people. People *like* me, really." Evers' agreeable manner and charming smile makes this easy to believe.

AIP publicity touted Evers as a "well-known TV cowboy," and "familiar figure to TV audiences in the title role of the lone cowboy in *The Wrangler*." How "well known" and "familiar" remains a point in question, however, since the show ran for less than three *weeks* (from August 4 to September 15, 1960)! Evers continued his film career after *Brain*, making about a dozen more movies over the next two decades, including the genre entries *The Illustrated Man* (1968), *Escape From the Planet of the Apes* (1971), *Claws* (1977; also known as *Devil Bear*), and *Barracuda* (1978). He also worked fairly steadily on television, making three TV movies, numerous guest appearances on shows like *Green Hornet*, *Star Trek*, and *Tarzan*, and even another series, *Channing* (which

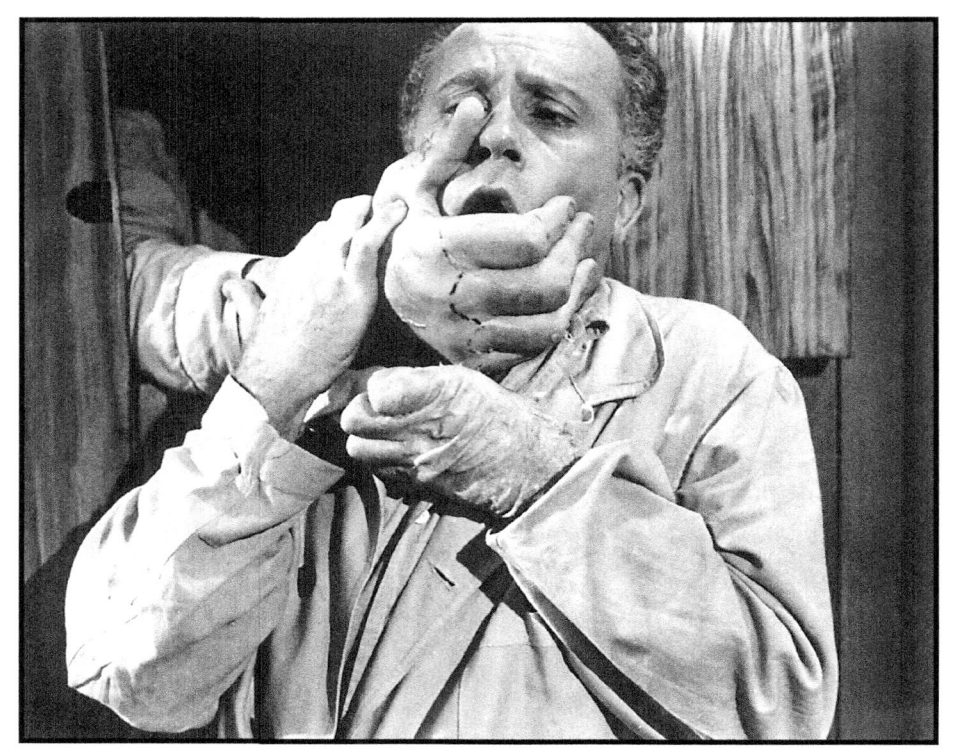

As Kurt, Leslie Daniel (who worked primarily as a dubbing actor) reaches new heights in melodramatics.

broke Evers' previous three week winning streak by running two full seasons in 1963 and '64).

Apart from these two players, most of the other *Brain* thespians emote as if they're performing 19th-century Grand Guignol (which may not be so inappropriate after all, since they are, in fact, doing a cheesy form of *20th*-century Grand Guignol). As Kurt, Leslie Daniel (who worked primarily as a dubbing actor) reaches new heights in melodramatics, speaking his ludicrous lines with a near-violent fervor while sighing and gesturing with a boundless theatricality. Though he's only got one good arm, Daniel waves it about and gesticulates enough for two. Of course, Green doesn't help by shooting scene after scene of Kurt pacing about, looking nervously around, and waffling in his convictions. Daniel's painful sincerity and over-the-top mannerisms, while far from any sense of normalcy, are indeed *fun* to watch. (And since nothing in this picture is "normal," Daniel's hyperdrive performance works.) Nevertheless, it all culminates in one of the most unintentionally amusing death scenes in the annals of cinema. After the closet creature pulls Kurt's one good arm from its socket, Daniel staggers about *for two solid minutes*, running his mutilated shoulder into doors and walls so he can drag it along the surface and leave a gory snail-track of blood. After smearing the lab wall with grue, he lurches upstairs, gasping and writhing all the while. He heads for the front door but can't get his remaining claw-like hand to close about the doorknob. After feebly beating at the offending portal in frustration, he wobbles across the room. His knees almost collapse so that he has to duck-walk over to the table where he topples into a chair. When Jan's taunting laughter wafts up from the lab below, he pushes himself up, nearly collapsing again so that he (once more) duck-walks over to the cellar doorway. He rests a moment, leaning on the door jamb for support, then totters a few steps backwards (as if to get a running start) before rushing through the opening. Now back in the lab, he unsteadily approaches Jan, raises his withered arm as if to strike, and gives a strangled gasp. The strain is too much and he stumbles backward where he slides down yet another wall. Now sitting on the floor, he clutches his chest with his deformed hand and his head suddenly flops to the side. After two full minutes of staggering, bleeding, pounding, and gasping, Kurt finally dies. This drawn-out demise is indeed a sight to behold—and one not to be missed.

The arm-removing "giant pinhead closet monster" (Green's appellation) was played by the exceedingly tall Eddie Carmel. A sometime Ringling Brothers and Barnum & Bailey Circus giant, Carmel's publicity listed him at 500 pounds and nine feet tall! While these stats may have been "heightened" just a bit, there's no denying the imposing impression he made as the hideous mutant behind the door. "He was a very fine young guy," remembered Green. "Every actor should be that easy to work with on the set. It was a shame he had this glandular problem." Sadly, this glandular problem, which made Carmel so suitable for his gigantic role in *Brain*, led to his early death in 1972 at the age of 36. After *The Brain That Wouldn't Die*, Carmel made no further significant big-screen appearances, though he did work sporadically in television commercials. He perhaps took some small inspiration from his sole movie monster role, however, for he later formed a short-lived rock 'n' roll band named "Frankenstein and the Brain Surgeons."

At one point, Jan sagely observes that, "People fear what they don't understand—and can't see." Green takes this axiom to heart and cleverly keeps the monster in the closet under wraps until the "biting" climax, letting the viewer's imagination conjure up something much more horrible than Eddie Carmel's mutant Zippy the Pinhead. "Radio was very important to me as a child," explained Green. "It makes you use your imagination and that's what I similarly tried to achieve in *The Brain That Wouldn't Die*." Of course, money (or lack thereof) may have had *something* to do with it. "We did have to use our special effects sparingly because of budget restrictions," admitted the director, "and that's why the viewer doesn't see the thing in the closet until the last five minutes of the film." Green periodically whets the viewer's appetite, however, by having all manner of grotesque grunts, wheezes, and slurping sounds emanate from behind the door. So while the monster's eventual emergence can't live up to our built-up expectations, Green quickly dispels whatever disappointment we may feel by assaulting—and shocking—our sensibilities with a piece of liver. And the creature's appearance certainly is *unusual*, with its oatmeal face, pointed bald head, off-kilter eye, and flaps of scarred, wattled flesh under its chin that make the poor wretch appear to sport some monstrous turkey-neck. "[Make-up man] George Fiala did a very good job," opined Green. "I was very happy with the result."

But what about that open ending, in which the closet monster simply carries Doris' drugged, naked body (demurely covered by a sheet of course) up and out of the burning lab, never to be seen again? "There was a thought that we would make a sequel," remembered Green. "I had an idea to pursue the situation further, but it never came about due to Carlton's death." In any case, it certainly remains one of the most enigmatic endings to a monster movie of that period—an eccentric climax completely in tune with the bizarre tone of the film.

After 13 days of guerrilla filmmaking in the fall of 1959, *The Head That Wouldn't Die* was finally in the can—and first-time filmmaker Joseph Green was quite pleased with his inaugural effort: "Since I wrote the script and directed it, I knew pretty well how it would fall into place. So when I saw the final cut, it really satisfied me that everything that I had planned, that we could afford to do, was done. So I was quite happy with it."

Actually, not *everything* planned was done. "There was a scene I wanted to do," admitted the disappointed director, "where a rat appears on the laboratory floor, scurries over the lab tables, and sees the blood circulating through the tubes to the head. It's late at night and the head is alone. The rat sniffs the blood, drinks a little, and then really starts to go into a frenzy. It starts toward the head which has been watching the whole scene helplessly. Suddenly, at the propitious moment, the scientists come through the door, chase the rat away, and save our heroine head from a fate worse than death. I could have made a hell of a scene out of that, but the rat simply wouldn't take direction! It simply would not stay within the area that was lit, and it was extremely important to get him to go to the table. We worked at it for two hours and we *still* had nothing on film. When you only have a 13-day shoot, you have to carefully evaluate the importance of every scene and how much time it is taking.... I hate to make it sound like a race, but that's exactly what a low-budget film is, a race against time." And so a potentially chilling scene was scotched by one resistant rodent. So go the trials and tribulations of low-budget moviemaking.

After the picture was finished, it took nearly three years before Green could see the fruits of his labors up in lights. "[Producer] Rex Carlton was very particular in the kind of distribution he wanted," explained Green. "And he wasn't desperate; he just held out and he got the kind of distribution deal he was looking for from the kind of outfit that could best do a first-class job on that kind of picture." The lengthy delay didn't seem to bother the director, however, for Green conceded that "[Carlton] was a smart man."

But even smart men can't always predict what others will do to their work, for AIP immediately lopped off 10 minutes of the picture's 81 minute running time in an attempt to decrease both the gore and sleaze quotients. Gone was the infamous liver scene, Kurt's drawn-out (and messy) death agonies, and a number of the voyeuristic "body-search" scenes (including the strippers' cat fight). Fortunately, these pivotal sequences (for "guilty pleasure" seekers, anyway) have been restored and can now be enjoyed in all their tasteless glory.

Producer Rex Carlton not only supervised low-budget pictures, but wrote many of their scripts as well, including the genre entries *Unearthly Stranger* (1963), *Nightmare in Wax* (1966; starring Cameron Mitchell) and *Blood of Dracula's Castle* (1967; with John Carradine). As the "money man" for *The Head That Wouldn't Die*, Carlton raised the needed capital quickly and efficiently. "Rex started to talk to 'angels' about the money for the film," remembered Joseph Green. "'Angels' are individual investors, and, in this case, our angels were mostly people who had invested in Broadway plays. Rex was very good at raising money."

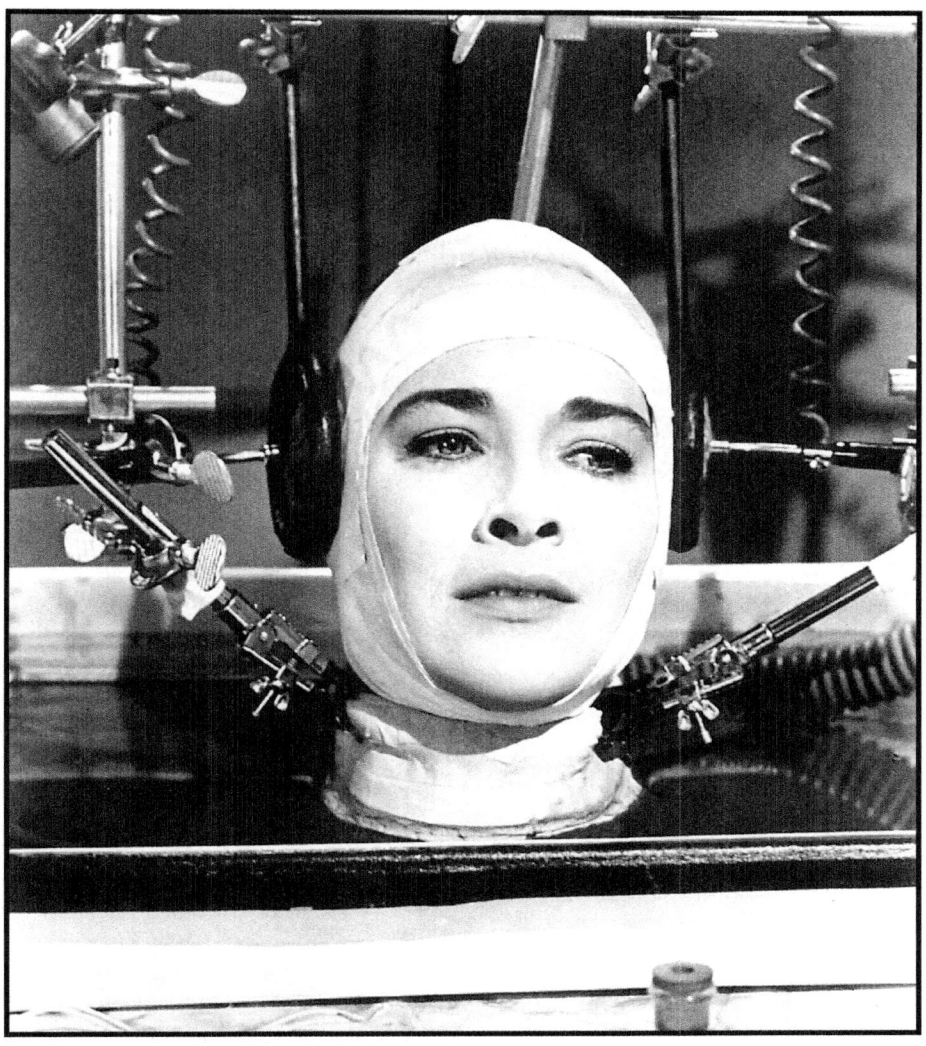

Call it what you will, but *The Brain That Wouldn't Die* remains about as far from boredom as a film can get—despite the fact that it is indeed the ultimate "talking head" movie.

    According to one source, however, this particular talent *may* have led to Carlton's early death (a suicide in 1968), for instead of continuing to seek out "angels," Carlton soon began consorting with "devils." The late Al Adamson, director of *Satan's Sadists* (1969), *Dracula Vs. Frankenstein* (1971), *Brain of Blood* (1971), and many others remembered (to David Konow in *Psychotronic* magazine) that "Rex Carlton was a very nice man and he helped me a great deal on a couple of pictures, but he had a problem. He borrowed some money from the mob and he was threatened by them because he couldn't pay them back. He had mob money in two pictures we made [*Nightmare in Wax* and *Blood of Dracula's Castle*] and he finally killed himself because of it—because he was afraid they were going to kill him anyway. But he was a very nice man,

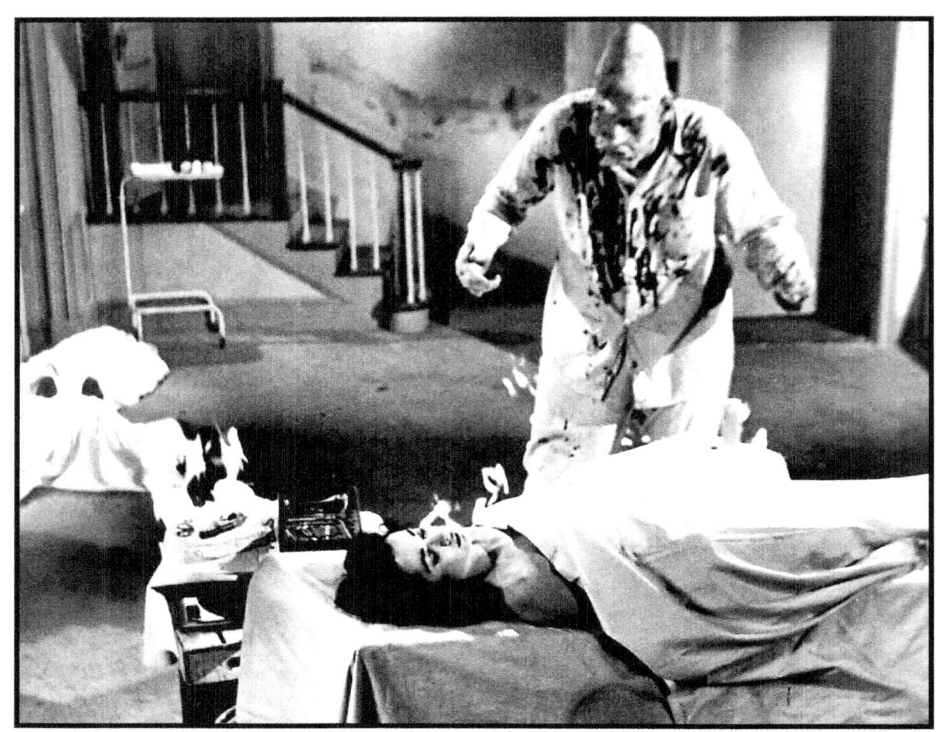

After the picture was finished, it took nearly three years before Green could see the fruits of his labors up in lights.

very cooperative, helped me any way he could. It was a real blow to have that man go through that." [NOTE: Sadly, Al Adamson himself came to a rather lurid end in 1995 when police found the 66-year-old filmmaker's body "entombed in concrete beneath his whirlpool hot tub" in his Indio, California home. Truth is indeed sometimes stranger than fiction.]

Not surprisingly, the official report of Carlton's death painted a different picture. *Variety* reported (on May 15, 1968) that "Police, who found a suicide note and an Italian automatic revolver beside the tub, reported he had made a previous attempt to kill himself. The note indicated 'things weren't going right,' for Carlton, who, according to police, apparently had been in poor health for some time." But whatever the circumstances, it's a shame Rex Carlton never lived to see how popular and appreciated his films (particularly *The Brain That Wouldn't Die*) have become.

The film was a fiscal success. "American International did very nicely with it worldwide," remembered Joseph Green. "At least in New York City it was combined as a double feature with *PT 109* and then they dropped *PT 109* and put it out just by itself." For most venues, however, *The Brain That Wouldn't Die* was supported by the inferior *Invasion of the Star Creatures* (a puerile bottom-bill sci-fi "comedy" that made *Brain* look like *Citizen Kane*).

What did the critics think of *Citizen Brain*, er—*The Brain That Wouldn't Die*? Most reviewers ignored it outright at the time of release, for it wasn't covered in any of the usual trade papers. Over the years, however, it has garnered some attention, usually from fan magazines and genre publications. Many modern reviewers (though by no means all) are quite attracted to its bizarre charm. Michael Weldon in *The Psychotronic Encyclopedia of Film* called it "a great, absurd movie." *Fangoria*'s Dr. Cyclops noted that "this 1963 [sic] zero-budget quickie kept me glued to the set.... *The Brain That Wouldn't Die* is unadulterated sleaze/exploitation/horror." Buddy Barnett of *Cult Movies* magazine observed that "*The Brain That Wouldn't Die* makes no promise which it fails to deliver. It throws buckets full of macabre nonsense at the screen without apology, a madcap whirlwind of horror."

Not everybody sees the plum in this celluloid pudding, however. Phil Hardy in *The Encyclopedia of Science Fiction Movies* complained that "Green's attempts to mix horror and Science Fiction fail because script and direction are all too obvious." Bill Warren in *Keep Watching the Skies!* concludes, "*Brain* possesses a kind of ripe ludicrousness that makes it almost watchable. But not quite." *Starlog*'s Tom Weaver dismissed it as "sleazy and dumb."

But one fan's sleazy and dumb is another fan's sleazy and *fun*. While some skeptics feel that this particular cinematic vessel should be christened "The Titanic," those viewers with an eye for the unusual and an ear for the bizarre should definitely sign up for a first-class berth.

And what does *Brain* creator Joseph Green think about his cinematic offspring these days? "I never thought of it as a cult classic, but it seems like as time goes on the reactions to the film are very favorable. So I'm pleased with it knowing I was able to do a union picture in 13 days for an extremely low, low budget. I'm proud of that."

Call it what you will, but *The Brain That Wouldn't Die* remains about as far from boredom as a film can get—despite the fact that it is indeed the ultimate "talking head" movie. For those viewers who maintain a sense of cinematic fun and love of the outlandish, *The Brain That Wouldn't Die* will forever remain *The* Movie *That Wouldn't Die*.

CREATURE WITH THE ATOM BRAIN
by David J. Hogan

Each time I step into my home office I'm happy to be greeted by a framed half-sheet poster from *Creature with the Atom Brain*, a film that, although perhaps not the best ever made, is surely one of the most entertaining. The poster is dominated by a vivid painting of an undead atomic zombie—forehead studded with a line of rivets—advancing toward the viewer with outstretched arms. The picture's stars, Richard Denning and Angela Stevens, embrace and cower in the background, and below the zombie is the figure of a beautiful young woman, clad only in a bathrobe and lying awkwardly supine—whether in terror or from some sort of seizure, I cannot be sure.

Columbia's promotional department went the whole nine yards with this vivid collage of images, but the cheekiest element of all, the one that makes me want to shout "Wowsers!" is one of the poster's tag lines: *Based on Scientific Facts!* Well, you can't argue with *that*. Scientific facts. No kid (or kid at heart) who took a look at this poster during the late spring of 1955 would have been able to resist.

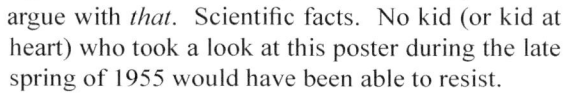

Creature with the Atom Brain was produced by that noted purveyor of scientific fact, Sam Katzman, by his Clover Productions B-picture unit for release by Columbia. Edward L. Cahn, one of the most prolific scare-film directors of the fifties and, like Katzman, a high-profile member of the scientific community, directed. The script was the work of Curt Siodmak, author of the 1943 novel *Donovan's Brain*, and thus a figure of no small scientific importance himself. It's clear, then, that *Creature with the Atom Brain* was brought to us by men capable of packing a remarkable amount of scientific credibility into the picture's brisk 69-minute running time.

Siodmak never was what Hollywood regarded as a noted screenwriter, but he did script some good (and sometimes very good) genre pictures in the forties: *The Wolf Man*, *Son of Dracula*, *Frankenstein Meets the Wolf Man*, *I Walked with a Zombie* (co-wrote), and *The Beast with Five Fingers*. In the fifties he went from highs (the original story for *Earth vs. the Flying Saucers*) to lows (writer/director credit on *Curucu, Beast of the Amazon* and on the deservedly obscure *Love Slaves of the Amazon*).

The plot Siodmak cooked up for *Creature with the Atom Brain* is classic comic book stuff,

Son of Guilty Pleasures

Professor Steigg is played by Gregory Gay, well known to serial fans as the title creature in one of Republic's lesser chapter plays, *Flying Disc Man from Mars* (1950). Photofest

fifties-style. Following the violent murders of a mobster and a district attorney, police medical examiner Dr. Chet Walker (Richard Denning) is puzzled, for the killers have used no weapons other than their hands, and have exhibited superhuman strength. The fingerprints they have carelessly left behind are oddly luminous. A blood sample Walker collects from one of the crime scenes is revealed to be not blood at all, but what Walker calls "a chemical composition."

Even more puzzling is something pointed out by Walker's friend, detective Captain Dave Harris (S. John Launer): The perpetrator's fingerprints found at both scenes belong to dead men! ("And I used to think Scrabble was tough," Dave muses.)

The killers are just two of a small army of atomic zombies created by Professor Wilhelm Steigg (Gregory Gay) and controlled by Frank Buchanan (Michael Granger), a burly gangster who has illegally returned to the States after being deported. At his trial, he vowed revenge upon the DA and every associate who turned against him. The gruesome killings, then, are part of a carefully orchestrated plan.

Dr. Walker—equal parts imagination and student of Michael Faraday—insists that each victim has run afoul of "a creature with atomic rays of superhuman strength—and that cannot be killed by bullets." The authorities buy this syntactically challenged ex-

The zombie climbs to a window, pulls aside thick security bars as if they were licorice, and plunges its heavy arms through the glass. Photofest

planation, but Walker's scheme to use radium-seeking trucks and planes to locate the zombies' energy source is stymied when Buchanan uses his undead minions to unleash a terrible wave of sabotage against the city.

Tragedy hits close to home when Walker's friend, Captain Harris, is murdered and made ambulatory again as an atomic zombie. Yet it is the undead Harris, brain-damaged following a car crash yet still hungry for radium, who unknowingly leads Walker and a small army of cops and soldiers to Buchanan's lead-lined mansion at the film's climax.

Perhaps you're saying, *Swell, but what about the scientific facts? What about 'em, huh?* Well, get this: When Chet meets with the city's civic and military leaders and invokes the name of Michael Faraday, he alludes to more scientific fact than the average American child absorbs in 13 years of public education.

Faraday was a 19th-century British physicist who revealed the link between electricity and magnetism, and who eventually discovered the phenomenon of electromagnetic induction. Other research led him to discover the foundations of metallurgy; electrical wave theory and conductors; and the boggling (and quite accurate) concept of "field theory": the assertion that space, rather than being "nothing" is actually a medium that supports the full range of electric and magnetic forces.

So full of scientific fact was the life of Michael Faraday that his surname became a scientific term: a *faraday* is a unit of electricity used in the study of electrochemical reactions. Furthermore, a *farad* is a unit in the meter-kilogram-second system of physical units of electrical capacitance, that is, the ability to hold an electrical charge.

Although Faraday's most notable experiments revolved around the nature of electricity and magnetic fields, the one cited by Dr. Walker—and well understood by the dotty Professor Steigg—involved electric current passed through the severed leg of a frog. When electrically charged, the leg moved—an apparent miracle that stunned lay people of the 19th century. Dr. Steigg elaborated on this, one of Faraday's lesser demonstrations, to create his atomic zombies.

And thus, ladies and gentlemen, we have *scientific fact*.

Much of the pleasure of *Creature with the Atom Brain* derives from its heedless combination of stylistic elements of police procedural, bizarre yet oddly plausible science fiction, and physical action as it was expressed in the style of the great serials of the forties. Walker's relationship with Dave Harris is grounded in friendship, but when the two are discussing the case, they're all business. Clipped dialogue sprinkled with heavy-handed, sardonic humor is Siodmak's way of establishing that the fellows are "real" cops, toughened by years in the trenches. At the scene of the first murder, for instance, the ill-fated DA McGraw (Tristram Coffin) notes that the killer left "six grand" untouched in the victim's safe. Harris doesn't miss a beat: "Maybe he didn't want to get into a higher bracket." Yessir, this guy's as hard as nails.

The fact that Walker figures out what's going on just a few minutes after arriving at the scene of the first murder is risible, to be sure, but also is Siodmak's way of demonstrating that Steigg and Buchanan are going to have a fight on their hands because Walker is 100 percent pro.

Siodmak had particular fun (or difficulty) with the story's scientific elements; I can't think of another science fiction thriller of the period that's as choked with inane gobbledygook. Dr. Walker tosses off impressive-sounding but essentially meaningless jargon as blithely as a duck shakes off water: "Sodium hydroxide," he explains to Dave as he fiddles with zombie blood. "Absorption bands"; "Let's put it in the centrifuge"; "amygdala stimulation"; "amygdaloid stimulation" (take your pick); and my favorite: "It throws the beam to the right dextrous!" If Captain Harris is the quintessential detective, Chet Walker is Joe Science.

DA McGraw (Tristram Coffin) is accosted in his own garage by a zombie who silently lowers the door and lifts McGraw from the seat by his neck. Photofest

The film could have been pretty heavy going if not for the energy and imagination brought to it by director Ed Cahn and cinematographer Fred Jackman, Jr., who built mood as successfully as they depicted wild violence. A brief pre-title sequence (a reasonably rare device for 1955) is spookily atmospheric, as a burly, nattily dressed zombie (Karl Davis) shambles along a well-tended walkway outside a mansion. Viewed in long shot, the zombie is shadowed by the night and eerily backlit by an unseen street lamp. There's a suggestion of fog in the air, and when the zombie pauses it's interestingly framed by hedges and bushes. A human heartbeat pulses on the soundtrack with metronomic regularity: *bum-bum, bum-bum, bum-bum*. This is a moody and technically accomplished sequence that reaches out and pulls the viewer right into the story: *Bam!*, you're hooked.

The sequence continues after the titles, establishing a neat sense of menace inside the mansion as an employee quietly pads about, switching off lights and bringing the night inside. The zombie continues to approach the house, which we observe via a subjective camera angle, and then via the same view, only now as seen on a TV screen that's being observed in a faraway lab by Steigg and Buchanan. A microphone operated by Buchanan is used to instruct the zombie and to relay Buchanan's voice through the creature's artificial voice box.

The zombie climbs to a window, pulls aside thick security bars as if they were licorice, and plunges its heavy arms through the glass. The target, a casino owner who once crossed Buchanan, recoils in alarm. "Who are you? What do you want?"

Much of the pleasure of *Creature* derives from its heedless combination of stylistic elements of police procedural, bizarre science fiction, and physical action. Photofest

The zombie shuffles closer, its face a blank, its voice a strangely disembodied monotone. "I told you I'd come back," it intones. "Remember Buchanan?"

"Wha—*you're* not Buchanan!"

"I don't look like him, but I *am* him. Don't you recognize the voice, Jim? I told you I'd see you die, and I will."

With this, the victim is grabbed by the throat and lifted off his feet. The camera discreetly pans to a wall, where the man's shadow writhes for a split-moment before the zombie snaps his spine like a bread stick. Lackeys who burst into the room as the zombie turns to leave empty their guns, punching smoking holes into the creature's back—an effect accomplished with explosive squibs, and genuinely startling for the period.

"Come back home," Buchanan instructs. "Come back home."

The later murder of DA McGraw is no less shocking. The fellow is accosted in his own garage by a zombie who silently lowers the door, plucks the steering wheel from the dashboard of the DA's car, and lifts McGraw from the seat by his neck. The camera holds on the car's cockpit, the DA's feet rising to the top of the frame. Following a horrible-sounding *crunch*, the body is released and crumples into the seat.

Cahn's quasi-circumspect approach to murder is effective because (to coin a phrase) it leaves something to the imagination. And the imagination, of course, conjures visions infinitely more horrible than anything that might have been devised by a special effects technician.

Other murders are depicted with similar cleverness. When a zombie dressed as a policeman relieves an officer who has been guarding Buchanan's turncoat ex-accountant, the door to the house swings shut; the camera remains outside, focused on the door. Then a man screams. The camera remains locked on the door as the real cop returns to the house and dashes inside, only to gag, grunt, and perish.

The death of still another target is depicted via a close-up of his hand slipping from a doorknob as a heavy knife plunges into his back (complete with wince-inducing sound effect).

Cahn's purposeful avoidance of on-camera grue cleverly sets us up for the explicitly violent climax, when the cornered gangster clobbers Steigg with a pipe wrench and sends the full complement of zombies to the front lawn to do battle with the gathered soldiers and police. Walker is astonished: "Those are the bodies that were stolen from the morgue!"—a line sufficiently pungent to remind you that you're not watching *Masterpiece Theatre*. (Another hint, early in the film, is a wildly overwrought newspaper headline: *DEAD MEN WALK CITY STREETS*.)

The creatures stride blithely through hand-grenade explosions, and are not fazed when machine-gun bullets rip through their chests and out their backs (another very startling use of squibs). The good guys are flung about like rag dolls, and the carnage is stopped only after Dr. Walker enters the house, engages Buchanan in a rousing, kinetic fistfight, and begins to smash the hell out of Steigg's equipment. The lab explodes but Buchanan recovers sufficiently to level his revolver at Walker. The mobster is stopped—for good—when he is strangled by the undead Dave Harris. Has Harris been moved to kill Buchanan for radium, or because he retains a dim memory of his fondness for Walker? We never know.

Creature with the Atom Brain was produced on a strict budget, but is far less poverty stricken than many other Katzman pictures of the fifties. Nighttime exteriors were expertly shot outside and at night (thankfully, day-for-night shooting was avoided), and a plentitude of daytime exteriors are well used as establishing shots and as settings for whole sequences. On-location car chases that culminate in leaps for life (two more staples of the serials from which the picture took a lot of its style) are in abundance.

Further, Cahn had the luxury of covering scenes in long shots, two-shots, and close-ups, which gave editor Aaron Stell a nice variety of footage to work with. The result is a lively, briskly paced film that avoids the visual monotony that sinks so many other low-budget thrillers of the period. In one particularly well-edited sequence, shot simultaneously from two angles (another luxury seldom enjoyed by Mr. Cahn), Dave's car jumps the curb outside Buchanan's house, the nose plowing into the lawn, the back end popping up like a jack-in-the-box. Stell expertly combined footage from the two p.o.v.s, giving the audience a dynamic moment that literally propels us into the next setup.

Casting is another plus. Richard Denning was one of the most consistently appealing sci-fi heroes of the fifties, battling *The Creature from the Black Lagoon*, *The Black Scorpion*, the robots of *Target Earth!*, and the atomic mutant created on *The Day the World Ended*. *Creature with the Atom Brain* offered him a focal, quite verbal role, and Denning ran with it. He spouted Siodmak's garbled science with complete conviction, and gamely plowed his way through some clumsy exposition. His inherent likeability and slick acting style brought the illusion of sense to lines that would have defeated a lesser actor.

Dave (S. John Launer) sits limply on the sofa while Penny (Linda Bennet) innocently notes, "Gosh your hand is cold." Photofest

Denning benefited because Siodmak took pains to establish that Chet Walker isn't just a cop, but a family man, as well. Chet's scenes with his wife, Joyce (Angela Stevens), are brisk and well-played, and have a ring of truth about them. The Walkers have a young daughter, Penny (the enthusiastic but rather too cute Linda Bennett), and one gets the impression that they've been married for quite a while. But that doesn't stop Chet from grabbing Joyce and soul-kissing her when she enters the bedroom to awaken him, or from happily swatting her pretty rump when she bends to retrieve the morning paper from the front stoop. They embrace at other moments, as well, giving the impression that they're a lusty, physical pair who aren't merely in love, but who have an easy, cheerful fondness for one another.

This aspect of Siodmak's characterization of Joyce is pleasing, but other elements of her personality are dated and, to modern eyes, insulting. She exists mainly to cook Chet's dinners (which he never has time to eat), mix his martinis (which he never has time to drink), and look after his child (whom he seldom has time to parent). Although Chet is clearly crazy about her, he has doubts about her intellectual capabilities: When Dave Harris shows up to discuss the zombie case, Chet shoos Penny *and* Joyce from the room! Later, when Joyce offers a suggestion about the investigation, Dave and Chet look at her as they might regard a dog who has done something unexpected but thoroughly worthless. Chastened, Joyce retreats to the kitchen.

Worst of all is when the zombified "Uncle Dave" (who can speak with a deadened version of his own voice rather than Buchanan's) is admitted to the house by Penny, who innocently notes, "Gosh, your hand is cold." Dave sits limply on the sofa while Joyce calls to him from the kitchen, telling him he sounds terrible and is probably coming down with a cold. Then she inadvertently spills the beans about Chet's plan to entrap a zombie and follow the creature back to its source. Boy, you just can't tell a woman *anything*.

Columbia contract player Angela Stevens began her screen career about 1952, and worked in film (mainly Westerns) and TV until at least 1960. She was an appealing, pretty blonde who happened to be a competent actress, and who should have had the opportunity to work more frequently, and in better vehicles. Her career could not have been satisfying for her—other than *Atom Brain*'s Joyce Walker, the only role that is likely to be of interest to B-film buffs is her appealing turn as the wife of one of the Three Stooges in a 1952 two-reeler, *He Cooked His Goose*.

Stevens played Joyce Walker with charm and good humor—and with a nice sense of urgency, as well. When Penny unexpectedly screams from the living room, Joyce dashes from the kitchen, the picture of motherly concern. Dave is gone and Penny sits on the edge of the sofa, clutching her favorite doll, which has been torn apart by Uncle Dave. Although Dave's assault on the doll makes little logical sense, the moment is effective, nonetheless, and successfully elevates the horror to a focused, personal level.

S. John Launer, a small-part film and TV actor often cast as a judge or a businessman, is fine as Dave, bringing just enough cheek and understatement of style to make the character believable. Dave is serious about his work, but not so serious that he can't find moments of amusement. His relationship with Chet is a professional one that, we plainly see, has grown into friendship many years before. So close are the two, in fact, that Joyce brings a good-natured jaundice to her assessment of the relationship. When Penny asks, "How come you never got married, Uncle Dave?", Joyce pipes up, "He'd be a bigamist, Penny. He's already married to your father."

The fact that Dave is fond of Penny is a little tug on our heartstrings that makes his fate particularly affecting. When the real Dave is eliminated, destroyed, we feel bad.

Michael Granger was another Columbia contract player who, like most small-part actors of the fifties, got his biggest, juiciest roles in second features. His burly physique; pockmarked, olive complexion; and deep, smoothly menacing voice made him ideal for roles as hoods, caliphs, police prefects, and similar quasi-exotica. He's quite good as Buchanan, underplaying every line to discomforting effect, and moving his heavy body with the slow, easy assurance of an unflappable schemer who is not to be trifled with. When Steigg complains in an early scene that his creations are being used to kill people, Buchanan quietly corrects him: "Not just people. *Particular* people. And when we're through, there'll be nothing we can't do or have."

Later, when Steigg presents the undead Dave to Buchanan (following a nasty operating-room sequence in which an electrode-studded control device is inserted into Dave's skull), the mobster fearlessly steps nose-to-nose with the creature, places his fingers on its shoulder, and gives Dave a firm, exploratory shove. Satisfied, he slips a huge knife into the waistband of Dave's pants.

Professor Steigg is played by Gregory Gay, well known to serial fans as the title creature in one of Republic's lesser chapter plays, *Flying Disc Man from Mars* (1950). The Germanic accent he brought to the role of Steigg, and his suggestion of the character's essentially amoral nature, are sufficient to conjure memories of the Nazi Party

Richard Denning was one of the most consistently appealing sci-fi heroes of the fifties. Photofest

(an organization which, the viewer can reasonably suppose, had included Steigg as a member, and probably an enthusiastic one). But the professor is not entirely unsympathetic. He claims he wants his creatures to be used "for the benefit of mankind," and struggles constantly with the implications of his alliance with Buchanan, who has financed his work. Worse, Steigg has radium poisoning, which brings him excruciating pain and prompts him to make an unwise foray out of the house and into the city, in search of medicine.

Character actors fill out the remainder of the cast. Tris Coffin, hero of the last great Republic serial, 1949's *King of the Rocketmen*, is suitably no-nonsense as DA McGraw; the look on the character's face when confronted in his garage is less one of fear than of profound disbelief, as if such a thing should not be possible in his professional, well-ordered world.

Gruff Pierre Watkin (Perry White in Columbia's 1948 and 1950 *Superman* serials) is marvelously dense and obtuse as the city's mayor. "I don't see the connection!" he snaps when Chet discusses Faraday's frog leg. Later in the scene, Mr. Mayor whines, "Of all things to happen under *my* administration!"

Karl "Killer" Davis, playing the zombie seen in the pre-title sequence, was a former professional wrestler who had appeared as himself in the celebrated tug-of-war sequence in *Mighty Joe Young* (1949). Balding and tree-trunk thick in middle age, Davis was intimidating in the extreme, not least because of the curious flatness of his gaze. Davis also can be seen as a crooked wrestler in the "No Holds Barred" episode of *The Adventures of Superman*, and as a zombie (again!) in Ed Cahn's 1957 cheapie, *Zombies of Mora Tau*.

Special mention must be made of Paul Hoffman, cast as Dunn, Buchanan's one-time enforcer who now wishes to go straight. When it's suggested to him that he be jailed for his own protection, Dunn protests, "I can't go to jail! My wife'll think I've gone back to packin' a rod!" It's a dated, absurdly false bit of dialogue made all the more amusing by Hoffman's raspy, overemphatic delivery. When he faces off later in the picture with a zombie who claims to be Buchanan, Dunn gives the creature a fishy stare: "You're nuts! *You* ain't Buchanan!" (He pronounces the last as "Boocannon," another unintentionally jocund touch.)

Special make-up is limited to the aforementioned stipple suggestive of rivets, drawn with grease pencil on a raised line of putty that horizontally bisects the zombies' foreheads. Jack Erickson's special mechanical effects, notably those fabulous bullet hits, are better than anyone has a right to expect. Destruction attributable to zombie sabotage—a grand montage of crashing trains, exploding aircraft, and sundered factories—is stock footage, some of it lifted from—what else?—Columbia serials.

Columbia staff composer Mischa Bakaleinikoff, without peer in his ability to fashion scores from bits and pieces of the studio's library music (including snippets of his own compositions), provided appropriate mood and menace, utilizing a repeated four-note motif to herald Zombie Trouble. Many scenes are augmented by the tinny, overemphatic brass that is a Bakaleinikoff trademark.

The June 22, 1955 issue of *Variety* described *Creature with the Atom Brain* as a "[h]orror programmer for lower-case bookings," and noted that the film had "minor entertainment values.... Up to a point, the picture plays with sufficient conviction to meet release demands adequately...." The reviewer cites the generous use of stock footage, and concludes, "Technical assists are standard."

These are not unfair comments, but they are considerably less fond than I would like. Granted, according to critical standards that regard, say, *Roman Holiday* and *High Noon* as good films, *Creature with the Atom Brain* is not a good film. But then, it never overreaches its ambition, either. It has no pretensions to meaningful themes or complex characterizations. As nicely as they are played, the characters are creations of a sort of shorthand, as if Siodmak discovered their personalities on file cards marked "Hero," "Wife," and so on. And although the picture tells a story, it does so incidentally, because all it really wanted to do was sell a shtick, a gimmick, an exploitable notion. And it does that very well—entertaining us, surprising us now and again, pushing our Scare Button and our Gross-Out Button, making us laugh when we're supposed to and even when we're not.

FRANKENSTEIN CONQUERS THE WORLD
by David H. Smith

Hardly anything was going right for Frankenstein's Monster in the 1960s.

Aside from scattershot releases from England's Hammer Films, the patchwork brute spent the better part of the decade as the butt of jokes on television sitcoms, shimmying his butt in a number of "nudie cuties" ("See Frankenstein do the twist with Miss Hollywood!"), or landing on his butt on several Mexican wrestling mats, grappling with masked super-heroes. It was all quite a comedown for the onetime King of the Monsters, and really quite sad in the light of his historic lineage. It would take a culture far removed from that lineage to turn the tide.

Since near the dawn of Japanese history, storytellers called *kataribe* have spun folk tales for younger generations using the ancient legends of dragons and ogres. For more than 40 years, the modern equivalents of *kataribe* have toiled behind the scenes of Japan's Toho Studios, producing dozens of science-fiction and fantasy films, featuring a menagerie of gigantic monsters and hordes of extraterrestrial invaders.

Occidental audiences wildly embraced these colorful adventures, even crudely reedited and dubbed as they were for foreign consumption. The popularity of the imported Godzilla series of films paved the way for rival studios' Gamera movies, tales of nuclear Armageddon, and countless anime features. Toho created its own mythology with its monsters, instilling them with a kind of grandeur that American movie producers seemed unwilling (or unable) to in their own tales of nature run amuck.

As the success of their exported product increased, Toho began to look more toward targeting the foreign market from the outset of production. While its indigenous legends of fire-breathing dragons had been subtly combined with the nuclear horrors their nation had suffered to produce *Gojira/ Godzilla, King of the Monsters*

(1954/1956), Toho wanted to utilize a wholly Western concept in one of its films, and only one theme intrigued company executive Tomoyuki Tanaka (1910-1997) enough: Frankenstein.

Frankenstein, or, the Modern Prometheus has been enormously popular and continuously in print in many languages since it was first published in the early 19th century. The story has inspired plays, poems, and parodies, as well as other stories, novels, and dozens of movies. *Frankenstein*'s popularity is partly because it is the first modern myth. It shows a dark side of science, out of control and out of touch with true human values. Victor Frankenstein's experiment attempts to defeat death, but his creation kills everyone he loves. Frankenstein is sometimes compared with politics, nuclear science, genetics, and other agents of change to warn against experimenting with things we do not understand.

It was unusual the Japanese would consider making a Frankenstein film.

That the Japanese would consider a Frankenstein film is unusual enough. Save for corneas and kidneys, organ transplants have long been a volatile issue in Japan, where taboos remain about cutting into bodies. In fact, the only heart transplant in Japan was performed in 1968; it failed, and the surgeon was accused of seeking frivolous fame.

Nevertheless, rumors of a Frankenstein film from Toho first emerged in the Western fan press in the first part of the sixties. Early on in the decade, special effects innovator Willis O'Brien (1886-1962) had been unsuccessful in raising the finances to film a story he had developed called *King Kong vs. Prometheus*, which would revive the artisan's 1933 stop-motion model triumph. O'Brien probably felt safe in selling the idea to Universal staff producer John Beck, whose resume of films included *The Countess of Monte Carlo* (1948) and *Harvey* (1950). When Beck took the concept across the Pacific and stood by, allowing it to be bastardized into *King Kong tai Gojira/King Kong vs. Godzilla* (1962/1963), O'Brien's exciting vision of the great ape battling a giant monster (called a "Ginko") constructed from animal parts was almost unrecognizable. It would go on to become the highest grossing *kaiju eiga* (Japanese monster movie) in Toho history.

Toho was still intent on producing a Frankenstein film with appeal to audiences homegrown and worldwide. Shinichi Sekizawa (b. 1921), at the time one-half of the studio's team of science fiction writers, submitted an unfinished screenplay in early 1963 called *Frankenstein vs. the Human Vapor* as a proposed sequel to *Gasu ningen dai ichigo/The Human Vapor* of 1960. In Sekizawa's treatment, the Vapor Man seeks out a mad scientist to revive his girlfriend killed in the auditorium explosion finale of the first film. It turns out this very scientist has found and resuscitated the original Frankenstein Monster, who becomes involved in the ghoulish scheme.

of the Horror Film   41

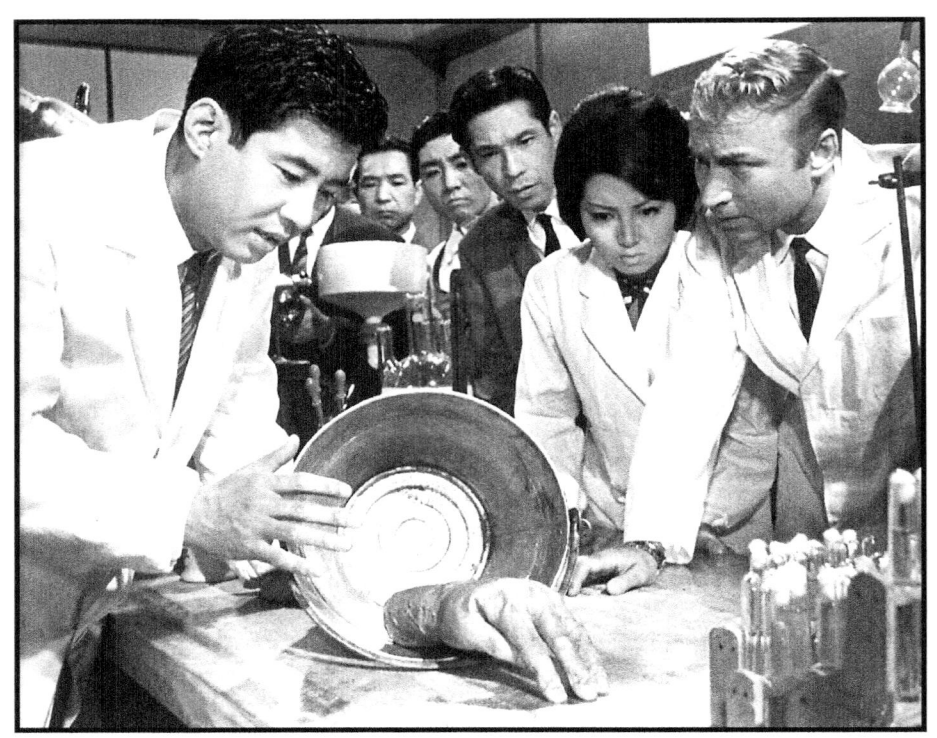

Kawaji (Tadao Takashima), Sueko (Kumi Mizuno), and Bowen (Nick Adams) scrutinize the still-living remnant of Frankenstein's escape.

Another peculiar title bandied about was *Frankenstein vs. the Giant Moth*, intended as a sequel to *Mosura/Mothra* (1961/1962), but this never went beyond advance publicity stages. Sekizawa's writing counterpart at Toho, Takeshi Shimura (b. 1912), submitted *Frankenstein vs. Godzilla*, wherein the gigantic fire-breathing reptile was to be cast against type (at the time) as a force for good, taking on a rampaging giant Frankenstein Monster.

When a set of intriguing photos of a 60-foot Frankenstein Monster battling an octopus showed up in the United States to ballyhoo the impending release of *Frankenstein vs. the Giant Devilfish*, enthusiasts were alternately intrigued by and mortified at the changes to the character.

Frankenstein Conquers the World, as it was finally entitled, was released stateside in the summer of 1966. As half of an American International Pictures double-feature with *Tarzan and the Valley of Gold*, the movie was actually produced (with sustentative financing from America) the year before in Japan as *Furankenshutain tai Chitei kaiju Baragon* or, roughly translated, *Frankenstein vs. the Subterranean Monster Baragon*.

Uniquely, for the first time in a Japanese monster movie, an American actor topped the bill from its inception. This was done specifically with an eye toward U.S. distribution rather than, as in the past, the film being sneakily reedited to include new American stars to hoodwink audiences reluctant to shell out for foreign fare. Earlier examples of this chicanery include *Jujin Yukiotako/Half Human* (1955/1958) and *Daikaiju Baran/Varan the Unbelievable* (1958/1962).

Frankenstein Conquers the World even spawned a sequel, *Furankenshutain no kaiju—Sanda tai Gairah/The War of the Gargantuas* (1966/1970), that, before U.S. release, had scenes inserted that eliminated the continuity between the two. It was as though Toho realized its mistake in changing the world-famous creature so drastically. The reviews for *Frankenstein Conquers the World* were scathing upon its release, and even in the years since, critical opinion hasn't changed all that much.

Why this continued loathing of a movie, now more than 30 years old, when other, decidedly worse offerings line video stores' shelves or receive incessant replay on premium cable TV channels?

There is a hostility toward anything deviating from the norm, in almost all facets of life and, as it pertains here, in entertainment. "Few people welcome change," wrote John McCarty in *The Modern Horror Film*, "and film critics tend to welcome it less than most." Casual filmgoers and continuity sticklers alike expect clichés when the name "Frankenstein" is invoked: thunderstorms, angry villagers, lab pyrotechnics, etc.

Now, these clichés can be hackneyed, or they can be skewed slightly for shock effect on intended audiences, but they must be employed to satisfy this zeal for convention. *Frankenstein Conquers the World*, to its critical undoing, strayed so far from what audiences and critics expected that only disdain was left.

Now, I'm not blind to the movie's failings. Fundamentally, *Frankenstein Conquers the World* is a goofy film and, structurally, it's an awkward film. But, thematically, it's a relevant film; historically, it's an original film; technically, it's a good film; commercially, it's an exploitable film; traditionally, it's an honest film; and ultimately, it's a fun film.

The beating heart of the Frankenstein Monster is sent ("nestled in a liquid") by the Third Reich to its Pacific ally in the closing months of World War II. At a military

The doctors cower before the fast-growing Frankenstein.

hospital, Japanese scientists are confident that, by gleaning the secret of immortality from "this palpitating thing," they "might learn to process or grow any section of the body" in hopes of saving lives. Obviously, the dissertation given by the scientist-in-charge (Takashi Shimura) provides the first ammo that detractors of *Frankenstein Conquers the World* choose to fire. Here, the Japanese come across as altruistic medical men, never mind the attack on Pearl Harbor, the Bataan Death March, Corregidor, Saipan, Iwo Jima, and Okinawa.

Also, the differentiation between Frankenstein the scientist and his monstrous creation, blurred over the years by a public's fragmentary knowledge of the novel and by misleading movie titles *(Frankenstein Meets the Space Monster, I Was A Teenage Frankenstein*, et al.) is wholly eliminated. "They sewed Frankenstein together and activated it—they stimulated his heart with electricity," the scientist relates, naively perpetuating the misnomer.

The military hospital's location in Japan is revealed in the next scene, as air-raid sirens whine, then a massive explosion turns the city into an inferno of flame, super-heated wind, and radioactive dust. It is Hiroshima.

In a Murphy's Law farrago of science fiction and reality, the U.S. had chosen to bomb Japan rather than Germany out of concern that a dud recovered in Germany might advance the Nazis' knowledge of how to build such weapons. The Monster's heart made the transcontinental trip just in time for an inoculation of radioactive *deus ex machina*.

After the U.S. airburst a second atomic weapon over the seaport city of Nagasaki, Japan surrendered; at the time, *Life* magazine prophetically wondered if a "Frankenstein monster" had been created with the atomic bomb.

With an establishing shot of the familiar Atomic Dome, the film cuts to 20 years later, at the Hiroshima International Institute of Radiotherapeutics, where the film introduces Dr. James Bowen (Nick Adams) as he makes his rounds. He graciously accepts an embroidered pillow from one patient who, like her fellow *hibakusha* (bomb survivors), is a moribund survivor of radiation exposure from that fateful day.

The institute Bowen and his associates Sueko (Kumi Mizuno) and Kawaji (Tadao Takashima) work at and their research are, remarkably, based on fact. There was an Atomic Bomb Casualty Commission in Hiroshima established after the war, a joint undertaking of the National Academy of Sciences and the Japanese government. A team of Japanese and American scientists did actually carry out extensive research on how the bursts over the two cities continued to affect the health and life spans of residents.

A feral child (Sumio Nakao) has been seen in the area lately, carrying off a small dog and dismembering a rabbit in an elementary school classroom. Bowen and Sueko, intrigued by the allegations of his gamy diet and tales of his first being sighted amid the ruins of the Hiroshima military hospital, assist some gun-toting rabble in cornering and capturing the wild boy in a seaside cave.

The two scientists take the boy back to their hospital, where they and Kawaji examine him. The child actor wears a rubber forehead piece, suggesting the proverbial Universal Frankenstein Monster. The dialogue here is particularly disliked by purists, as the trio of doctors conjecture, with the news media, on the child's origins.

Somewhat oblivious to the boy's sloe-eyed features, Bowen argues their patient is not Japanese, but "distinctly Caucasian." The *gaijin* scientist is excited by another aspect of their subject: "His body has received radioactivity, and this is the important part: he did not succumb to atomic disease. Instead, his body is building up a strong resistance to radiation." One shudders to think of the sadistic radiological tests conducted to ascertain these results.

Elsewhere in Japan, the foreman of an oil refinery (who coincidentally was the submarine officer who delivered the bodiless living heart to Hiroshima) catches a glimpse of a monstrous horned dinosaur emerging from beneath the earth, causing mass destruction.

The boy has now grown to the size of an adult (Koji Furuhata). Holding clipboards and looking perplexed, the doctors observe their subject watch a *Shindig*-style rock 'n' roll TV show. One of the onscreen dancers' wails of joy enrages the "monster boy" and he pitches the television out the window. (The scene was reprised in 1970's *Trog*.)

The "boy's" astonishing growth, theoretically from the radiation, means the scientists have to confine him for his own safety (!) chained to a basement wall by a wrist manacle. About 10 or 12 feet tall now, the "boy" sits in a huge cell behind iron bars (this was obviously filmed in a pre-Amnesty International era). The stolid Kawaji even thinks of him as more gorilla than anything else.

The out-of-work refinery foreman has incongruously put the mystery of the "boy's" past and the Frankenstein heart together, urging the scientists to confer with an ex-Nazi doctor practicing in Frankfurt. The Occidental actor (Peter Mann) who played the Ger-

The dinosaur displays his ungainly jumping ability with a leapfrog over Frankenstein.

man scientist in the movie's opening scene reprises his role, now sporting a conspicuous rubber bald skullcap to show the passage of years.

As Kawaji interviews the old medico, the nazified tendencies of the *Deutscher*'s past become evident as he urges the Japanese man to cut off the "boy's" arms or legs to see if new ones grow to replace them, and, as a bonus, if the severed limbs also remain alive.

One of the biggest bones of contention with *Frankenstein Conquers the World* over the years has been the exact nature of the connection between the "boy" and the heart of the original Frankenstein Monster. Early, poorly translated press materials indicated a Japanese child, having survived the nuclear firestorm, came upon the organ in the rubble and ate it (this does explain the Asian physiognomy), becoming a giant by virtue of the blast's radioactive effects.

With due attention paid to the film, however, this is seen not to be the case. The German doctor clearly states growth of a new body occurs from the undying heart. Leslie Halliwell, in *The Dead That Walk*, casually dismisses the whole conundrum, saying the filmmakers justify the "boy's" appearance in an "evasively unexplained way."

Despite Bowen's and Sueko's humanitarian objections, Kawaji nevertheless sidles to the "boy's" cell toting a cart of surgical instruments. Such duplicity is uncommon on the part of Japanese heroes in these films; one could understand Toho studio heads foisting Adams, the "Ugly American," into the role of extremist instead of one of their own countrymen. Kawaji, almost caught *in flagrante delicto* by a coterie of TV reporters, suggests the klieg lights be turned off, as their glare aggravates the giant. Exhorting the "boy," the zealous director (Haruya Kato) gets himself crushed as the giant tears off his own hand (which crawls away) breaking free of his leash, and pushes the barred door out of its jamb.

Eluding a barrage of bullets, Frankenstein pushes through a concrete wall to the street outside and scampers off into the night. About 20 feet tall now, Frankenstein still wears the pajamas given him, although the fit has become a bit snug. Frankenstein bounds over low buildings and roadways to escape the city, causing several police cars to careen off a bridge in a fiery crash.

One of the great joys of *Frankenstein Conquers the World* are these scenes of urban rack and ruin, as an obviously human performer interacts with the miniature sets audiences had become accustomed to in the Godzilla films. Unencumbered by a puffy latex suit, with this giant monster there is a more natural and, dare it be said, real feel to it. Frankenstein's height, too, while impressive, is not on the stupendous scale of his vulcanized studio cousins. The movement of clothing and even hair makes Frankenstein all the more identifiable, with no trap door jaws and spiny dorsal fins wobbling around like gray balloons.

"Larger than 10 humans" by this point, Frankenstein escapes into the forests away from the city. Unable to conceive of a way to catch him (much less what to do with him if they could), the authorities decide Frankenstein will have to be killed, martial law is declared, and heavier weapons are called up. Evidence of Frankenstein's appetite increasing geometrically with his size is shown, first by mentioning a dog has been devoured, then by showing two farm women discovering the skeletal remains of a cow.

His hand regenerated, Frankenstein roams through the forest. His shoulders are now level with the tops of the trees, his tattered clothes stretched to their limits. Uprooting a tree to hurl at a large bird flying overhead, Frankenstein misses his target and, in a flawless sequence of special effects, the tree crashes into a woodland cottage, terrifying the residents luckily working just out of range.

Hungry and frustrated, Frankenstein digs a pit out of the soft loam to trap an enormous (at least twice the world record) wild boar snuffling nearby. With the military setting up operations near the forest, a lone tank begins to reconnoiter the area. The heavy machine crashes through the leafy camouflage into the booby trap; in the U.S. version, the scene ends there, but for the Japanese audiences a bit of slapstick ensues as the shaken soldiers are nearly mowed down by the charging boar.

Bowen, Sueko, and Kawaji contemplate the why's of reports on Frankenstein's location near a remote mountain, deciding their monstrous subject "instinctively seeks a climate like that of Frankfurt, where his ancestors [sic] came from." When Kawaji scrutinizes an atlas and proudly (and wrongly) announces the Japanese mountain range is in the same latitude as Frankfurt, reality goes out the window just as surely as that TV set did earlier.

Confusion begins to reign as the dinosaur (Haruo Nakajima) glimpsed at the refinery disaster reemerges to trash a mountain lodge, killing everyone there. Frankenstein is blamed for the carnage, of course, despite the great distance separating his reported locale and the lodge.

Seen in all its glory, Baragon (unnamed in the U.S. version) is somewhat disappointing in design. The quadruped dinosaur is plainly unsuited for underground bur-

The dinosaur blasts Frankenstein with lightning bolts from his mouth, an effect displayed nowhere in the film.

rowing—the forepaws should have been large, splayed things; the goggle-eyes should have been tiny and nearly blind from the darkness, or oversized to compensate for the lack of light.

Almost as indemnification for this monster's shortcomings, Toho composer Akira Ifukube (b. 1914) produced some of his finest film scoring to accompany Baragon's rampage. With the scene set at night, the music is dark and brooding. There is a chilling leitmotif: three extended notes descending the scale, as if tolling "Frank-en-stein." To the Frankenstein film cognoscenti, it sounds like an inverse of Frank Skinner's ascending three-note theme used in *Son of Frankenstein* (1939), itself recycled in *House of Dracula* six years later.

Bowen and Sueko champion Frankenstein's innocence long enough for the rumors of a subterranean monster to be bandied about. There is a perfunctory effort to explain Baragon's survival since the Mesozoic era, as well as a scientific rationale for his glowing extremities (both theories inapplicable to higher life forms), but the doctors fail to convince their colleagues and the media that such a monster is actually responsible for the destruction.

When the doctors' efforts to stabilize Frankenstein's locale through food supplies run short of cash, they decide to venture into the foggy forest on foot to try to save the giant before the military blows him to bits (the possibility of each piece regenerating into another full-fledged monster was addressed in the sequel). Kawaji shows his true colors to Sueko and Bowen at last, planning to blind Frankenstein with chemical grenades so his heart and brain can be salvaged intact for research.

Kawaji demonstrates the power of his grenades by lobbing one at a nearby hillside, where, by the serendipity of all good (and bad) monster movies, the burrowing dinosaur just happens to be. Violently awakened, it bores out of the earth and charges the hapless scientist who, along with Bowen, futilely pitches more grenades. Sueko stumbles as the three run away, and is about to become Purina Dinosaur Chow when Frankenstein intervenes.

Frankenstein is larger than ever and completely prehistoric, with tufts of hair growing haphazardly on his body, wearing the skins of animals for clothes. There is a foreshadowing shock of orange in his black hair (à la one of the combatants in *The War of the Gargantuas*). Frankenstein and the dinosaur wrestle, with the reptile ineffectually blasting the heroic giant with some sort of heat ray from its mouth. Save for the dinosaur's leaps, which look like the empty costume being jerked into the air with wires, the battle is well choreographed and exciting.

Frankenstein is larger than ever and completely prehistoric, with tufts of hair growing haphazardly on his body, wearing the skins of animals for clothes.

Bowen, Sueko, and Kawaji drive to a nearby village and warn the citizens of the impending danger. Frankenstein stops the dinosaur before it can enter the village, stuffing a boulder into the animal's mouth, then luring it away from the terrified populace.

Frankenstein runs to the cave he has been using as a shelter and lights two tree trunks in the embers of his campfire. He charges back to the battle, brandishing them like torches—a far cry from his Universal predecessor's dread of fire.

The torches are ineffective against the dinosaur and serve only to accidentally ignite a surrounding stand of trees, which swiftly spreads into an inferno. The two giants continue their fight, leaping upon one another and tumbling. Frankenstein sees the fire eating away at the forest, uproots a tree, and begins beating at the flames. The remainder of the film is lit in a tremendously effective, hellish orange.

The dinosaur comes up behind Frankenstein, who somersaults over its bony, ridged back, and grabs its tail. With the army now joining the three scientists, they all watch as the reptile furiously digs to escape, with Frankenstein holding on in the ensuing hurricane-force winds and backwash of loose earth.

Managing to slip away, the dinosaur pops out from underground a short distance away. Frankenstein grabs the beast in a headlock and forces its jaws apart. Snippets of

The struggle between Frankenstein and the octopus is short-lived, with the latter dragging the exhausted "boy" beneath the waves.

Godzilla's familiar contrabass bellow are mixed in with its roars at this point. Frankenstein adjusts his handhold and twists the monster's neck, breaking it with an audible snap. He picks the carcass up and drops it to reassure himself of his opponent's death.

Standing over the remains, Frankenstein howls his triumph. An earthquake opens a rift under the two, and both sink into the earth.

"Frankenstein is finally dead," Sueko mourns.

"He can't die," Kawaji counters. "His heart will live on forever. One day again we will hear of him."

This is the ending familiar to American viewers of *Frankenstein Conquers the World*, whereas in Japan a wholly different finale and several minutes' running time followed. Instead of the seismic *coup de grace*, in Japan, Frankenstein hefts the dinosaur's remains and flings them down into a canyon. The tentacles of a monstrous octopus writhe from behind some rocks. Going to investigate, Frankenstein comes upon a monstrous sea beast crawling from the nearby ocean, which envelops him in its slithery arms.

Special effects for Toho had markedly improved in just a few years, as this octopus is hardly the rubbery puppet (wrapped in cellophane for a "wet" look) that grappled with the big ape of *King Kong vs. Godzilla*. In fact, the thing's appearance is so effective that it is no wonder publicity shots of the pair's battle were used to advertise the film; when those reached the U.S., however, they served only to confuse fans and vex researchers.

The struggle between Frankenstein and the octopus is short-lived, with the latter dragging the exhausted "boy" beneath the waves. It's thoroughly anticlimactic, and, although author Robert Marrero thought its deletion was "another fine example of the West's splice and dice mentality" in *Godzilla King of the Movie Monsters*, American International was probably wise in doing so.

Interviewed in *Filmfax* #45, American co-producer Henry G. Saperstein said the octopus footage was cut because of "the different tastes of Japanese and American film audiences." Likewise, a scene of Sueko stopping to pray at a memorial to the victims of Hiroshima, with Bowen self-consciously standing aside, was cut as well.

Further evidence of AIP's influence is hinted at in company co-founder Sam Arkoff's autobiography *Flying Through Hollywood By the Seat of My Pants*. There, the wheeler-dealer tells of his unscheduled vacation in Japan during *Frankenstein Conquers the World*'s production after dealing with the finagling Italian co-producers of *La Vendetta di Ercole/Goliath and the Dragon*. Inasmuch as the sword and sandal epic was made four years earlier, Arkoff's recollections seem somewhat fuzzy.

For all its detractors, *Frankenstein Conquers the World* does still have its devotees. Phil Hardy, in *The Encyclopedia of Science Fiction Movies*, said it was "one of the most inventive reworkings of the Frankenstein myth." John Stoker wrote in *The Illustrated Frankenstein*, "The plot was ingenious.... As a comic-strip [the] script worked fairly well."

Despite its (to date) unavailability on licensed home video, *The Blockbuster Guide to Movies and Video 1995* hailed it "a must for '60s Japanese horror fans." Kenneth Anger, writing about Nick Adams in *Hollywood Babylon II*, mentioned it as a "goose-flesh epic that deserves mention, if only for its name."

James Van Hise was noncommittal in *Hot Blooded Dinosaur Movies*, saying it was "easily the most bizarre version of Mary Shelley's creature ever brought to the screen," sentiments shared by Gene Wright in *The Science Fiction Image*.

Like many other writers, Tom Weaver performed a hatchet job on the movie. In the fifth issue of *Movie Club*, he condemned its meaningless title and proceeded from there. True, taken literally, the title chosen by AIP may deserve some nit-picking; however, looking at it figuratively, the title shows now that Mary Shelley's monster had, with this release, been interpreted on film by every culture; Frankenstein had truly conquered the world.

Typical for the time, the U.S. ad campaign was wildly overwrought. Posters showed a decidedly more brawny giant with a freighter tucked under one arm, catching a fighter jet with his free hand, and knocking over a suspension bridge to boot. Poor, beneficent Dr. Bowen is depicted aiming a machine gun at him.

Genre expert nonpareil Stuart Galbraith IV, in his exhaustive *Japanese Science Fiction, Fantasy and Horror Films*, wrote that, despite dull stretches, *Frankenstein Conquers the World* was "nearly saved by its interesting premise and the fine performances of Adams and Mizuno."

The performers are, indeed, among the strongest points of *Frankenstein Conquers the World*. Nick Adams (1931-1968), a successful television and big-screen actor for years (even nominated for a Best Supporting Actor Oscar for *Twilight of Honor* in 1963), signed a multi-picture deal with Toho in 1964 after actor David Janssen (1930-1980) had second thoughts about working in Japan and backed out of a similar contract.

Despite the culture shock, Adams took to Japan like a duck to water. Of *Frankenstein Conquers the World*, Adams seemed to enjoy the production, telling an interviewer, "I must say I enjoyed it very much.... I was the guy in the middle who had to fight the monsters—sort of like the referee in a [Sonny] Liston–[Cassius] Clay dancing lesson."

Adams acted as the token American in *Kaiju daisenso/ Monster Zero* (1965/1970), the sixth in the Godzilla series, and in *Kokusai Himitsu Keisatsu: Zettai zetsumei/The Killing Bottle* (1967), a straightforward spy tale. Director Ishiro Honda (1911-1993) remembered Adams as "a very passionate actor with some very good ideas."

For all its detractors, *Frankenstein Conquers the World* does still have its devotees.

Scary Monsters magazine, in a review of *Frankenstein Conquers the World* by Kent R. Daluga in its seventh issue, said that, besides Adams, the "film had a brilliantly talented Japanese cast." Heading up that roster was the attractive Kumi Mizuno (b. 1937), "the true Diva of the Toho film," so christened by *Markalite Magazine* editor August Ragnone in *Kaiju Review* #8. Denying the romantic rumors with Adams as "unfounded studio gossip," Mizuno was the favorite actress of director Honda, and is familiar to American audiences for her wide range of starring roles in other imported monster movies, including two in the Godzilla series. Similarly, shifty second lead Tadao Takashima (b. 1930), misspelled Takao in the American credits, was another face well-known to stateside audiences via his role in *King Kong vs. Godzilla* and others. In writer Martin Tropp's lofty *Mary Shelley's Monster*, Takashima was erroneously credited with the role of the Frankenstein Monster.

In the small role of the WW II research scientist was esteemed actor Takashi Shimura (1905-1982), who had had leading roles in the acclaimed films of director Akira Kurosawa. As a character actor in genre parts, Shimura is best known as the eminent paleontologist in the first two Godzilla films; he also had parts in several other Toho science fiction epics as well as in the acclaimed ghost anthology *Kwaidan* (1964).

The role of Frankenstein was played by Koji Furuhata, an actor in the Shin-Geki Theater, whose only other film role seems to have been in *L'Amour a Vingt/Love at Twenty* (1962), an unwieldy international compendium of love stories made by youthful directors from France (Francois Truffaut), Italy (Renzo Rossellini), Japan (Shintaro Ishihara), Germany (Marcel Ophuls), and Poland (Andrzej Wajda).

Furuhata is perhaps the most unjustly unrecognized actor to ever play the part of Frankenstein's Monster on film. Here he enthusiastically throws himself into the action scenes, but also quite capably handles the nuances of the monster's childlike personality. He coos and giggles like a baby over Sueko's dangling necklace in the lab, later mimes confusion and loneliness looking into a second-story apartment window, and finally, convincingly degenerates (but retaining his human and heroic nature) into a throwback as the movie proceeds.

Furuhata's lean physique seems a paradox of the muscular hulks Frankenstein Monsters are wont to be, but it suits the part here, and even evokes the image rendered in the source novel of a "being of a gigantic stature," capable of "advancing... with superhuman speed." Frankenstein here changes throughout the movie, both in size (the scale of the special effects props follows suit) and in appearance. He becomes more bestial as it goes along, and certainly more ugly, with thick veins wrinkling his neck and jagged buckteeth. By the time of the crowning battle with the dinosaur, dark lines are etched in his face, and his livid expression is one of constant rage. His is a genuinely fearsome monstrosity, as Bowen eulogizes at the finale, "[unable] to live in this world."

For an international co-production, and perhaps because of it, *Frankenstein Conquers the World* has a nice innate balance struck between the efficiency of the Japanese and the concern expressed by the American. Bowen regrets his country's nuclear action; in fact, with Adams' sincere acting, America comes off looking pretty good, and doesn't seem the veiled menace it usually does. As recently as *Gojira vs. Kingughidorah/Godzilla vs. King Ghidorah* (1991), the latter menace was in the service of time travelers from the future whose aim was to force Japan to buy foreign computers. Trade barriers, anyone?

The Japanese military in *Frankenstein Conquers the World* is shown not to be so emasculated as it has been in other Toho movies—American troops stationed in Japan, supposedly to protect the country from external threats, rarely do anything to ward off giant monsters. Here the military is competent, ready, and on the verge of success without relying on some last-minute, jerry-built mechanical contrivance.

During the early 1950s, a Japanese fishing vessel strayed too close to the Bikini atoll in the South Pacific during the detonation of an American nuclear bomb, and a fisherman subsequently died from the radiation. This was recalled in the first of the Godzilla movies; the title monster was a metaphoric reaction to the brutality of the nuclear age by its first victims, not the fatuous friend of planet Earth he devolved into.

Protests against scientists and scientific institutions grew during the Vietnam War era and, coincidentally, at about the same time as *Frankenstein Conquers the World*'s release. President Lyndon Johnson (1908-1973) recognized the public mood, telling a group of scientists gathered at the White House, "You and I both know that Frankenstein was the doctor, not the monster. But it would be well to remember that the people of the village, angered by the monster, marched against the doctor."

Most experts set the beginning date of science fiction with Mary Shelley's *Frankenstein, or, the Modern Prometheus* in 1818, a book that created a monster by serious extrapolation of known scientific theory. By the same token, the nuclear age officially began with the horrific destruction of Hiroshima in 1945, again the culmination of a brain trust working with theories of the time. "For all we know, we have created a Frankenstein!" NBC radio commentator H. V. Kaltenborn remarked when the Japanese city was destroyed.

The two horrors were united in *Frankenstein Conquers the World*, and made for a rousing, relevant, even thought-provoking movie. If Godzilla was an allegory for the terror the atomic bomb inspired, then the "boy" of *Frankenstein Conquers the World* can be seen as one representing the tragedy that ultimately results from its use.

At one point in the movie early on, Sueko begs to accompany Bowen to recapture their mutating charge.

"It's going to be dangerous," Bowen warns her.

"The boy is going to need me," she insists. "I have to go. I have to!"

Bowen grabs Sueko by the shoulders. "He's no longer a boy!" he declares, turning and leaving; Sueko begins to cry.

Coincidentally, the nickname of the atomic bomb dropped on Hiroshima was "Little Boy."

FRANKENSTEIN'S DAUGHTER
by Steve Kronenberg

My thanks to Midnight Marquee Press for the opportunity to sprint to the defense of one of my favorite guilty pleasures, the underrated and unfairly ridiculed *Frankenstein's Daughter* (1958). For a B horror movie fanatic, *Frankenstein's Daughter* has it all: Tacky, cheapjack production values, a delightfully smarmy mad doctor residing in a modern L.A. tract house, a truly insipid suburban teen rock band, and, best of all, *two*—count 'em—*two* monsters. Hammer fans aside, when I see the word "Frankenstein" in a movie title, I expect to see at least one mad doctor and one full-fledged, plug-ugly monster. *Frankenstein's Daughter* ups the ante on both of those crucial elements.

The film was released in 1958, obviously on the coattails of TV's *Shock Theater* package, AIP's Teen Monster series, and Hammer's resoundingly successful *The Curse of Frankenstein*. But unlike some of Hammer's subsequent monster-less Frankenstein fiestas, *Frankenstein's Daughter* has been critically pummeled over the years—and unfairly so. *TV Guide*'s listings invariably mention the film's "unintentional laughs" during its all-too-rare small screen showings. Phil Hardy's *Overlook Film Encyclopedia* (Overlook: 1994) describes the film as "...a decidedly shoddy teenage monster movie." In his book *Cult Science Fiction Films* (Citadel: 1993), Welch Everman likens the film to "rotgut kitsch." Maybe so, but like rotgut *whiskey*, *Frankenstein's Daughter* may not look good and may be hard to swallow—but a sustained dose is bound to put a smile on your face.

The film's plot is sophomorically simple: An unctuous descendant of the original Dr. Frankenstein (Donald Murphy) wants to follow in his ancestor's footsteps. He works for an enfeebled old chemist (Felix Locher) who has discovered a formula which regenerates dead tissue but causes startling disfigurement in whatever poor soul gets injected with the stuff. Our mad doctor, who insists on disguising his name as Dr. *Frank*, decides to slip a dose of the nasty home brew

Dr. Frank decides to slip a dose of the nasty home brew into some fruit punch, which he feeds to his employer's perky teenaged niece, Trudy (Sandra Knight).

into some fruit punch, which he feeds to his employer's perky teenaged niece, Trudy (Sandra Knight, who was married to Jack Nicholson at the time), turning her into a snaggle-toothed, bushy-browed, pop-eyed monstrosity. The mad medico then pieces together a real-live monster from scratch, and both monster and doctor are dispatched by the niece's over-age boyfriend (ubiquitous 20-something teen, John Ashley). It is the *execution* that makes the film such a delight—including some nasty surprises along the way.

The acting in *Frankenstein's Daughter* is mostly appalling, but two performances carry the show—and make it well worth watching. The film's best lines, scenes—and acting—are unarguably provided by Donald Murphy as the smarmy, arrogant Oliver Frank (enstein): "The name is *Frank*." Murphy's Frank is cold and calculating, but his chilly exterior belies his sheer joy as the film's resident mad doctor. Look at the delight in his eyes and his sleazy smile as he feeds his monster "fruit punch" formula to the hapless Trudy! Note his oily charm as he seduces sexy Sally Todd, who plays the town's resident teen tramp, Suzy Lawlor. Suzy decides to reject Frank's advances, only to watch Frank run her over with his car in a wild-eyed frenzy in order to obtain her head for his home-made monster. We savor Murphy's final moments of lunacy as he tries to seduce Trudy, is rejected again, then plans to *permanently* transform her into a monster: "You've always treated me like a monster. Now you're going to *be* one!"

Murphy is also delighted with his own patchwork Frankenstein Monster, calling it "magnificent" and embracing it as a killing machine whose female brain can be conditioned "...to take orders in a man's world!"

The other notable mad doctors of the late 1950s were played by Peter Cushing and Whit Bissell. It is pointless to compare Murphy's thespic talent with Cushing's.

The film's best lines, scenes—and acting—are unarguably provided by Donald Murphy (on the right) as the smarmy, arrogant Oliver Frank (enstein).

But Murphy compares most favorably with Bissell. In AIP's *I Was a Teenage Werewolf* (1957), and *I Was a Teenage Frankenstein* (1957), Bissell delivers credible, workmanlike performances, but they are neither as interesting or as fun to watch as Murphy's work in *Frankenstein's Daughter*. Murphy's Oliver Frank is truly a mad medico for modern times, as earnest, obsessed, and maniacal as any "classic" mad scientist, while possessing the arrogance, charm, and oiliness of a Las Vegas lounge lizard. Indeed, Murphy's smarmy cruelty was later perfected by Michael Gough in such films as *Horrors of the Black Museum* (1959), *Konga* (1961), and *The Black Zoo* (1963).

But Murphy's delightful histrionics would not work without a complementary performance by Wolfe Barzell as Elsu, the gardener who doubles as Frank's assistant. In the film, Barzell's Elsu verbally invokes the Frankenstein lineage and legend by telling Frank how he once obtained corpses for Frank's father. In fact, as a leering degenerate obsessed with Frank's mad experiments, Barzell resembles Dwight Frye's Fritz. But Barzell also echoes Bela Lugosi's Ygor in his desire to protect and shelter Frank's final, monstrous creation from the police and, ultimately, Frank himself.

The chemistry between Murphy and Barzell, as mad doctor and murderous assistant, is one of the grand delights of *Frankenstein's Daughter*. The relationship between both characters also ties the film directly to the classics—a connection which does not exist in the other "teenage" monster films of the 1950s.

Murphy's Oliver Frank is truly a mad medico for modern times, as earnest, obsessed, and maniacal as any "classic" mad scientist.

If only the rest of the acting in the film were as interesting and enjoyable as Murphy's and Barzell's performances. Felix Locher is atrocious as Carter Morton, Trudy's doddering uncle and Frank's employer. Locher looks enfeebled enough as Morton, but he acts and sounds as if he is reading every line from a gigantic cue card. Yet, Locher's garbled delivery and Germanic accent add to the film's fun. He gets to spout lines such as: "I somehow get the impression he's a-spying on him"; "You vill drive me to distraction"; "Nothing is going stop me from completing this experiment." Locher's enunciation makes Tor Johnson sound like John Barrymore by comparison. Yet, Locher's facial ugliness and foreign accent add to the film's dreary, grim tone.

Sally Todd, another low-budget fifties B girl, is almost as stilted as Locher. In such films as *Frankenstein's Daughter* and *The Unearthly* (1957), Todd specialized in playing sultry, tawdry bombshells who purr their way through a film, then come to a nasty and abrupt end. Todd was great to look at (her shapely derriere adorns the posters for *The Unearthly*), but when she opened her mouth to deliver her lines, her appeal suddenly diminished.

Sandra Knight may have been married to Jack Nicholson at the time she made *Frankenstein's Daughter*, but her husband's acting skills never rubbed off on her. Knight's performance in the film is simply awful, laced with melodramatic histrionics. Indeed, her best scenes show her running through the streets of Los Angeles in Harry Thomas' monster make-up. Knight teamed with both Nicholson *and* Boris Karloff in Roger Corman's *The Terror* (1963), an incomprehensible mess that was vastly inferior to *Frankenstein's Daughter*.

John Ashley fares little better as the film's hero, despite his somewhat interesting performance in AIP's *High School Caesar* (1958). As in most of his horror films, Ashley comes off more as a geek than a leading man. At least Todd, Knight, and Locher are fun to watch; Ashley's performance is merely dull.

The low-budget fun of *Frankenstein's Daughter* comes not only from its make-up, monsters, and madmen. H.E. Barrie's script is a joy to behold. In one scene, Murphy comes on to Knight as she prepares for an evening swim. When she rejects him, he asks her where she is going. Her reply: "Into the pool to take a cold swim. *And I suggest you take a cold shower*!" When Knight tries to tell Ashley that Murphy is turning her into a monster, Ashley responds with: "The day someone as pretty as you turns into a monster is the day the moon comes down in my backyard!" A hysterical woman who runs into Knight's monster describes her as "a terrible looking woman in a bathing suit!" And a newspaper headline following one of Knight's monstrous rampages blares: "Woman Monster Terrorizes City!"

But Frank's home-made female monster—the "Frankenstein's Daughter" of the title—is the film's crowning touch. The monster is played by Harry Wilson, who once dubbed himself "the ugliest man in Hollywood," and started out as Wallace Beery's double in the 1930s. Wilson is no Boris Karloff, nor is he even a Glenn Strange. But his jerky, robotic movements as the monster augment the creature's creepiness. Indeed, the transformation of Sandra Knight into a temporary teen monster is only a warm-up for the full-fledged real thing we see later on in the film.

The *real* monster's face looks as if its left side were ground down with a high-speed power sander. A bandage covers the entire head, and black rubber gloves and a shiny black rubber suit adorn the creature. The nose is split, broadened, and shows a nasty, bloody gash down the center that extends upward to the top of the forehead. The monster's swollen, protuberant lips are smeared with lipstick—the result of the make-up artist being told only at the last minute that Frank's creation was supposed to be female!

In Tom Weaver's *Interviews with B Science Fiction and Horror Movie Makers* (McFarland & Company: 1988), the film's director, Richard Cunha, states that he was disappointed with the final result of the monster's make-up, but money ran out before he could perfect the desired appearance of the creature. Cunha need not have worried. The monster's make-up is eerily, gruesomely effective. Jack Pierce's work always conveyed a strange sensitivity, symmetry, and yes, beauty. In *Frankenstein's Daughter*, the make-up is the polar opposite of Pierce's, denoting mutilation and corruption even more effectively than Hammer's Phil Leakey.

Still, the best make-up work in the film comes at the very end, when Frank receives a fatal facial with a thrown bottle of acid. The camera unflinchingly shows a close-up of Frank's bubbling, burning face just before he collapses and dies. The close-up of Murphy's acid-eaten face is the film's supreme shock moment. As far as I know, it is also the first scene of its kind. Before *Frankenstein's Daughter*, I can't think of another horror film that contains a scene as singularly gruesome. In Midnight Marquee's first *Guilty Pleasures* volume, David J. Hogan persuasively argues that the makeup in *The Flesh Eaters* was the first to show gory, gruesome mutilation. But *Frankenstein's Daughter* preceded *The Flesh Eaters* (made in 1960 and released in 1964) by two years—and I would match Murphy's acid scene with any of the make-up in *The Flesh Eaters*.

Murphy's delightful histrionics would not work without a complementary performance by Wolfe Barzell as Elsu, the gardener who doubles as Frank's assistant.

The question of exactly who performed the make-up chores in *Frankenstein's Daughter* may still be debatable. The film's credits list Harry Thomas as the make-up artist. Thomas was to 1950s B horror movies what Jack Pierce was to Universal's Golden Age. Thomas plied his trade for Ed Wood and AIP, among others. Yet, in his interview with Tom Weaver, Richard Cunha insists that Paul Stanhope designed the make-up for both Harry Wilson's monster and Murphy's acid scene. In that same interview, Cunha insists that Thomas' contribution consisted only of Sandra Knight's two monstrous transformations. On the other hand, in an interview in *Filmfax* #21, Harry Thomas insists that *he* designed and applied all the make-up for the film, even insisting that Murphy's acid-burned face was the most frightening make-up he'd ever done. John "J.J." Johnson's book, *Cheap Tricks and Class Acts* (McFarland & Company: 1996) also credits Thomas with the make-up chores in *Frankenstein's Daughter*. Johnson relates that Thomas took only five minutes in fashioning Murphy's acid-burned face, using hair gel stuck to wrinkled pieces of lens paper, then filling holes in the paper with chocolate. Johnson also notes that Thomas wanted to redo Harry Wilson's monster make-up, after learning that the creature was supposed to be female. In fact, according to Johnson, Thomas tried to persuade producer Marc Frederic to add a wig and redo the eyes, to make the creature look more like Sally Todd. Frederic's schedule and budget would not allow for the changes, so Johnson reports that Thomas used spirit gum, stretched cotton, plastic collodion, and liquid make-up to fashion Frank's memorable monster. Regardless of who did the make-up—Stanhope or Thomas, or both—*Frankenstein's*

Daughter exemplifies how gruesome and unforgettable make-up effects can be performed quickly and cheaply.

By the way, in the scene in which the monster catches fire and burns to death, the creature is played not by Wilson, but by George Barrows, whose ape suit was a mainstay of B movies in the 1940s and 1950s, including the infamous *Robot Monster* (1953).

The director of *Frankenstein's Daughter*, Richard Cunha, must be given his due for some of the film's quirky, creepy, bargain-basement delights. The scenes of Wilson's monster shambling his way through the tract house where Frank lives is as surreal as anything in *Plan 9 From Outer Space*. There is also a scene of the monster creeping down the steep stairway to Frank's basement laboratory, with a bare stone wall in the background, reminiscent of (but not comparable to) certain scenes in the original *Frankenstein*. And with the exception of a truly insipid teen dance party scene, Cunha moves the film along at rapid-fire pace with no dull spots.

Like Ed Wood and Herbert L. Strock, Cunha's reputation is that of a schlockmeister. But unlike Strock, who toiled for AIP, Cunha's domain was Astor Pictures, a bottom-dwelling studio that made AIP look like MGM. But *Frankenstein's Daughter* is scarier and more fun than any of AIP's other teen monster outings, such as *Blood of Dracula* (1957), *I Was a Teenage Werewolf* (1957), and *I Was a Teenage Frankenstein* (1957).

In *Interviews With "B" Science Fiction and Horror Movie Makers*, Tom Weaver discusses the fact that Cunha's canon of horror-science fiction films has been ignored for too long. In his introduction to the Cunha interview, Weaver notes that at one point Cunha was rumored to have disappeared in the Peruvian jungle, despondent over the bad reviews received by his films. In fact, Weaver's book reports that Cunha was running a video shop in Oceanside, California, and had directed television commercials after leaving the movie business in 1961. In addition to *Frankenstein's Daughter*, Cunha directed three other low-budget genre delights, all of which bear watching. There is the Frankensteinian *She Demons* (1958), featuring Nazi mad doctors, mutilated make-up, and then-Sheena TV star, Irish McCalla; *Giant from the Unknown* (1959), featuring B movie stalwarts Ed Kemmer and former heavyweight prize fighter, Buddy Baer. Cunha's *cojones* are probably best displayed in 1958's *Missile to the Moon*, in which the director actually attempted to remake the infamous *Cat Women of the Moon* (1954), though Cunha's film was decidedly superior to the original. But in my opinion, *Frankenstein's Daughter* remains Cunha's *magnum opus*.

Sure, there is plenty to laugh at in *Frankenstein's Daughter*: Cheesy production values, stilted dialogue, some God-awful acting, and overage actors trying to pass as teenagers. But the film also has a memorable mad doctor, a delightfully deranged lab assistant, *two* monsters with moxie, and a shining moment of unprecedented grue and gore. In addition to all those qualities, *Frankenstein's Daughter* is pure fun, devoid of the brooding, troubled, and depressed teenagers that inhabited so many fifties monster movies. "Rotgut kitsch?" In my opinion, *Frankenstein's Daughter* is the Dom Perignon of teenage monster movies.

THE GIANT GILA MONSTER
by Jim Doherty

As a child growing up in the sixties, I scoured the TV guide for every science fiction and horror film I could find. I was fascinated by them, and loved almost all of them with the blind, defensive kind of love a parent has for a child he thinks can do no wrong. I actually liked *The Cape Canaveral Monsters*, and was frightened by the turkey marionette in *The Giant Claw*. Yet, in my immature naiveté, I thought *The Giant Gila Monster* was incredibly bad. But oddly, I would go out of my way to watch it every time it was on, drawn to it by a power greater than Universal-International and AIP combined.

While preparing to write this piece, I watched the film over and over, expecting to find glaring flaws and laughable inadequacies to ridicule. I was not disappointed. However, I also discovered, lying in wait beneath the surface, more than a few termites of quality threatening to eat away at the foundations of crudity and amateurism on which the film would appear to be built.

With this revelation, the mystery of my fascination with this film began to unravel.

"Only Hell could breed such an enormous beast... Only God could destroy it!" proclaims the poster for *The Giant Gila Monster*. But don't worry, it won't be *all* doom and gloom, for the poster also promises "Rock and Roll Hits: *My Baby She Rocks*, *I Ain't Made that Way*, and *The Gila Monster Crawl*"! (Wowee, Skip, let's go!). The artwork depicts a giant scaly claw reaching down to crush a hot rod piloted by two hapless teens. On the surface, that actually sums up the film rather well. Released in 1959, it tried to cash in on just about every genre craze in vogue at the time. It's got the giant monster (or reasonable facsimile thereof), it's got hot rods, it's got rock 'n' roll. It even adds a few soap opera touches. In a peculiarly well-crafted script for a film of this ilk, screenwriter Jay Simms intertwines each of these elements in a surprisingly deft manner, each one relating to the other and somehow smoothly fitting into the story. Scriptwise, this film actually has a lot more going for it than many of its big studio cousins.

The film wastes no time in setting up its premise. Over a shot of a deserted, tangled wooded area somewhere "in the enormity of the West," an offscreen narrator sternly asserts that "it is in these lonely areas of impenetrable forest and dark shadows, that the gila monster still lives. How large the dreaded gila monster grows, no man can say." Well, no man has to say, for in the next scene, the viewer is shown how large it can grow. A pair of turtledoving teens, sitting in their hot rod, listening to rock 'n' roll music, are shoved into a deep chasm by a terrifying striped blur. Be warned that this is the most convincing effect in the whole movie, much more so than the prop man's arm dressed in a giant gila monster claw which attacks the camera in the next shot, turning the screen to black as the main title appears.

Two young lovers meet their doom at the claws of The Giant Gila Monster*!*

Let's recap. So far, there's been rock 'n' roll, a hot rod, and a monster... and that's only in the first minute! Wow, truth in advertising! This movie is going to be good!

After the credits, the scene shifts to Spook's Diner, where the young hero-to-be, Chace Winstead (Don Sullivan), is hanging out with his pals. Two other important players are also introduced in this scene. The first is Chace's girlfriend, Lisa, a foreign exchange student from France. The fact that she's French really has no bearing on the story, but it does add a little color to the character. (The most probable reason the character is French is because the producers managed to snare Lisa Simone, Miss France of 1957, for the role.) Harris, the friendly old town drunk (spelled C-O-M-E-D-Y R-E-L-I-E-F), played by Shug Fisher, also debuts in this scene. The kids are a little concerned that their friends Pat Wheeler and Liz Humphries haven't shown up yet (and they're not going to, as they were the unfortunate ravine crashers seen before the credits).

They're not the only ones wondering about their whereabouts. Pat's father (Bob Thompson) has called in the sheriff (Fred Graham). In a short scene between Mr. Wheeler and the sheriff, several points are made clear. 1.) Mr. Wheeler is the B.M.O.C. in this town. He owns the oil field (where a good number of the townspeople probably work). By the size of his palatial mansion, it's apparent he's rolling in dough. (Well, at least it's palatial in the exterior shot. The inside is just a small dingy set.) In a town where everyone is on a first-name basis, the fact that the sheriff calls him Mr. Wheeler is a good indication of the man's position. 2.) Mr. Wheeler thinks Chace Winstead is a bad influence on the other kids: "He's older than the others. Sets 'em all wrong. Why, he's got more influence on Pat than I do." The jealousy hinted at in that last line is probably all that's behind Wheeler's anger; he really has nothing else to pin on Chace. The whole concept of the important dad not being able to communicate with his son, and not wanting him to marry someone beneath his station (a point brought up in upcoming scenes), is quite similar to a plot thread in *Peyton Place*, released two years earlier. 3.) The sheriff is pro-Chace: "Chace Winstead does more about keeping them in line than getting them in trouble than I know. He's supported his mother and sister ever since his dad was killed on one of your drill rigs. Your son could take a page out of his book, Mr. Wheeler." This kind of mutual respect and friendship between peace-loving hot-rodders and the lawman is a staple item of many hot rod films of the period, including *Hot Rod Girl* (1956) and *Motorcycle Gang* (1957). It is also a major contributor to the script of *The Blob* (1958).

Following up on the idea that Pat and Liz might have eloped, the sheriff pays a call at Compton's Garage, where Chace works. After asking Chace a few questions, including the possibility of Liz being pregnant (another popular theme of the day, famous from films like *A Summer Place* and *Blue Denim*), the sheriff rides out to the home of Liz's parents, a small dwelling, not much more than a large shack with nice siding. As the sheriff pulls up, the audience is informed of the Humphries' occupations as farmers in a very efficient, if not very subtle, way as a farmhand drives through the foreground on a tractor. In a brief conversation with Eb and Agatha Humphries on their front porch (actually the same set used as the interior of Mr. Wheeler's house, just slightly redressed, and of course, not matching the exterior long shot in the least), it becomes clear that Eb doesn't find the elopement idea very plausible ("Ma, the likes of Wheeler ain't marryin' our kind of folks"). The Humphries' unassuming attitudes and friendliness are in direct contrast to Mr. Wheeler's anger and self-importance. Their concern for their daughter and Eb's final (probably ad-libbed) lines as they go back inside ("We've gotta quit worryin' this way. We've gotta trust in the Lord. We've gotta pray") puts the audience

As a favor to the sheriff (Fred Graham), Chace (Don Sullivan) makes a thorough search of the neighboring territory for any traces of Pat and Liz.

on their side. In a comedic tag to the scene, the sheriff stops Harris, who is passing in his car, and asks to smell his breath. Although unnecessary to this scene, it does set up the idea that Harris can usually be expected to be drunk, which will figure into later scenes.

Back at Compton's Garage, Mr. Compton (Cecil Hunt) returns and complains to Chace about the "hot" load he just brought back with him in his truck—four quarts of nitroglycerin. Now even an idiot can pretty much tell that the nitro is somehow going to be important later in the film. However, the script is careful to make the nitro's presence plausible. It seems that Mr. Wheeler is sinking a new oil well and wants the nitro handy in case of fire when it comes in. Chace also pre-explains his later dexterity with the nitro by saying, "You know, last winter when [oil well] number 21 came in, I made a hundred bucks with that stuff. Dad showed me how to use it. It's not so bad, as long as it doesn't get nervous." An unintentionally funny moment now occurs as Chace takes the dangerous nitro out to the storage shed for safe keeping, then doesn't bother to lock or even close the shed door.

A side note here. The overabundance of Mobil products in the garage scenes (Mobil fan belts, Mobil oil filters, and signs for Mobilgas, Mobiloil, and Mobil Tires) gives the distinct impression that some local Mobil dealer pitched in a few bucks in exchange for giving his products the high-visibility treatment.

After all this setup, the action is finally about to begin... almost. There's been a car wreck just outside of town. At the crash site, the sheriff and Chace observe that the skid marks are at a 90-degree angle to the road, as if the car had been pushed off the road sideways. There's blood on the front seat, yet there's no body anywhere to be found. As a setup for an upcoming scene, the discussion switches to Chace's little sister, Missy.

"The doctor says she'll be able to start walking again pretty soon, and it took all the money I had to make a down payment on her braces," says Chace. The whole idea of Chace's sister needing leg braces is really irrelevant, but, just as the French accent adds a touch of character to the role of Lisa, this provides a good moment of development for the character of Chace.

Meanwhile, a hitchhiker has a deadly encounter with the big gila, which the audience finally gets to see in full... all two feet of it. By far, the film's worst component is the special effects work. According to the film's pressbook, *Gila Monster* director Ray Kellogg worked as a "special effects wizard" at Twentieth Century-Fox for 30 years, and "according to Hollywood film editors, scenes in [*The Giant Gila Monster*] are his finest achievements." These great achievements consist entirely of tabletop miniature photography, credited to Ralph Hammeras and Wee Risser. Never are the miniatures and the live action combined in a single shot. Further exacerbating the bargain basement feel is the fact that no matter what shot the gila monster is in, no matter how it is lit, or what miniature props are used, the "monster" is always obviously fake. Plus, the way the shots are inserted into scenes is often ambiguous or disorienting. It's usually impossible to tell whether the monster is coming or going, whether it's on this side of the road or the other, whether it's 20 feet away or 200. One gets the impression that the filmmakers grabbed a camera and got as many shots of the little gila monster as possible—gila monster staring, gila monster flipping its tongue out, gila monster thinking about being cast in a film with better effects—and then randomly inserted them as they were needed. Close scrutiny will also reveal that on more than one occasion, the uncooperative gila was given a little help to move him on his way. There are several shots where it is quite obvious that the monster is being shoved by hand, its front legs either dragging through the dirt or not touching the ground at all.

In an ensuing scene, the monster forces a speeding car to swerve off the road. Conveniently, Chace is driving by soon after the accident, with the service station tow truck. "Are you all right?" he asks. Getting out of the car, the middle-aged driver (Ken Knox), obviously quite sloshed, replies, "Dad, I'm superb! Seven to a box, no corners. I'm a round hound!" "Sorry I asked," Chace retorts.

Chace tows the car in and fixes the fender as the guy sleeps it off, or tries to at least. It's a little hard to doze off while Chace is banging out dents in the next room, singing a little rock ditty, *My Baby She Rocks*... no accompaniment, just Chace and his trusty ball-peen. (And this is what the poster referred to as a rock 'n' roll hit?) As luck would have it, the guy Chace towed in is none other than Steamroller Smith, the coolest disc jockey around, who tells Chace to look him up when he's town. Boy, fate sure works in mysterious ways.

As a favor to the sheriff, Chace, Lisa, and a couple of their friends make a thorough search of the neighboring territory for any traces of Pat and Liz. While investigating a long ravine, Chace discovers evidence of a large animal having dragged something through it. Stopping at a stream for a sip of water, Chace spits out his first mouthful, exclaiming, "Oooo, that's bitter. Must have an awful lot of mineral in it." Once again, the script neatly interjects a tidbit of important information, without putting it up on stage under spotlights. Around this time, it vaguely appears that the gila monster is stalking Chace and Lisa. (As was pointed out earlier, the camera angles and editing make it difficult to tell exactly where the monster is in relation to the characters.) But

Chace pulls out his little banjo-uke and mesmerizes the rocking teens with a few haunting choruses of *The Mushroom Song*.

not to worry, for just as the jumbo lizard is licking its lips, the sound of their friends' car horn summons Chace and Lisa back. The friends have found Pat and Liz's car in the ravine a few miles back, minus Pat and Liz of course.

That evening, Mr. Compton is delivering a load of fuel oil in a tanker truck when the gluttonous lizard appears. Upon seeing the monster, Mr. Compton, as one would expect, screams. Then the tanker, for no real reason apparent on the screen, turns over into the roadside ditch and explodes. (In an upcoming scene, the sheriff asserts that the truck was pushed right off the road, judging by the tire marks, which again are at a right angle to the road. However, due to some poor effects planning, there is no gila monster anywhere near the truck as it suddenly tumbles into the ditch.)

Meanwhile, back at the Winstead household, Chace returns home to find his mother waiting with a surprise. Lisa has bought Chace's little sister Missy her leg braces. Missy (Janice Stone) tries to walk across the room to Chace, but falls after a few steps, crying and disappointed because "I've been practicing all afternoon, and walked all the way twice." To cheer her up, Chace instantly decides to sing a song. Grabbing a nearby ukulele-sized banjo, Chace launches into a cute, if rather out of place, little religious number entitled *The Mushroom Song*. Missy smiles politely through lyrics of mushrooms, meadows, birds, and gardens that are sad until the Lord creates a girl and a boy, and instructs them all to "laugh, children, laugh." (No wonder this song wasn't mentioned in the poster's list of rock 'n' roll hits.) Ironically, it is during this happy song that the viewer sees the most horrifying element in the film: close-ups of Missy. Whoever cast this actress must have been blind to the fact the she looks frighteningly like a male midget. Her helmet-head hair style is extremely reminiscent of that of Davey's

The Giant Gila Monster attacks the dance hall.

little sister Sally in the *Davey and Goliath* animated films, her eyebrows are thick and dark, and thanks to the unflattering lighting, she appears to have a mustache.

Fortunately, the scene soon ends as a report of the oil truck sends Chace out to investigate. At the wreckage (which impressively uses a full-size burning truck!), the sheriff clues Chace in on some important oddball info. "You would have no reason to know about this, but there's been a lot of livestock missing lately. One here, one there. That doesn't make headlines... but now it's people." About the crash, the sheriff ponders, "What batters a car around like it was a toy?" (Apparently, Missy, the mustachioed midget, is not suspected.)

The following day, Chace cashes in on Steamroller Smith's indebtedness and gets him to spin records at their platter party that night at Hardy Hay's barn.

But that evening, disaster strikes again. Harris is driving his old Model A, swigging down some hooch, when he decides to play a little "beat the train" at a railroad crossing. This scene contains one of the film's best continuity gaffes. The first time the train is shown, it's a diesel locomotive. In its next appearances, it magically changes into two different freight train engines. Harris beats the train at the crossing, but his thrill of victory is short lived, for just ahead, the giant gila monster has destroyed a railroad trestle over a ravine. Harris comes to a quick stop as he spots the oversized gila lounging across the road ahead. He rubs his eyes in disbelief (as the reflection of a cameraman with a wonderfully shiny watch is seen in his windshield). Just then, the magic train, which has now been transformed into a beautiful Lionel, derails very unrealistically into the ravine. Apparently, everyone aboard the train was asleep, as it takes several seconds after the crash for anyone to finally scream. The smell of burning plastic fills the air as the voracious gila heads back toward the smoldering toy train. (Considering what old model trains are worth today, this was probably, in retrospect, the film's most expensive effect.)

Harris heads back into town to tell the sheriff about the destruction of the miniature train by the bus-sized beast, but the sheriff is skeptical because of Harris' 180-proof breath. However, he does call Chace to request that he bring over a book on reptiles. When Chace drops it off on his way to the dance, the sheriff explains that he's been talking with a zoologist about animal growth. The sheriff's theory, based on the zoologist's information and the testimony of Harris and some of the train wreck survivors, is that a gila monster has been turned into a giant by an out-of-whack thyroid or "pituitory" (sic) gland, caused by a change in diet. (Ah ha! Remember Chace's earlier throwaway line about the water having "an awful lot of mineral in it"?) How refreshing it wasn't caused by the standard nuclear mutation. As Chace ponders the horrible possibility of his friends and Mr. Compton ending up as giant gila monster excrement, the sheriff offers the sage advice, "Try and forget about it for now, and have some fun, will ya, boy?"

At the dance at the barn (which incidentally, looks just like a barn on the outside, but suspiciously like a clean, bare sound stage inside), Chace unveils the surprise M.C. of the evening, Steamroller Smith, who plays a couple of rockin' numbers before putting on a mystery record by "a fella that dropped by at KILT the other day. We got a little pick-up group together, and cut a demo disc." After playing a whopping 32 seconds of *I Ain't Made That Way* (another one of the "rock 'n' roll hits" misleadingly mentioned on the poster), Steamroller interrupts it to ask if anyone can identify the singer/songwriter. Guesses range from Elvis to Kate Smith, but only Lisa has the real answer. That's right, "Chace did it!" When asked why he didn't tell anyone else, Chace replies, "Well I didn't know if it was anything I'd want to admit to." If he didn't want to admit to that song, what happens next is without explanation. Steamroller announces, "At the station the other day, Chace played me another little song. It's kind of different from this one [You can say that again], but with a little coaxing, he might give you a little preview of it." Encouraged by the crowd's applause, Chace pulls out his little banjo-uke and mesmerizes the rocking teens with a few haunting choruses of *The Mushroom Song*. At first the crowd seems to dig its rhythm, and starts to rock back and forth. But after a quick cutaway, showing the gila monster approaching the outside of the barn, the teens are suddenly standing catatonically, either entranced by the song's inventive freshness, or just wishing it would end. Some try halfheartedly to sing along, resulting in a kind of zombified group murmur. Fortunately for everyone involved, the huge gila takes this opportunity to crash through the barn wall, or more accurately, have its head shoved through the balsa wood miniature wall by some prop man. (Please note that the model wall changes quite noticeably from shot to shot.) Everyone begins to panic, prompting Chace to yell a very ineffective, "Don't panic!" The recently arrived sheriff pumps a few rifle rounds into the rambunctious reptile, managing to frighten it off. Chace, abandoning his banjo-lele, hops into his hot rod with Lisa and heads back to the garage with the brilliant notion of using the four quarts of nitro to dispatch the beast. Driving back toward the barn with the nitro jiggling all over the front seat, Chace discovers that the insidious beast has doubled back and hit the home of the Blackwell family, where Missy was spending the night! The house is a shambles and deserted. Hoping to find the Blackwells and Missy, Chace cuts across a deserted bumpy field. Amazingly, they are not blown up, and within seconds, he finds Mrs. Blackwell and Missy *running* across the field (apparently Missy has made a miraculous recovery). Lisa hits the dirt with

The amount of screen time directly related to the monster's attacks is only about seven minutes, or roughly 1/11 of the film's running time.

Missy, as Chace speeds off toward the nearby giant gila. Setting his speeding roadster on a collision course with the murderous monster, Chace leaps to safety just in time to see his car plow into the beast and go Ka-plooey! The great beast is made to pay for the lives it has taken, as well as the destruction of the Tonka oil truck and the Lionel Express. Chace is despondent over the loss of his "brand new, 100 percent completed hot rod," but the sheriff opines, "The railroad will be glad to buy you a new one," in repayment for destroying the giant train derailer. As the monster roasts, everyone heads home, safe and happy.

The amount of screen time directly related to the monster's attacks is only about seven minutes, or roughly 1/11 of the film's running time. This helps the film succeed in more ways than one. The most obvious reason is that the effects are so laughable, they deserve as little screen time as possible. The more important reason is that this is not primarily a story about a giant gila monster; it is a story about the everyday lives of the people in this small town, and how the imposition of this monster affects those lives.

Some of the most interesting films to watch are those which create their own world in which the story unfolds. Very few have done this successfully. *Blade Runner* was one, with its unique view of a future that was somehow familiar, yet not familiar, a sort of retro/future amalgam... something unlike that to which audiences were accustomed. It succeeded in creating that world so distinctly, that the privilege of just being able to experience it is almost as satisfying as watching the storyline unfold. Other films which have also achieved this to a great degree are *Dragonslayer*, *Edward Scissorhands*, and especially *Eraserhead*. Unwittingly, *The Giant Gila Monster* accomplishes the same

If viewed as a normal dramatic film that just happens to have a monster in it, *The Giant Gila Monster* is surprisingly well crafted,

thing. Without intentionally trying to do it, the producers have captured the aura of a small hick town of the late fifties. Of course, when the film was released in 1959, nobody would have noticed that. But looking back from a modern perspective, the film vividly recreates that world for people who might have missed it the first time around. Everything feels real (with the exception of the monster of course), because in many cases, it is real. The low budget did not allow the film to "go Hollywood." The outdoor scenes, shot at Cielo, Texas, genuinely look like the middle of nowhere, most of the actors probably wore their own clothes, the hot rods were rented from local Texas drag race enthusiasts, etc. It all blends together to create an inherent sense of reality unmatched by big-budget Hollywood films of the period.

The direction by Ray Kellogg (who later would permanently stain his career by directing a film far more ridiculous than this one, *The Green Berets*) is restrained, yet oft times inventive, with some subtle, unobtrusive dolly work. He tells the story simply, a pattern also followed by others working on the film.

The script, as has been pointed out, also emphasizes the ordinary and the simple. The monster is not explained by some nuclear scientist, but instead is figured out by everyday people using little more than common sense. The characters are down to earth, and possess more depth than one would anticipate in this kind of film. The dialogue is natural, and well suited to the characters (the hip slang for the disc jockey, the folksiness of Harris, etc.).

The acting in the major roles is, for the most part, also commendably natural, with the distinct exception of Bob Thompson's wooden portrayal of Mr. Wheeler. Don Sullivan, veteran of TV roles on *Death Valley Days* and *M Squad*, and later star of *The Monster of Piedras Blancas,* is fine as Chace; he's not overtly cute or manly, he's just an average guy. His singing voice, when he gets to use it, is also pleasant in the same unassuming way. A minor question though: Why is Chace about the only person in the film without some degree of a Southern accent, especially in light of the rather thick ones displayed by his mother and Missy?

The teenage partygoers express shock at the arrival of the new guest.

Naturalness is also the key to Fred Graham's portrayal of the sheriff. Through his friendly, fatherly demeanor, he indicates that the sheriff is dedicated to his job, yet he's also one of the locals. He knows everyone by name, and his concern for them is genuine. Graham's role in *The Giant Gila Monster* is one of his largest. He is more commonly seen in smaller supporting roles, including appearances in *The Fighting Kentuckian* (1949), *Angels in the Outfield* (1951), and *20,000 Leagues Under the Sea* (1954). He also worked as a stuntman, perhaps most memorably in 1938's *The Adventures of Robin Hood*, taking the climactic fall for Basil Rathbone.

Even Lisa Simone peppers her performance with some wonderfully subtle techniques. Her shining moment comes in a brief scene where she secretly meets Chace to tell him that Mr. Wheeler (who happens to be her sponsor in the foreign exchange student plan) has threatened to send her back to France if she continues to see Chace. As Chace tries to reassure her, her concern, confusion, and ultimate belief in Chace's reassurance and love is conveyed through a stream of subtle averted glances, short thoughtful pauses, a moment of distracted playing with Chace's jacket collar, a tender look at Chace, and the slightest trace of a smile just before they kiss. Previously, Miss Simone had had roles in French television shows, Italian films, and some American TV shows like *The George Burns and Gracie Allen Show*.

Shug Fisher did comedy and country singing stints in live tours with Roy Rogers and The Sons of the Pioneers, as well as roles in films, including a bit in *Mister Roberts* (1955).

Although Wilfrid Cline's photography of the cheap indoor sets is generally nondescript, the outdoor photography, especially the excellent day-for-night shots, adds immeasurably to the film's atmosphere. Although probably more by accident than design, the outdoor scenes were filmed in the fall. The trees are almost bare, the sky is usually gloomy. One can almost feel the autumn chill in the air. This adds a wonderful, almost palpable aura of bleakness to those scenes.

Guitarist and composer Jack Marshall (known primarily for his theme for *The Munsters*), contributes an odd yet perfectly suited musical score. Several years earlier, Marshall wrote the music for the Robert Mitchum opus, *Thunder Road*, and some of its compositional techniques (such as the prominent use of electric guitar, and the incorporation of other composers' songs) served as good practice for *The Giant Gila Monster* (in which Chace's songs were written by the star, Don Sullivan). Marshall makes the most of his small budget by using small ensembles that never number more than six or seven musicians. For instance, the theme heard under the main title, and resurrected during scenes showing the monster, is a textbook fifties' sci-fi "Ooo-wee-ooo" scary melody played by the eerie theremin (or very similar-sounding electronic instrument), over a background of subdued tympani and snare drum, bass guitar, and minor chords strummed on electric guitar, accented by a few scattered notes on the piano and flute. Yes, it's pretty sparse, but it conveys that same bleak quality as the outdoor photography, and is especially effective during the scene in which Chace and the sheriff examine the place of the hitchhiker's disappearance, where the theremin takes a short, lonely solo.

The Giant Gila isn't a very fearsome monster.

Missy's "oh so cute" music is played by celesta and flute. The love theme for Lisa and Chace is sort of an easy listening piece for soft electric guitar, bass, and sultry sax.

Fifties rockabilly music is associated with the teens, usually heard as source music played on a jukebox, the radio, or at the platter party, although a particularly smokin' piece (similar in use and spirit to Marshall's *Thunder Road* chase) is used for Chace's exciting nitro run at the end of the film. As the film reaches its final confrontation between good and evil, the musical styles merge, with the monster theme played against the driving rock 'n' roll beat. A little musical recap ends the film. A mournful reprise of the monster's theme is heard over a shot of its burning carcass, Missy's celesta music returns for a few seconds as Chace walks over to her, the rock 'n' roll appears as the kids from the barn dance show up at the gila bonfire, and the dramatic buildup of guitar, tympani, and sax for the end title culminate in a brief quote of *The Mushroom Song*'s final three guitar chords. There are some symphonies that don't have as good a thematic wrap-up as this.

Taken as a whole, *The Giant Gila Monster* is not a great monster film. It does not sport a particularly fearsome monster, nor does it make the greatest use of the one it has. However, if viewed as a normal dramatic film that just happens to have a monster in it, the movie is surprisingly well crafted, from the subtextural nuances of the script to the natural feel of the acting, photography, and direction. Everybody contributes something which melts into the overall aura of this movie.

Hopefully this chapter will help give the better elements of *The Giant Gila Monster* some overdue recognition. As for the monster itself, a quote from one of Missy's scenes probably offers the best advice:

Missy: "Laughing is important, isn't it, Chace?"

Chace: "It sure is, and you know, I never felt more like laughing than I do right now."

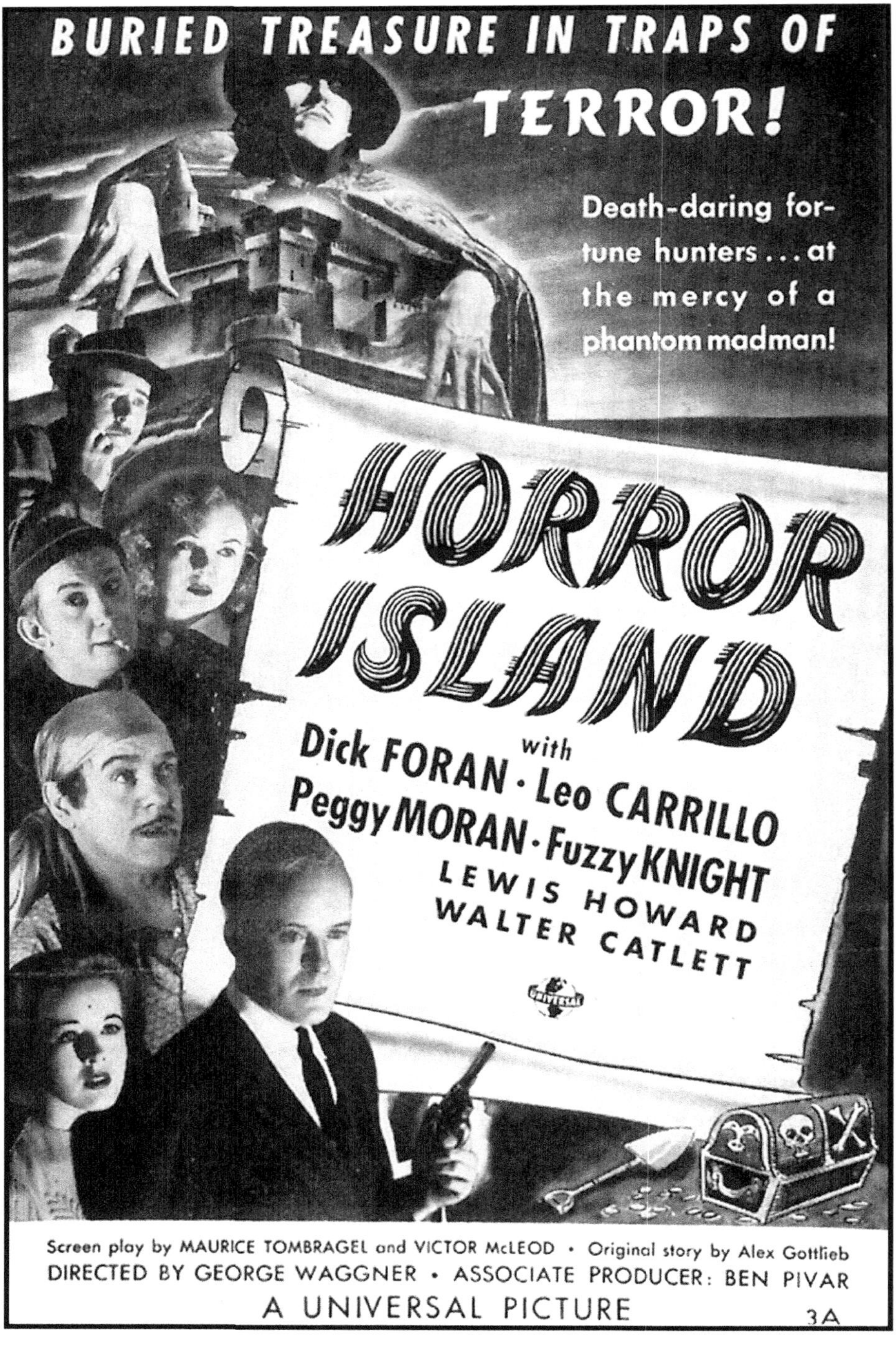
BURIED TREASURE IN TRAPS OF
TERROR!
Death-daring fortune hunters . . . at the mercy of a phantom madman!
HORROR ISLAND
with
Dick FORAN · Leo CARRILLO
Peggy MORAN · Fuzzy KNIGHT
LEWIS HOWARD
WALTER CATLETT
Screen play by MAURICE TOMBRAGEL and VICTOR McLEOD · Original story by Alex Gottlieb
DIRECTED BY GEORGE WAGGNER · ASSOCIATE PRODUCER: BEN PIVAR
A UNIVERSAL PICTURE
3A

HORROR ISLAND
by John "J.J" Johnson

If there's one place in this world I could go to escape the frenzied pace of society and the pressures it brings, I would choose Pier Five and a boat called the Skiddoo. Imagine a life in which mounting bills are tossed out a porthole, where one has nothing better to do than tip beers, dream up fortune schemes, and hang out with our old salty chums, Bill Martin, Stuff Oliver, and the Skipper? In our spare time we'd draw anchor and steam over to a haunted island once owned by Morgan the Pirate to hunt for buried treasure.

For those of you who've never beheld this obscure little horror-whodunit, I dare say you won't mate with it as I have. There is virtually no real *horror* in *Horror Island*. The characters are clichéd and the madcap mystery hijinks bring to mind an episode of the cartoon *Scooby Doo*. Most film critics pass the movie off as mindless fluff. *Halliwell's Film Guide* summed it up as a "Feeble little mystery with very little interest in who done what to whom." *Creature Features* author John Stanley was a little kinder calling it "outmoded but fun." Even my closest friends ridicule this obsession I harbor for *Horror Island*. My answer? Forgive them father, for they know not why I watch.

Horror Island is not just some treasure island lark masquerading as supernatural terror. It's a state of mind. Morgan's Island is my sanctuary, the Skiddoo is my womb, and Bill, Stuff, and the Skipper are my male-bond buds for life. Like Bill Martin says, "Riches, ghosts, a haunted castle on a deserted island! How does that grab you!" Well, it grabs me just fine.

For those of you who have seen this film, but can't get past a trite plot, a hackneyed cast of characters, a one-legged pirate with a penchant for winking at the camera, and a title boasting of horror, yet delivering something vastly different, please pardon my ravings.

Horror Island is based upon an original story by Alex Gottlieb called *Terror of the South Seas*. The plot is centered around the popular theme of uncovering lost loot from the infamous Welsh buccaneer, Sir Henry Morgan. Screenwriters Maurice Tombragel and Victor McLeod embellish Gottlieb's "Morgan's gold" premise with a variety of "haunted house" genre mechanisms such as a ghost castle with sliding panels, trap doors, and secret passageways, not to mention a lame reference to Agatha Christie's *Ten Little Indians*. It would seem the writers had in mind to throw every horror-mystery element ever conceived into their story pot and then boil it senseless. Suffice it to say, *Horror Island* leaves no gimmick unscalded.

Any good thriller must have an exciting musical score to set the tone and *Horror Island* opens with a rousing title theme borrowed by Vienna-born composer Hans J. Salter from *Seven Sinners* (a 1940 Universal South Sea naval romp starring John Wayne and Marlene Dietrich). As the stirring score works its magic, an atmospheric island shot of the fog-enshrouded ghost castle (a nifty, and rather large miniature representing Morgan's secret haunts) can be seen behind the superimposed opening credits.

The film begins with a wonderful low-angled shot of the peg-legged skipper (Leo Carrillo) at night, tottering down an eerie wharf studio set. This brief sequence alone

Stuff (Fuzzy Knight), the Skipper (Leo Carrillo), and Bill (Dick Foran) check out the treasure map.

certainly conjures up familiar images of the drunken sailor with gunny sack gear slung over his shoulder, drifting down by the waterfront docks on a moonlit eve.

As the camera stops momentarily at a dark alley way, out from the black emerges the mysterious cloaked figure known as "The Phantom." While the Skipper stops to peak inside Bill Martin's pier office window, the stalking phantom moves in for a closer look. From behind the skipper steps a dark figure who rests a hand on his shoulder in one of the film's rare shock scenes. The startled skipper (and audience) breathe a sigh of relief as the hand turns out to belong to an old pier watchman (Eddy Chandler).

Being the garrulous seaman that he is, the skipper foolishly volunteers his idea to uncover "buried treasure" to the disbelieving, yet affable, official. "I think you've had a nip too much," suggests the watchman. "You better run along and let the night air sober you up." And with that, the skipper is sent on his merry way to Pier Five and Bill Martin's boat, the Skiddoo. The night watchman continues his rounds, passing an alley where the eavesdropping phantom skulks in the shadows.

The following segment, my favorite of the film, commences with a zoom shot that slowly hones in on the Skiddoo, followed by a harmonious dissolve inside its warm cabin interior where Bill (Dick Foran) and Stuff (Fuzzy Knight) are engaged in discussion about bad credit and future dreams. For me, there is no other visual sequence in cinema with such strong associations. You see, I love to wander down by coastal piers in the evening hours. There's a friendly, almost familiar feeling as you stroll past row upon row of yachts and small craft gently rocking to the rhythm of the surf. Moonlight draws distinct forms as it dances across cluttered decks, shadowing old crab pots, overturned buckets, draped netting, and rusty chains. One senses something snug, almost sheltered about the warm flickering glow that shimmers behind drawn curtains and cabin portholes.

The bantering heard within this cozy cabin nook lends key insights into the characters of Bill Martin and Stuff Oliver, who are portrayed by handsome leading man, Dick Foran, and perennial side-kick performer, Fuzzy Knight.

Bill Martin's current inspiration, "Canned stuffing for Christmas turkeys," seems a little far fetched to Stuff who responds, "Why don't we give this whole business up and get ourselves jobs like other people?" Foran counters, "Now you don't wanna spoil a beautiful record, do ya? Two thirds of my class has been out of work since I left Princeton." Stuff comes back, "You mind if I get a job, I didn't go to college."

It's interesting to note how art and life intermingle here because Dick Foran was, at one time, actually enrolled at Princeton. Foran's father was a very successful New Jersey businessman who went on to become a senator. His son's aspirations, like that of the character he portrays, were far less grandiose. Originally Foran wanted to be a geologist (perhaps to uncover some kind of hidden treasure), yet like the character he plays, Foran never really finished his goal, electing instead to follow the allure of show business life—a quick-buck scheme that did prove successful.

While Bill Martin seems to be blessed with good looks, intelligence, and confidence, he's really nothing more than the consummate slacker. His loser sidekick Stuff Oliver, however, exemplifies the practical voice of reason. Stuff worries about paying the ever-mounting bills, "back rent on the store, three months payments on this boat," while Martin merely "files them with the rest of their bills," by tossing them out the porthole.

Bill Martin, in a sense, represents that spark in each of us that yearns to rebel against the traditional nose-to-the-grindstone work ethic. Who cares if we don't live up to our grandest expectations? Martin plays that corner-cutting gambler in us all that dreams of the quick buck and a life of leisure by the age of 35.

Though most of us will never realize that flight of fancy, the dream, or at least the pretense of it, can be achieved vicariously through the film. This is what *Horror Island* and movies in general, offer. Escape! Why do you suppose I spend half my leisure life watching film? While most people venture to the outdoors to commune with nature, I usually escape society by voyaging back in time to my own private Cinema Paradisio. I don't relish the idea of dealing with responsibility, the unknown, and death. Film, however, has properties of escape that seem quite inviting. Motion pictures offer us exciting plots, unique settings, and a chance to feed vicariously off an existence different from our own. On the other hand, movies lend us the stability of an outcome that never changes with each subsequent viewing. There's something mighty comforting about a conclusion one can count on, and few things in life are as predictable as a whodunit you've seen over 100 times. The notion of chucking it all in and heading down to the Skiddoo seems damn right appealing. Hungry? Just toss a crab pot astern or poke your fishing rod in the water. Bored? Steam on over to Morgan's Island with a pretty lass in tow. Just give me a bottle of booze, a good friend, my own boat, and I'll show you heaven.

Oddly enough however, I'm not sure Bill and Stuff realize the life they're leading now is the life they are dreaming of. For the sake of the plot, their happy-go-lucky reality takes a sharp turn starboard when a distant call for help brings our two pals on deck. The serious moment is given some levity when Stuff comments on the outcry by saying, "That must be one of our creditors." In the following shot, we witness a wrestling match in which the Phantom heaves the peg-legged skipper off the dock and into the drink (a scene actually played out by stuntmen, with Ed Parker hurling either Dale Van Sickel or John Burton into the studio tank.) While Bill and Stuff rush to the rescue, cinematographer Elwood Bredell demonstrates a keen eye for lighting as the rippling water reflects on the side of the Skiddoo.

Now safely on board, the skipper begins yelling, "my leg, my leg," momentarily shocking his two new guardians, who breathe a sigh of relief after realizing that the missing limb is only a loose peg leg floating in the harbor. "I would rather lose my good one than that one," jests the skipper. "Solid mahogany, I carved it myself out of a old piano. Very musical. Every time someone plays the spring song, I get a touch of sciatica or rheumatism."

After Stuff fetches the wooden shank, the audience quickly becomes acquainted with this affable scalawag suffering from a hypercongenial personality. This is one seaman who can really spin a yarn—a perfect companion for Stuff and Bill. If only all handicapped (excuse me—mahogany challenged) pirates were so gregarious. Come to think of it, most are.

In a film already saddled with one sidekick, one could make a solid case for the skipper's presence being merely a character contrivance to appease children. No doubt Leo Carrillo was encouraged to play his role over the top. Still, you have to wonder if the producers thought Leo was as funny as Leo thinks he is. His characterization of the bemused Skipper in 1941 certainly wasn't any great stretch as Carrillo worked in a number of comedy relief roles as a genial Latin in films like *The Gay Desperado* (1936), *Rio* (1939), and *Captain Caution* (1940). If Carrillo's comic performance seems more suited to off-Broadway than a motion picture, his extensive work as a newspaper cartoonist and a comedian both in vaudeville and the stage might offer an explanation. Carrillo was also known as a master dialectician and his talent in that area certainly wasn't wasted for *Horror Island*. The skipper's improper use of pronouns, fowled up clichés, and mis-used verbs makes him all the more quirky (like he needed it). More often

Did the producers think Leo Carrillo was as funny as Leo thinks he is?

MAP-SOCKS HOME PICTURE'S PLOT!

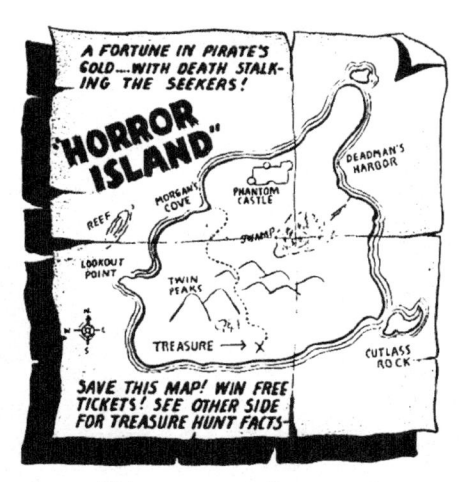

A FORTUNE IN PIRATE'S GOLD....WITH DEATH STALKING THE SEEKERS!

"HORROR ISLAND"

SAVE THIS MAP! WIN FREE TICKETS! SEE OTHER SIDE FOR TREASURE HUNT FACTS

Shades of buccaneer Captain Morgan! This picture fits the lucky treasure map stunt. Blow up illustration (at left) of map describing the location of pirate treasure on Horror Island. Illustration is designed so that map may be torn in half with complete copy remaining on portion which will be your throw-away. Imprint back of latter with theater ad and instructions as to how holder may win prize.

Flood town with halves of map, only a few of which will match the roughly-torn edges of the one posted in theater lobby. In this way you can control number of prizes. This map stunt serves two purposes. It gives exhibitor a punchy contest as well as aticket-selling throw-away!

than not, Carrillo's lilt-laden performance as the lovable old mariner is so broad you'd swear he was straining to make up for an unclever script all by himself. To say he's a ham would be optimistic. To call him a pandering swine would be more accurate. In one sequence, Martin has the Skipper dressed up as a walking advertisement for "Buried Treasure Inc.," a $50 per person weekend excursion to Morgan's Island to hunt for treasure. That shot of Carrillo dressed in pirate's garb (which may have inspired Andre Agassi at Wimbledon 1995?) clearly demonstrates his irrepressible personality. In what I now refer to as "the Wink Seen Round the World," the Skipper squints one off in grand gesture, no doubt calculated to titillate the admiration of young moviegoers. You gotta love that wacky buccaneer!

Upon returning to the Skiddoo, our trio encounters an intruder on board who turns out to be an unwelcome relative of Martin's. Cousin George (John Eldredge), a smoothy (sporting a thin mustache—the mark of mendaciousness in most forties whodunits), announces his interest in buying the house—which just happens to rest (rather improbably) on Martin's privately owned island. How the family of a slacker like Bill Martin ever came in possession of an island in which a "museum" landmark of such historic importance resides, is a mystery to me. Far more puzzling than the one we're about to see.

With his interest now piqued, Bill spurns George's offer and takes the map to a dockside expert named Jasper Quinley (played by mousy actor Hobart Cavanaugh) to determine its authenticity. Professor Quinley terms the map a "skillful imitation," and his insistence that "literally hundreds" of people fall for these "worthless treasure maps" spurs yet another scratchdream for Martin.

Once Bill's treasure cruise scheme is hatched and their car is loaded up with supplies, Martin gets side swiped by Wendy Creighton (played by Peggy Moran), the beautiful love interest of our story. This pure, natural, mid-Americana beauty seems an odd choice to play a rich, spoiled socialite, especially with her Iowa farm girl accent shining through like a K-Mart beacon. Moran retired from the screen following her 1942 marriage to filmmaker Henry Koster, who went on to direct several fine features like *The Bishop's Wife* (1947), *Harvey* (1950), *The Robe* (1953), and *Mr. Hobbs Takes a Vacation* (1962). When you consider Moran's frenetic acting career, over 20 productions with hectic shooting schedules in just four years, it's no wonder Peggy opted for housewife over movie star.

After a little fencing and flirtation, Bill manages to finagle a trip from Wendy and her hang-around boyfriend, Thurman Coldwater. Now here's a cold fish for you. The name says it all. He's a smug, pampered gigolo type who lives off hand-outs from wealthy women. As he aptly suggests, "Thurman Coldwater's the name, and if you want to leave anything to me, I'll accept it." You can't help but despise this foppish snob. Like Cousin George, Coldwater has the narrow mustache of dubious distinction, and it's quite obvious this tired-blooded playboy has never worked a day in his life. How he's managed to procure a babe like Wendy Creighton is beyond me. His limp wristed wave good-bye, wimpy white pants, and cute little yachtsman cap certainly conjure forth a bizarre image of some blue-blooded sea ninny from Frisco Bay. Actor Lewis Howard gets the nod as the cavalier Coldwater who could use a double Geritol.

He's certainly no stranger to jet set roles with kindred portrayals in pictures like *San Francisco Docks* (1940), *Seven Sweethearts* (1942; which also featured Peggy Moran), *I've Always Loved You* (1946), and *In a Lonely Place* (1950).

With Wendy and Thurman signed on as a bet for a thrill-filled weekend, Martin, Stuff, and the Skipper continue to round out their first cruise party with a number of clichéd characters including Jasper Quinley, Cousin George, and a rough looking couple who turn out to be a pair of fugitive crooks known as Rod "Killer" Grady and his gun moll Arleen. Grady is portrayed by Ralf Harolde, a feisty character actor distinguished by a tough, gravelly voice and a surly demeanor. Former Ziegfeld Follies dancer, Iris Adrian, gets the nod as Arleen. Adrian is known for spirited character performances, usually in comedies playing dumb blondes, chatty chorus girls, and hood molls as in *Horror Island*.

The last person to sign on is a pompous union watchdog named Sergeant McGoon, played by scatterbrain, comic character actor and experienced vaudevillian, Walter Catlett. In one of my favorite, subtle comedy bits (a rarity for *Horror Island*), McGoon confronts the Princeton huckster saying, "You're guilty of false and misleading advertising! Your ad says that you got ghosts." Martin responds, "Yeah and they all got union cards."

Once this motley can of mixed nuts finally arrives on the island, the haunting and taunting quickly commences. The first "thrill" of the evening occurs when a crossbow, mounted on a "mechanical man," accidentally releases a large arrow that very nearly impales the Skipper. This is followed by yet another mishap involving a suit of armor which teeters and then topples toward Wendy, who is saved, or, rather tackled from behind (actually head butted in the ass), by a lunging Dick Foran. Aside from the fact it's a rather tactless way to save a lady, the scene is made more (unintentionally) ridiculous when Foran pops up from the rear ending with his little captain's cap still perched atop his head. And speaking of permanent fixtures, one wonders if Stuff will ever remove the stocking cap that's apparently sewed onto his scalp.

From now until the climax we are treated (or rather mistreated) to a series of nocturnal nonsense like eerie warnings, sleepwalking, fainting spells, and the ever-popular corpse tally. Also added to the evening venue are some menacing poses by the Phantom (played by Foy Van Dolsen), more lunging head butts by Bill Martin, and of course, yet another tumbling suit of armor filled with the dead body of Cousin George. How someone is able to take the time to stuff a body inside a suit of armor is beyond me. Logic, however, is not a strong suit of *Horror Island*.

Many a fan has wondered how George Waggner, director of the classic monster opus *The Wolf Man* (1941), could

Added to the evening venue are some menacing poses by the Phantom (played by Foy Van Dolsen).

have apparently sunk so silly with *Horror Island*. The answer is simple. Waggner is a competent, efficient filmmaker, but he's no James Whale. When examining a list of his film credits like *Man Made Monster* (1941), *The Climax* (1944), *The Gunfighters* (1947), *The Fighting Kentuckian* (1949), *Destination 60,000* (1957), *Pawnee* (1957), *Fury River* (1959), and *Mission of Danger* (1959), all one can see is a big letter B.

    This New York born, World War I vet often ran his productions like a military campaign. In the acclaimed book *Universal Horrors* (by Tom Weaver, Michael Brunas, and John Brunas) actress Susanna Foster (*The Climax*, 1944) described Waggner as "a very stoic, stiff-upper-lip kind of person." *Horror Island*, like so many of his movies, was made during a very tight production schedule. According to the authors of *Universal Horrors*, the picture was ready for trade previews just 23 days after shooting began, and Waggner worked his cast and crew till midnight in the rain and cold just to finish on time. Actress Peggy Moran talked about the toll of their frenetic production pace in the Brunas/Weaver collaboration. "I remember going home and being so exhausted I couldn't eat dinner. My mother would rub my back and I would start crying just from being so exhausted."

Though the cast and crew of *Horror Island* may have run themselves ragged making the film, onscreen the characters look as though they're having a ball. Despite the hasty schedule the cast manages to impart the proper enthusiasm to keep the story infectious, and the production appears slick. One element which never fails to amaze me is how authentic and expansive the dock sets look for a movie filmed entirely at Universal Studios. Then again, director George Waggner was fortunate to have surrounded himself with an elite production team headed by art director Jack Otterson and set decorator Russell A. Gausman. That tandem should ring a bell as they teamed up to create several brilliant Universal sets like the elaborate expressionistic castle in *Son of Frankenstein* (1939), the musty archaic tombs in *The Mummy's Hand* (1940), and the uncanny indoor forest in *The Wolf Man* (1941) which Waggner directed that same year. Otterson and Gausman made the most of the film's $93,000 budget by combining left over sets from *Tower of London* (1939) together with Waterfront Street on the studio backlot. The in-house water tank at Universal proved an adequate representation for both Pier Five and the waters surrounding Morgan's Island, while the Carfax Abbey stone staircase from *Dracula* (1931) came in handy for ghost castle interior shots. Their knack for improvising sets combined with the silky cinematography of Elwood Bredell (and his keen lighting sense) provided Waggner with the power to squeeze great production value from every dollar spent.

Despite its strong visual presence, *Horror Island* will never score high on any comedy-horror hall of fame list, though it does exude a dumb familiar charm. I'm sure by now you're wondering how any reasonably astute film fan could possibly choose such a shopworn albatross as their all-time favorite film. I admit it's pretty corny stuff, but there are reasons for my misguided loyalty and devoted affection, and the first has to do with setting.

I've always enjoyed stories that are set around water, even as a kid. Many's the day I came home from school to sit with a steaming hot bowl of Beefaroni to watch Gilligan's Isle. In a quick glance at my all-time top-50 list you'll see several oceanic oddities like *Dead Men Tell*, *Father Goose*, and *Truth About Spring*. *Horror Island* and I, like meditation and water, are forever wedded.

But what is it about islands, a dockyard, and the sea that I find so soothing? In his screenplay adaptation of Melville's classic novel *Moby Dick*, Ray Bradbury wrote, "Choose any path you please and ten to one it carries you down to water. There's a magic in water that draws all men away from land. The sea's where each man, as in a mirror, finds, himself." Like Ishmail of old, I too share a deep fascination for the sea. You can lose yourself and your burdens when staring out into the ocean. Who knows. Perhaps it rekindles some warm, subconscious memory of a safer, more carefree world inside our mother's womb? Water sustains us, refreshes our existence, and as Melville would say, it "reveals the image of the ungraspable phantom of life."

Another possible answer for my devotion to *Horror Island* has to do with the chemistry of its characterizations.

Thelma Ritter (in *Rear Window*) once suggested, "People with good sense belong where they're put," and the kooky cast of *Horror Island* certainly do agree with their roles. Leo Carrillo, the lovable mariner whom Universal put such faith in, came from a distinguished family of Spanish dons and Italian navigators. His great grandfather, Carlos Antonio Carrillo, was the first provisional governor of California, and in 1837, he once negotiated a peace treaty (after the Battle of Cahuenga Pass) on the very site where Universal Studios was built.

Like Carrillo and his ancestors, actor Dick Foran has also shared a great love for the sea. When attending Princeton, Foran spent his summers working as a seaman on freighters visiting South American countries and the West Indies.

John Nicholas Foran (alias Nick Foran then eventually Dick Foran) was a Western singing hero in several shoe-string productions at Warner Bros. Though possessing classic good looks, he seldom portrayed the archetypal strong leading male. Foran's warm, friendly smile is seasoned with a blowhard's finesse and daring man's tomfoolery. He was once considered for the handsome suitor role in *The Wolf Man* (1941), until the lords of casting realized he had too much charisma for the part. The role eventually fell to the suitably bland Patric Knowles.

A good share of Dick's film work occurs in male-bond-oriented actioners like *Fort Apache* (1948), *The Atomic Submarine* (1959), and *Donovan's Reef* (1963). In a similarly successful character formula to *Horror Island*, Foran starred as one half of a wacky archaeological buddy team in *The Mummy's Hand* (1940).

For *Horror Island*, the camaraderie between Bill Martin and Stuff is wacky as well, yet genuine. These two are not your typical tag-team heroes. They are flawed, a little greedy, somewhat foolish, but basically good people. In other words, they're a lot like us. Though they act like a match made in heaven, it does seem a little strange for a dashing young Princeton grad to be chumming around with a dockyard drifter like Stuff. Now I'm not saying we have two Midnight Cowboys on Pier Five, but one wonders what they do have in common. Bill is confident, cocky, and carefree while his loser pal is anything but bold.

Stuff Oliver is a stuttering dolt with little to show and even less on the ball. We've all met a Stuff sometime in our life. He's the one boy caught with his pants down in the stalls when 7th-grade girls raid the boys' bathroom. He seldom keeps friends, he never wins the girl, he always gets ridiculed by jocks, and he invariably earns C's. Stuff

In *Horror Island*, the camaraderie between Bill Martin and Stuff is wacky as well as genuine.

is the kind of boy who drops his lunch tray, gets hit on the head with the tetherball, and could never field a ground ball to save his life. Like an old mouseketeer, Stuff is forever out of step in whatever direction life chooses.

So who is the man behind the social misfit. Born John Forrest Knight, this Fairmont, West Virginian known as "Fuzzy" Knight, is hardly a nobody. Believe it or not, Fuzzy graduated from the University of West Virginia with a degree in law. An accomplished vaudevillian, musician, singer, and nightclub bandleader, Knight's forte was comic relief, especially as a stuttering sidekick for Western stars Tex Ritter and Johnny Mack Brown.

In 1939, on the set of *My Little Chickadee*, Fuzzy Knight and Dick Foran met for the first time, and two years later in *Horror Island*, they began what some might suggest as the beginning of a beautiful friendship and one that lasted up till Fuzzy's death in 1976. Have you ever had a drinking buddy? Ever swear off work, women, or responsibility? If you know what I'm talking about than you'll understand my fondness for old Bill and Stuff. The ultimate slacker and the perennial loser prove the point that opposites do indeed attract.

It must seem quite bizarre for any connoisseur of film to expound at length upon the subtle nuances of a briny fluffball like *Horror Island*. It's true, there are setting elements and character compositions to delight my escapist id, but nostalgia is the vital ingredient in any true guilty pleasure.

It must seem quite bizarre for any connoisseur of film to expound at length upon the subtle nuances of a briny fluffball like *Horror Island*.

Although the precise date and time has faded from memory, many of the warm details of my maiden voyage to *Horror Island* remain intact and unshakable.

On a warm, summer day in July my sisters, Gayla and Luanne, and I relished an evening alone to ourselves. Nothing but the very best would do for this divine occasion. We delighted in Lu's famous Tollhouse chocolate chip-oatmeal cookies for dinner and Gay's rootbeer floats for dessert. My sisters and I rarely got along. Dad used to refer to us as a brood of "bee-stung tarantulas with ulcerated fangs," but tonight it was all for fun, and fun for all. With a brimful pan of popcorn crackling on the stove and a red hot game of hearts waiting for us on the bed, all that we needed was a late night chiller to complete the occasion.

As we scanned the *TV Guide* for possible thrillers, the Gods of programming delivered unto us what looked like a fiendishly delicious treat. So that night we staved off the anticipation with card games à la hearts, war, and king's corner until *Horror Island*, the film with the goosepimply good title, came on. Minutes before the film began, we pushed their twin beds together and settled in, cloaked with a large bedspread and armed with bowls of buttered popcorn. As the film began, our expectations seemed secure as the mysterious caped Phantom darted in and out from the waterfront alley. As the story moved along, it soon became quite evident that *Horror Island* would not include any bloodthirsty island monsters as the title implied.

A peg-legged pirate joining forces with a lazy Princeton huckster just wasn't cutting the suspense mustard at first, and we demonstrated our disappointment with jeers and popcorn missiles. Before long our derisive energy reserves dissipated, and soon we found ourselves catching interest for the characters and the infectiously juvenile plot.

Somehow, possibly through the principles of cinematic osmosis, we eventually became thoroughly immersed in this buoyant little mystery romp, and by film's end, we were all smiles and ice cream. Though we may not have understood all the divine ramifications of the moment, the elements of an unforgettable evening were all present. Good snacks, fun games, lights out, and the most important of all—no parents.

In all honesty, any film we might have selected would have been memorable on that eve, but happenstance placed before us, or rather me, a symbol of my soul. I am inexorably mated to this movie. Like a fond tune or a familiar aroma, I will always associate *Horror Island* with childhood bliss. Life seldom gets that perfect.

Horror Island is my favorite stuffed animal, my warm fuzzy, my special childhood memory. Webster's defines nostalgia as "a longing for things, persons, or situations that are not present," but I regard nostalgia as the essence of life.

As Melville might suggest, any time I grow hazy about the eyes, or feel like knocking men's hats off in the street, I know it's high time to revisit *Horror Island*.

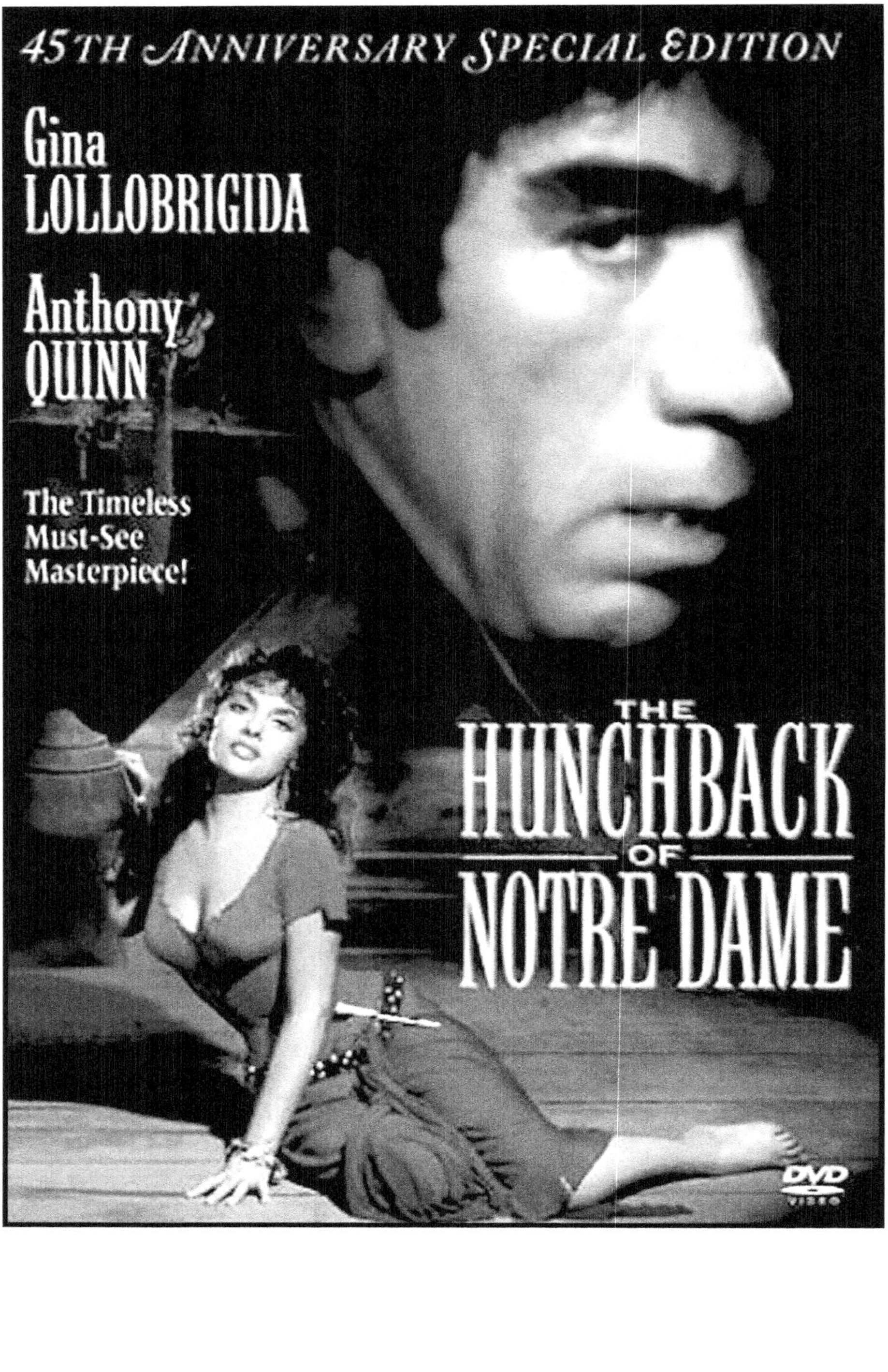
45TH ANNIVERSARY SPECIAL EDITION
Gina
LOLLOBRIGIDA
Anthony
QUINN
The Timeless
Must-See
Masterpiece!
THE
HUNCHBACK
OF
NOTRE DAME
DVD

THE HUNCHBACK OF NOTRE DAME
by Don G. Smith

In 1957, when Robert and Raymond Hakim launched their French and Italian co-production of Victor Hugo's classic novel *The Hunchback of Notre Dame*, the title had already been filmed 10 times: *Esmeralda* (1906, U.S.A.); *Notre Dame de Paris* (1911, France); *Notre Dame* (1913, U.S.A.); *The Darling of Paris* (1916, U.S.A.); *The Darling of Paris* (1917, U.S.A.); *Esmeralda* (1922, England); *The Hunchback of Notre Dame* (1923, U.S.A.); *Dhanwan* (1937, India); *Nav Jawan* (1937, India); and *The Hunchback of Notre Dame* (1939, U.S.A.). Of course, the two films now considered classics are the 1923 version starring Lon Chaney and the 1939 version starring Charles Laughton. Chaney's incredible make-up, his powerful emotive performance, and the magnificent sets highlight the 1923 version, while direction, thematic scope, and memorable performances distinguish the 1939 version.

The low esteem with which the critical community holds *The Hunchback of Notre Dame* (1957) is apparent from the fact that it neither exists in professional video format nor appears on television. Not only that, it is routinely maligned when discussions turn to film versions of Victor Hugo's 1831 novel. Leonard Maltin's 1996 *Movie and Video Guide* assigns the film 2 1/2 stars, opining that "Quinn makes a valiant try in the lead role, but film misses scope and flavor of Victor Hugo novel." Phil Hardy's *Overlook Film Encyclopedia of Horror* concludes that the "the amorphous international co-production, tarted up with some mild torture scenes involving Lollabrigida's Esmeralda, is embarrassingly awful by comparison with the Chaney (1923) and Laughton (1939) versions...." Until recently the film has remained virtually unseen since 1957.

So why is this film one of my guilty pleasures? Please don't fear that I am going to proclaim it superior to the 1923 and 1939 versions. My fondness for the film does not overpower my critical judgment to that extent. What I will do is argue its considerable merits. As most people understand, a guilty pleasure is usually a function of time, place, and circumstance. The same film, viewed at another time, in another place, and under different circumstances would probably not impress us nearly as well, would not burn itself indelibly into our memory as only a first or very special love can do. Yes, guilty pleasures are often equivalent to our first loves. In the dew of youth we loved intensely and now those days are gone. Perhaps, thereafter, we never loved so well again. Years later, our buddies might ask with amazement how we could have loved that person we loved so intensely, and we can only answer that "you had to be there." I was seven years old in 1957 when I first saw ads in the newspaper for *The Hunchback of Notre Dame*—ads proclaiming the film "The World's Supreme Shocker" and featuring Anthony Quinn as the grotesque Quasimodo grabbing Gina Lollobrigida's Esmeralda the gypsy. Looking back, I can see that Allied Artists considered their film a potential box office smash. For example, they went all out promotionally, producing a large format 16-page pressbook and arranging the release of both an Avon paperback tie-in and a Dell comic book tie-in—evidence of the confidence that fuels a major push.

Esmeralda (Gina Lollobrigida) seen with Gringoire (Robert Hirsch) represents wild, innocent freedom.

So why didn't it all work out? Why is *The Hunchback of Notre Dame* (1957) considered such a dud? A fair examination of the film will reveal flaws, but the flaws are minor compared to its overall merits.

As the film opens, the credits are superimposed over close-ups of a giant church bell majestically clanging. Then a narrator tells us of Victor Hugo's having been inspired to write *The Hunchback of Notre Dame* after discovering, scrawled on a wall of Notre Dame, the very sad word ANAYKH, meaning evil destiny. What despairing soul must have left that one word as a legacy? This indeed sets the tone for the film, as it does for Hugo's novel.

The next scenes establish certain thematic contrasts and introduce us to the main characters. The time is 15th-century Paris during the celebration of The Feast of Fools. Gringoire, a poet, is attempting to present his play to a raucous mob of commoners as Clopin, the king of beggars, insolently mocks the proceedings from the sidelines. When the crowd refuses to listen and begins tossing vegetables at the actors, Gringoire gives up, sighing "How can poets compete with fools?" Though Gringoire is a poet, he is not a very successful one. In fact, as he admits later, he became a poet because he was unsuccessful at everything else. Still, he is refined compared to the jeering mob. Clopin, on the other hand, is shrewd, cunning, and comical—a quick-witted beggar who feigns being crippled in order to make his living. His past has taught him that education and refinement are inconsequential next to the struggle for survival. And in that struggle, though it has hardened him, Clopin is a master.

The play dispersed, Esmeralda the Gypsy and her goat Djali perform for the appreciative crowd. Glaring at her from the sidelines is Claude Frollo, an alchemist in the robes of a priest. It seems that her dancing and singing disturb his "work." In reality, her sensuality, her freedom, and her dark beauty arouse his sexual appetites and tempt his spirit, causing him to war against himself. When Esmeralda at one point looks up into Frollo's disapproving face, she is momentarily shocked by the evil and danger she senses. As Frollo tries to clear the noisy throng from the square, he is roughly handled, and has to be rescued by his servant, Quasimodo, the grotesque, nearly deaf, hunchbacked bellringer of Notre Dame.

Esmeralda represents wild, innocent freedom. Frollo, on the other hand, represents the frustration and anger of sexual repression. The film does not so much blame The Church for Frollo's dilemma as much as it suggests that Frollo was unsuited for the priesthood. After all, his greatest interest is alchemy, certainly a worldly pursuit. Then there is Quasimodo, the nearly deaf, disfigured bellringer. We learn only two things about him at this early juncture: that commoners simultaneously ridicule his appearance and fear his strength, and that he is devoted to Frollo as a dog is devoted to its master.

To me, the main characters in this film represent parts of all of us. We war within ourselves, lash out when we feel wronged, and long for freedom and sensuality in the shadow of moral principles. Each character in this film is alive because each character is part of us. That is what great literature is all about, and this film translates Hugo's great novel to the screen intact.

The first of three key scenes in any faithful version of *The Hunchback of Notre Dame* is the crowning of Quasimodo as King of Fools. A high point of the Feast of Fools is the crowning of the ugliest man as King. After several ugly commoners have competed for the "honor," Esmeralda spies Quasimodo and encourages the crowd to crown him king. Quasimodo at first does not comprehend as the crowd drapes a robe over his shoulders and places a crown on his head. After all, because the people often tease him cruelly, he does not trust them. But when they place in his hand a whistle so shrill that even he can hear it, he becomes positively exuberant. The crowd then hoists the joyful Quasimodo onto a makeshift throne and carries him through the streets in mock procession. Frollo, however, quickly cuts short Quasimodo's joyful "reign" by halting the throng, knocking the crown from Quasimodo's head, and shaming him. Like a dog, the bellringer goes down on one knee, silently and uncomprehendingly begging forgiveness.

Quinn's transformation from happy "freak" to shamed animal is powerful, establishing the hunchback as a human being, something the jaded crowd cannot or chooses not to understand. All the while, Frollo maintains the outer serenity of a saint doing God's work in the face of adversity as the Devil gnaws at his peace of mind.

When night falls, revelers mock Frollo's sourness, proclaiming that "the night belongs to lovers." Of course, Frollo knows that only too well as his mind and testicles churn in torment. Frollo is in the process of further castigating Quasimodo for allowing the crowd to make a fool of him when he spies Esmeralda walking the streets alone.

Quasimodo (Anthony Quinn) is so physically ugly yet so spiritually beautiful; Esmeralda is a woman of virtue.

"My faults are like your face," Frollo tells the bellringer. "Ugly! We are brothers—your face and my soul. Get her!"

I am moved in this scene by the contrast of ugliness and purity. Quasimodo is so physically ugly yet so spiritually beautiful while Frollo is exactly the opposite. How often life is like that. How often we ourselves are like that!

Acting on his master's orders, the reluctant Quasimodo pursues Esmeralda, all the while unsuccessfully trying to calm her with promises that she will not be hurt. Esmeralda's screams attract the attention of a squadron of soldiers led by Captain Phoebus, who orders his men to arrest the hunchback as he sweeps Esmeralda into his saddle and spirits her away to safety. When Quasimodo is in custody and the situation under control, Phoebus suggests that Esmeralda meet him later at a disreputable inn, but guessing his intentions, Esmeralda, though fascinated by him, playfully runs away.

These scenes further establish Quasimodo as Frollo's "pet." Though his conscience tells him otherwise, the bellringer cannot disobey the man who has given him protection throughout his unfortunate life. The scenes also establish Esmeralda as a woman of virtue. Though she is immediately attracted to Phoebus, she will not compromise her principles for a night of pleasure. Yes, she is wild and innocent, but she knows who she is and will not give herself to someone only for physical pleasure. Though Esmeralda

After his beating, Quasimodo cries out, "I'm thirsty!" Only Esmeralda feels sympathy for Quasimodo because he is a fellow human being.

does not know it, Phoebus is engaged to be married to a young lady of the upper class. Unlike Esmeralda, Phoebus would readily betray that engagement for a few hours of physical pleasure with a beautiful woman. As the film unfolds, the contrasts continue to abound. And it is partially the power of these contrasts that make the film engaging and worthy of attention.

The second key scenes in any faithful version of *The Hunchback of Notre Dame* are the ones in which Quasimodo undergoes his punishment for the "crime" of having attempted the kidnapping of Esmeralda. Rotating on a pillory while he is whipped by an official tormentor, Quasimodo endures that acute pain as he has endured all the insults in his life—with acceptance. This time, however he partially understands why he is being hurt. He knows that it has something to do with Frollo and Esmeralda. After his beating, Quasimodo cries out, "I'm thirsty!" Of course, this only encourages the crowd to taunt him even more. Only Esmeralda feels sympathy for Quasimodo because he is a fellow human being. When she gives him water to drink, her kindness is forever imprinted on his memory. All the while, Frollo watches from a distance, allowing Quasimodo to take the punishment for his (Frollo's) sin. In a sense, Quasimodo becomes a Christ figure, and Frollo stands in as the unappreciative sinner. The fact that Frollo is a "man of the church" creates an unpleasant but interesting irony, especially when we remember Frollo's conclusion that his soul and Quasimodo's face are *one*.

The next morning, before her death sentence can be carried out, Quasimodo recalls Esmeralda's kindness and carries her into the sanctuary of the church.

In the next scenes, Esmeralda's charitable nature is reemphasized when she saves Gringoire from being hanged by Clopin's gang of beggars. She does this by agreeing to marry the poor poet, though she rightfully explains to him later that her life-saving gesture does not entitle him to a place in her bed.

Esmeralda herself becomes a victim, however, when she succumbs to Phoebus' entreaties and meets him in a tavern. Frollo observes their tryst and stabs Phoebus with Esmeralda's knife, precipitating her arrest. Under torture, she confesses and is sentenced to be hanged. The next morning, before the sentence can be carried out, Quasimodo recalls Esmeralda's kindness and carries her into the sanctuary of the church. Quinn lifts Lollobrigida over his head and proclaims sanctuary—the "law" that the church is off limits to secular justice.

The pressbook claims that Quinn worked out in a gym for two hours daily in preparation for his role as Quasimodo. Actually, based on Quinn's general physique, he probably worked out regularly anyway. In the film, while it is true that Quinn was burdened by a 25-pound hump on his back, he does not perform physical feats requiring strength superior to that of Chaney, Sr.'s performance. In fact, a stunt man handles the most rigorous acrobatics. Quinn did possess an impressive physique, but he did so both before and after his performance as Quasimodo.

After being rescued by Quasimodo, Esmeralda is touched by the hunchback's tenderness and faithfulness. As Quasimodo says after he has inadvertently frightened Esmeralda, "All my life, I've been ugly. People have stoned me and laughed at me.

When the beggars finally manage to take Esmeralda from the church at the time the troops arrive, she is killed by an arrow.

I've been hurt, but to frighten you makes me sad." Quasimodo is accustomed to physical and emotional pain inflicted on him by the mob, but the pain he feels for causing his loved one discomfort is the greater pain by far! These scenes further establish both Quasimodo and Esmeralda as sympathetic human beings. Esmeralda, however, cannot forget Phoebus, who lied to her about his freedom to engage in a love affair. Duped by his feigned sincerity, she asks Quasimodo to bring Phoebus to her. Looking forward to a marriage promising riches, he, of course, refuses.

When King Louis XI, encouraged by the vindictive Frollo, temporarily revokes the sanctuary of Notre Dame and allows government troops to mount an assault on the church, the stage is set for the great climactic battle of Notre Dame—the third sequence of scenes necessary in any faithful version of the novel.

The battle of Notre Dame—Quasimodo's energetic attempt, through a variety of violent means, to protect Esmeralda from intruders—is quite effective. In fact, *Time* magazine wrote that "when the fighting is over, Quinn's Hunchback has broken all records for Notre Damage!"

When Esmeralda's people attempt to rescue her before the troops arrive, Quasimodo mistakes them for soldiers and rains carnage upon them. When the beggars finally manage to take Esmeralda from the church at the time the troops arrive, she is killed by an arrow. Discovering his error, Quasimodo throws the villainous Frollo from the upper gallery of the cathedral, after which he steals into the crypt and embraces the corpse

Quinn's performance as Quasimodo does not capture the frenetic passion of Chaney nor the deep sadness of Laughton.

of the woman he loves. Several years later, when the bur-ial vault is re-opened, two skeletons are discovered in close embrace. When an attempt is made to separate them, the skeletons crumble to dust. ANA-YKH indeed! The evil destiny is the unfairness and ultimate tragedy of life itself. We are born, we struggle, and we die. If we are lucky we love and are loved in return.

Neither the 1923 nor the 1939 version is true to Hugo's novel. In fact, both earlier versions cheat unforgivably! On the other hand, the 1957 film is true to the novel and works both thematically and emotionally. Lollobrigida is exciting as Esmeralda and Alain Cuny is perfect as the brooding Claude Frollo. Cuny, incidentally, would go on to give a chilling performance in Fellini's *Satyricon* (1969). As a bonus, Georges Auric's musical score is suitably majestic and sad. So I return to my original question: why is the film so maligned? The answer is three-fold.

First, most people have never seen it. Yet they brazenly assume that its rarity is a result of poor quality. In addition, those who have seen it have seen only a bootleg video version (rare enough in itself). Unfortunately, the 1957 *The Hunchback of Notre Dame* loses much of its scope when reduced to video. Not only that, but many of the remaining Technicolor negatives have altered with time and no longer offer the brilliant color of the original prints. Mirimax recently corrected some of these problems by releasing a print on video.

Second, though Quinn is a fine actor, his performance as Quasimodo does not capture the frenetic passion of Chaney nor the deep sadness of Laughton. The difficulty does not lie so much with Quinn as it does with the superiority (at least in this case) of those to whom he is compared. Quinn, after all, had given a great performance in Fellini's *La Strada* (1954) and had won an Academy Award for his performance as Gauguin in *Lust for Life* (1956). In addition, he would go on to earn Academy Award nominations for his fine work in *Wild is the Wind* (1957) and *Zorba the Greek* (1964). Having seen Quinn on stage in *Zorba the Greek*, I can personally attest to his great skill to move an audience. Perhaps some of the blame can be laid at the feet of director Dellanoy, who does not elicit Quinn's greatest acting.

Still, let me repeat—Quinn gives a fine performance, and if we judge the film on its own merits, his performance is impressive.

Explaining his approach to the role, Quinn said:

> You live with a character all day. You probe his thoughts and reactions. It isn't easy to shed the mood, like the costume, at the end of the working day.... I sensed that the feeling of being completely different from one's fellows would bring an individual a terrible feeling of isolation. It could even develop into a psychopathic shyness that would cause an individual to completely withdraw from the world.... On shipboard, between New York and Paris, I awoke one morning to find that my face was swollen three times its normal size. I was frantic, because no diagnosis could be made on the high seas, I hid in my stateroom. I refused to see my friends. I learned what it meant to look repulsive. I knew what it meant to fear people and be alone.
>
> In France, I went to a dermatologist. He diagnosed the case as a skin infection, probably contracted in a barbershop.

The third problem with the film is its budget. Despite being filmed in France, the whole affair has an inexpensive look manifested as rather unconvincing long shots of the cathedral and as medium-range shots that fail to convey the grandeur of the setting. As Quinn admitted later, "Those French studios are so tiny the producers had to rent two sound stages: one in Paris, and another half an hour from the city. What's more, the real Notre Dame could not be shown; they built a special and larger replica because they used Cinemascope—and used extra-wide lenses."

So *The Hunchback of Notre Dame* (1957) is my guilty pleasure. But do I really feel guilty? Not at all. It led me to the literature of Victor Hugo. It shaped my 7-year-old personality and helped me to develop a tolerance and sympathy for the different, as long as the different was itself humane and moral. It helped teach me compassion, and it remains one of the defining moments of my life. If only more films could make such claims!

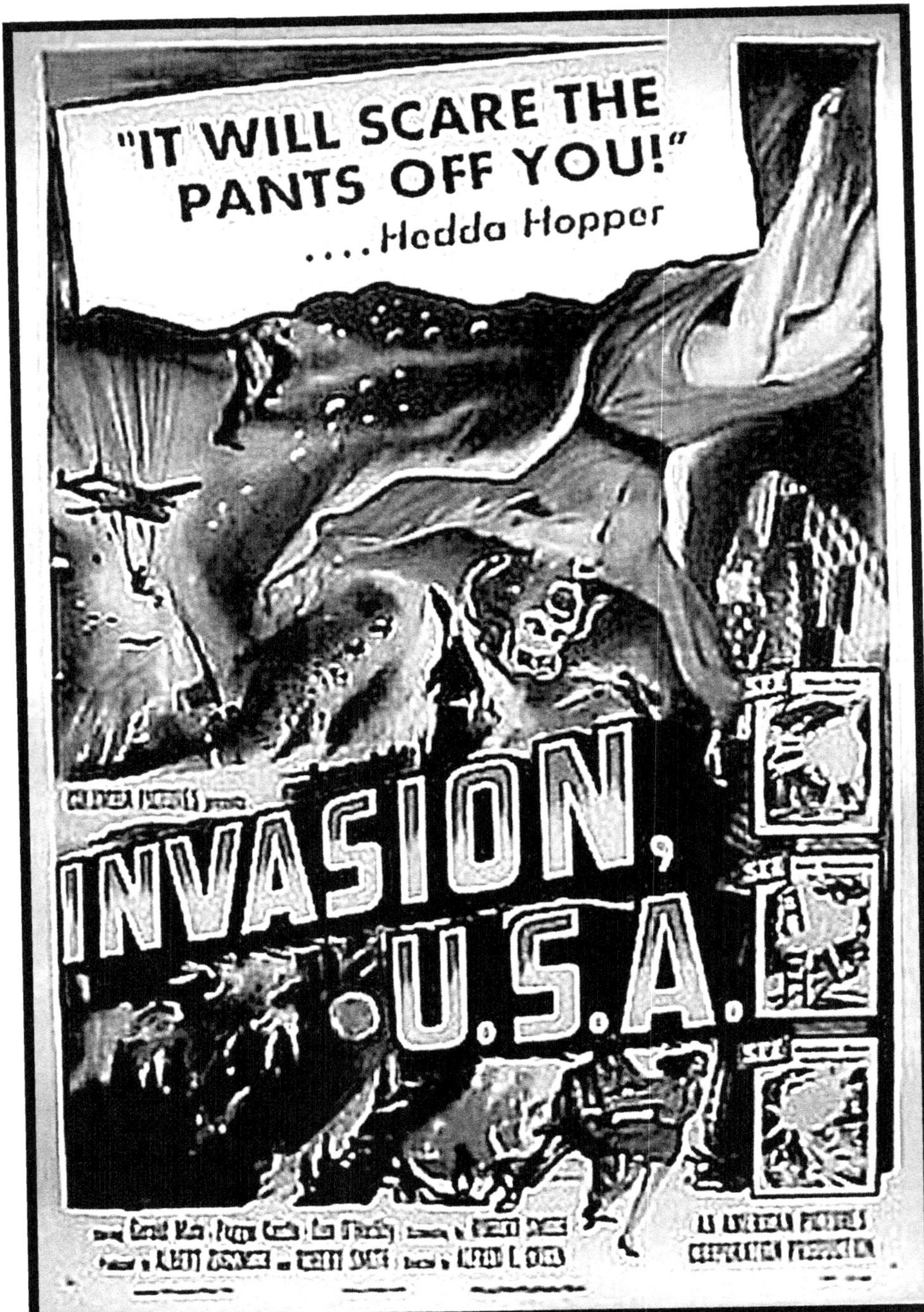
"IT WILL SCARE THE
PANTS OFF YOU!"
....Hedda Hopper
INVASION,
U.S.A.

INVASION U.S.A.
by Bruce Dettman

For a decade still wistfully referenced as carefree and uncomplicated, a cultural and economic nirvana of festive backyard barbecues, cheap gas, and little crime (murderers, rapists, and malcontents of the period such as Charles Starkweather and Caryl Chessman being comfortably pigeonholed as natural anomalies along the same lines as two-headed chickens or Siamese Twins), the 1950s was in reality a great morass of contradictions and simmering stews of social and political paranoia. Selective memory can work just as effectively on mass canvases of recollection as on those reflecting one's personal universe. It is undoubtedly comforting to believe that those 10 years of economic prosperity that offered more people than ever electric toasters, wall-to-wall carpeting, Hula Hoops, and Ozzie and Harriet (the latter reflecting a domestic oasis where the ultimate household dilemma was deciding which flavor of ice cream Ozzie should bring home to Ricky and David) were unsoiled bliss wedged in between World War II and the turbulent sixties that followed. In truth, that later decade and the social unrest, assassinations, and political chicanery which characterized it, did not spring independently or emerge as an isolated phenomenon connected to no other time or place, but was rather the outgrowth and extension of much that had gone on previously. The sixties might have been an explosion, but the fifties, rife with international tensions in the Mideast, Africa, and Korea, not to mention a domestic arena marred by the insidious machinations of Senator Joseph McCarthy, were surely the slowly burning fuse that ignited it. It should also not be forgotten that while such TV juveniles as Beaver and Wally, Bud, Kitten, and Princess, and Dennis the Menace cavorted about on the small screen with nothing more pressing on their minds than marbles, prom nights, and getting their allowances raised, the real life children of the decade were continually reminded that at any second as they watched *Superman* or bought a jar of Silly Putty, they could—and very well might be—reduced in a micro-second to nuclear silt. Of course, there were no pop psychologists in that era, at least not the garden variety sort that descended in flocks on America's children when the Challenger went down or the Gulf War exploded on CNN. Consequently the children of the 1950s had to grin and bear it. The Ruskies were something like algebra, acne, and mowing lawns. You didn't like the fact that they existed but you lived with it. As a possible salvation, teachers told you to duck and cover in school, to drop beneath your desk and ram your head between your legs as part of something my school district called a "disaster drill" but, of course, we knew better. We knew about the flash that could instantly blind you and the melting waves of heat and the deadly radioactivity. We also knew that the chance this gesture would protect one against a hundred megaton bomb was about as likely as getting a date with Annette Funicello, but at least the drills were an improvement on dividing fractions or diagramming sentences or studying the War of 1812. We went along with the joke.

Personally, I don't recall being unduly concerned about nuclear annihilation until the Cuban Missile Crisis of 1962 when I suddenly came to the realization that there were more pressing issues in life than perfecting my hook shot or putting the proper detailing on my Aurora model of the Creature From the Black Lagoon (I was never content with the tone of green I used for his scaly body). I devoured articles on bomb shelters in magazines like *Mechanics Illustrated* and eventually tried to persuade my father to dig one in our backyard, but logic (his, not mine) won out. "You're in school," he reasoned through my frantic pleas. "Your brother is at school and I'm at work. That leaves only your mother and she wouldn't want to go on living without us, would she?" At the time it made a crazy sort of sense, not that we consulted Mom about it. For the record, my mother's big concern in the fifties was not Khrushchev or the bomb, but my spilling Welch's Grape Juice on the beige living room carpet. All else paled next to this disaster.

So our family did without a bomb shelter (we made do with two rows of canned goods in the garage—mostly Campbell's Tomato Soup) and as a consequence I experienced more than my share of private nightmares about being roasted in a nuclear war. Outside of newspapers my main reference to things atomic and mushroom-shaped came from TV (*The Twilight Zone* was good for at least one atomic-related episode per season) and the movies I caught each Saturday at the horror double-feature downtown. Serious films about the Third World War didn't seem to interest either the public or the major Hollywood studios. Perhaps it was thought that avoiding such a grim subject might just make it go away. In any case such first-rate efforts as *On the Beach, Dr. Strangelove*, and *Failsafe* were delayed a few years for Frances the Talking Mule, Doris Day, Tammy, and other staples of the 1950s to run their celluloid courses.

It was therefore left to bargain-basement film producers and quick-buck artists, many already in the horror and science-fiction field, to trade in and exploit this theme. What this batch of pictures may have lacked in quality it more than made up for in variety and quirkiness. There was *The Last Woman on Earth* (1960), a Roger Corman cheapie about a love triangle among survivors of an atomic war; *Rocketship X-M* (1950), which showcased how atomic war on Mars had reduced the surviving inhabitants to vicious, rampaging mutants; and *World Without End* (1956), the story of spacemen who inadvertently break through the time barrier only to discover the Earth of the future following atomic oblivion. Atomic touches figured in *Beyond the Time Barrier* (1960), *The Time Machine* (1960), and *Terror From the Year 5,000* (1958). There was even a comedy of sorts called *The Atomic Kid* (1954), but as gullible as I might have been at five, I still couldn't buy even Mickey Rooney at his spunkiest surviving a hit at ground zero.

Atomic testing didn't stop with humans either. It set free *The Beast From 20,000 Fathoms* (1953) from its arctic confines, drove the giant octopus from *It Came From Beneath the Sea* (1955) to the surface where it took umbrage at several San Francisco landmarks before being blown into about fifty thousand calamari steaks, and also turned up in the careers of *The Giant Behemoth* (1959), the oversized locust from *Beginning of the End* (1957), the blood-sucking mollusks from *Attack of the Giant Leeches* (1959), and numerous other genetically altered aberrations.

Still, with the exception of these over bloated reptiles, mammoth mollusks, and poorly rear-projected insects munching on too much uranium, perhaps the oddest—and one of the earliest—of atomic bomb films, one which bizarrely mirrored the unreasoning paranoia and manufactured fears of the early 1950s, yet which presented its case with the sophistication and finesse of a Bowery Boys double feature, was Alfred E. Green's oddball, hysterically manipulative *Invasion, U.S.A.*, produced in cooperation

A small crowd of strangers gather in the afternoon to kill time in a downtown Manhattan bar. (Peggy Castle and Gerald Mohr seated in center.) Photofest

with American Pictures Corporation and released by Columbia Pictures in 1952. I am not kidding when I suggest that if I were asked to place one film in a time capsule that would accurately reflect the mood of that bygone decade, *Invasion, U.S.A.* would be a very likely candidate. In philosophy, crazy-quilt execution, topsy-turvy style and substance, it stands as testimony to the rampant political and philosophical excesses that earmarked America of the period.

Its plot is as simple and direct as its message.

A small crowd of strangers gather in the afternoon to kill time in a downtown Manhattan bar. There is an out-of-town factory owner (Robert Brice) and his beautiful but directionless cousin (Peggy Castle), an Arizona cattleman (Ed Mulfory), a bombastic politician (Wade Crosby), a television newsman (Gerald Mohr), and a strange individual who calls himself Mr. Ohman (Dan O'Herlihy). The reporter conducts an on-the-scene interview asking everyone for their opinions on the controversial issue of a universal draft. Across the board the reaction is a selfish one, with each expressing the feeling that government is already encroaching too heavily on their lives. The factory owner protests that the military has unsuccessfully tried to get him to change his product from tractors to tanks, which would make him lose profits. The politician explains that the people want peace.

Enemy planes penetrate air defenses on the East Coast and A-bomb New York, obliterating much of the city. Photofest

Suddenly a televised report announces that strange planes have been sighted over Alaska. The patrons react with indifference until a second broadcast reveals how they are actually attacking and that the "Red Alert" is on. The bar empties as each individual is now intent upon getting home and doing something about the situation ("Can you imagine those guys attacking the United States of America!?").

Scenes depict a group of the enemy strategizing over an enormous map of the United States, the President of the United States lamenting initial losses and promising the citizenry that for every bomb dropped on America three have been taken to the enemy's homeland.

Meanwhile, the Pacific Coast falls. San Francisco is in foreign hands (defended by what appears to be no more than two anti-aircraft guns) and the industrialist has been brutally murdered by the invading hordes. Hoover Dam is destroyed and our rancher and his family drowned. Men try to enlist but it is too late to train them. What is desperately needed is equipment and weapons ("We did not provide a strong enough army to protect ourselves").

Finally enemy planes penetrate air defenses on the East Coast and A-bomb New York (the enemy pilots, releasing their deadly cargo, actually say "Bombs avay") and obliterate much of the city. Officials contact the Pentagon begging for help to guard their states but they are turned down. The enemy land effortlessly in Washington D.C.

The enemy land effortlessly in Washington D.C. and attack Congress in session, mowing down elderly politicians with machine guns. Photofest

and attack Congress in session, mowing down elderly politicians with machine guns including the senator from the bar who had been soft on military spending (he falls near a statue of George Washington). Back in New York the newspaper man and girl are brutalized by two enemy soldiers who eventually kill the reporter, then try to rape the girl, but she breaks free and hurls herself through a window.

Suddenly we are back in the bar where all of this started. As it turns out the whole thing, the entire nightmare of the war, has been the result of mass hypnosis created by Mr. Ohman. Was it a dream, one of the groups asks. "It is unless you do something to stop it," he replies.

Invasion U.S.A. is not so much a movie with documentary footage and training films occasionally inserted for cost efficiency as it is documentary footage and training films with a meager story included. For every new scene legitimately shot for the picture, there are interminable stretches of dark and grainy film, most of them culled from World War II dog fights and sea battles, not to mention pointless (save as time fillers) moments of G.I.s doing nothing in particular. The footage is badly edited, with little thought given to continuity or flow, and is often good for a lot of unintentional laughs (a friend of mine insists that during an aerial confrontation a shot of a World War I bi-plane actually turns up and, although repeated viewings have failed to substantiate this, I did spot what appears to be a propeller job). In one scene, repeated several times, where the pilots at an Air Force base have been warned to scramble to engage enemy

Gerald Mohr (seated left), the silky-throated Bogart look-alike of numerous B mysteries and thrillers, comes off more cocky and breezy than intense as the newsman. Photofest

planes which are just about to drop atomic bombs on the installation, the footage shows airmen and crewmen leisurely strolling across the field totally oblivious to the nuclear detonation about to befall them.

Director Alfred E. Green, helmsman of over 60 films, began his career in silents dating back to the teens. His credits are a mixed bag. There were early classics like *Disraeli* (1929), a whole string of adventure and mystery films in the thirties including a Nero Wolfe film *The League of Frightened Men* (1937), and a Philo Vance whodunit *The Gracie Allen Murder Case* (1939). He sprang back the next decade with a few successes such as *The Jolson Story* (1946) and *The Fabulous Dorseys* (1947), but was at best a competent if unremarkable professional who worked fast and cheap. How he inherited *Invasion U.S.A.* or what he must have thought about it is anyone's guess, particularly as I have no inkling of his political bias. He certainly pulled out all the stops with stereotypical characters and situations so over the top that suggesting they *border* on parody is to give them their highest compliment. The only thing that can be said for Green's direction is that somehow, even with the inclusion of those endless documentary clips and hackneyed dialogue between actors who obviously don't care, he does manage to keep things moving. *Invasion U.S.A.* may be many things—nonsensical, moronic, hilarious, stunningly stupid—but never boring!

The performances are, much like the film itself, inconsistent and erratic and reflect great extremes of energy and sincerity. Gerald Mohr, the silky-throated Bogart look-alike of numerous B mysteries and thrillers (not to mention supplying the voice of the Scorpion in the serial classic *The Adventures of Captain Marvel* and being Philip Marlowe on the long-running radio series) comes off more cocky and breezy than intense as the newsman chronicling the downfall of America. Peggy Castle, blonde, feline, and much more alluring than any of her roles (*Target Zero, Son of Bell Star, Back From the Dead*), seems only mildly interested in a world crumbling around her. Dan O'Herlihy, always an interesting actor (*Adventures of Robinson Crusoe, The Desert Fox, The Cabinet of Dr. Caligari*), though listed third in the credits, has only a few minutes onscreen as Ohman, but given the theatricality of the part comes off credibly. It must not have been easy for him. Rugged and dependable Robert Brice lends convincing muscle as the no-nonsense industrialist, and it's certainly a novelty (and a great movie trivia question) to find TV's first two Lois Lanes, Phyllis Coates and Noel Neill in the same film, but never the same scene. For the record, when I met with the charming (and incredibly unchanged) Ms. Coates in 1993, she professed to having absolutely no recollection of having appeared in this film. One could hardly blame her. The rest of the cast are pretty much nonentities although the always reliable William Schallert has some good moments as a television newsman, and old-timer Tom Kennedy as Tim the bartender is a harmless comedic diversion.

In the matter of performances, no write-up on *Invasion U.S.A.* would be complete without reference to the villains of the piece. Although never identified by nationality and decked out in tight fitting, goose-stepping uniforms undoubtedly left over from some WWII film, the heavy Slavic accents and references to their leader leave little to the imagination. The guilty country is only referred to by both the President of the United States (portrayed by an uncredited actor whose face is only depicted in silhouette) and the participants as "He" as in "What do you think He is up to?" or "Where do you think He will strike next?"). One might expect such silliness in one of those Republic or Columbia serials of the late 1930s, but by the fifties this is just more hokiness in a film drowning in the stuff. Incidentally, I am particularly fond of an actor named Aram Katcher, initially depicted as a lowly window washer, who turns out to be not only a spy for the enemy but apparently one of their leaders (again the writers seem to have watched too many of those old cliffhangers). His mugging, screaming fits, and cliché-ridden speeches about the "people's army" would make him a standout in any case, but the fact that he is such a dead ringer for the immortal Dwight Frye only makes him more endearing.

There are so many unintentionally hilarious moments in the film that trying to single out a few would be next to impossible. Perhaps my personal favorite, if I must choose, comes near the film's conclusion when Washington D.C. is being attacked. A lone soldier has been stationed on guard duty (the Pentagon cannot spare more than one trooper to protect the nation's Capitol). He takes note of a group of G.I.s approaching (the enemy is cleverly wearing American uniforms) and challenges them to identify their unit. The result is the following exchange:

> That's an Illinois Division, isn't it?
> Yes.
> Ever go see the Cubs play?
> Cub is a young animal, a bear.

Invasion U.S.A. **is such a preposterous and comic book exercise that very few saw it and, of those who did, even fewer probably took it seriously. Photofest**

Invasion U.S.A. was the first film produced by Alfred Zugsmith, whose career would include such divergent projects as *Written on the Wind* (1956), *The Incredible Shrinking Man* (1957), *High School Confidential* (1958), and *Fanny Hill* (1964). Zugsmith, who lamented the $127,000 budget and seven-day shooting schedule he had to work with on *Invasion U.S.A.*, nonetheless is reported to have thought it "a good job."

Jack Rabin's special effects are inconsistent and only marginally effective although one can imagine the meager funds he was forced to work with. Most of the explosions are simply the result of flashes printed over pre-existing documentary footage, although the A-bombing of New York is handled with some degree of effectiveness. Across downtown Manhattan, a giant animated mushroom cloud, spreading its lethal heat and radioactivity, fans out over the familiar jagged skyline. However, the film's writers, Robert Smith (*Beast From 20,000 Fathoms*, *Girls' Town*) and Franz Spencer (*Masquerade In Mexico*), seemed not to have grasped the terribly devastating power of the bomb because only one building away from ground zero, victims, discovered under rubble, make it through without any visible signs of injury. I've always wondered if any survivors of Hiroshima or Nagasaki saw this film.

The film's composer, Albert Glasser, always seemed to be working on horror and science-fiction films. His resume reads like a history of the genre during the 1950s. A partial list of these would include *Indestructible Man*, *The Amazing Colossal Man*,

Invasion U.S.A. opening in New York

Earth vs. the Spider, and *Saga of the Viking Women and Their Voyage to the Waters of The Great Sea Serpent*. Not surprisingly, his score for *Invasion U.S.A.*, heavy on horns and drums, has a heavy, very strident military feel to it.

All of the crude editing, the jerry-rigged construction of the film, the anemic directing, the half-hearted performances, all of these ingredients, while painfully embarrassing and slipshod, simply pale next to the aggressively manipulative nature of the script and the primitive message of the film, which is about as subtle as, well... an atomic bomb. Military preparedness and a sensible appeal to the general public for caution and reasonable vigilance is one thing. However, this sort of blatant propaganda and mindless manipulation, particularly coming in the midst of a reactionary decade where such a mentality and perspective often saw lives and careers ruined, is quite a different matter and can be a very frightening and dangerous thing. Fortunately, *Invasion U.S.A.* is such a preposterous and comic book exercise that very few saw it and, of those who did, even fewer probably took it seriously. More the pity since as unintentional parody, in my opinion at least, it has never been equaled.

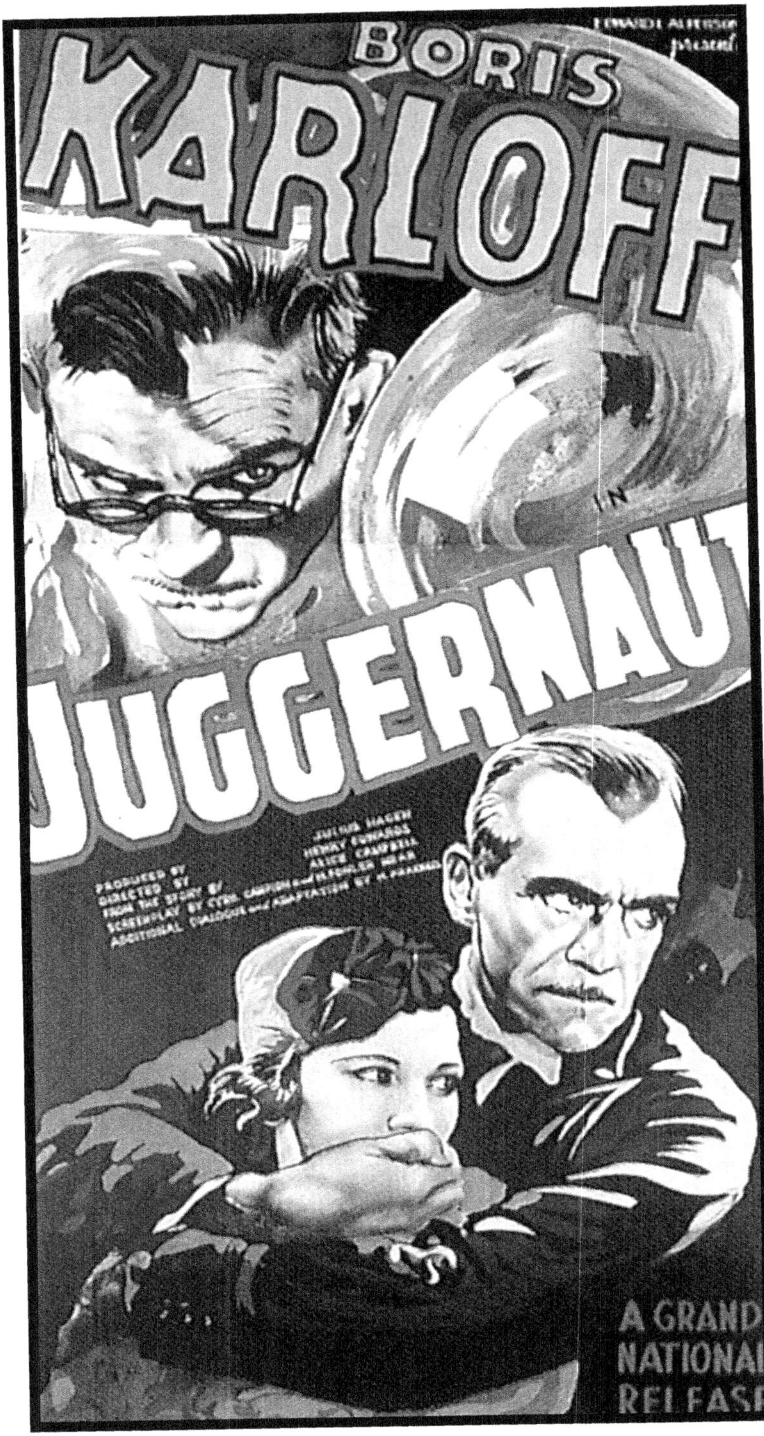
BORIS
KARLOFF
IN
A GRAND

JUGGERNAUT
by Nathalie Yafet

Juggernaut seems to be a film that is fashionable to lambaste. Peter Underwood is the only Karloff biographer (*Karloff*, Drake Publishers, 1972) who gives the film some credit, calling it "an excellent thriller." The others either politely ignore it, say as little as possible, or are merciless in their attacks. Scott Allen Nollen, in his biography (*Boris Karloff*, McFarland, 1991), is the most vicious, saying that, "Karloff... merely affects a few melodramatic, scowling facial expressions and utters a few lines of banal dialogue—creating one of his worst cinematic performances." Tom Weaver also skewers the actor (*Poverty Row Horrors!*, McFarland, 1993), declaring that, "... he's so phony and exaggeratedly sinister in... *Black Friday, The Climax* and *House of Frankenstein*... He's even *worse* in the British *Juggernaut*... playing a murdering doctor seeking a paralysis cure." (One can only speculate as to what Mr. Weaver's agenda was since these films have nothing to do with his subject matter!) Milder digs include "a minor melodrama..." (Michael R. Pitts, *Horror Film Stars*, McFarland, 1981); "a ponderous B crime drama" (Beverly Bare Buehrer, *Boris Karloff*, Greenwood Press, 1993); and "ordinary crime thriller..." (Denis Gifford, *Karloff: The Man, The Monster, The Movies*, Curtis Books, 1973).

Contemporary reviews, however, were mixed. Bland Johaneson of the *Mirror* (July 16, 1937) stated, "Mr. Karloff is interesting in the role which demands that he look intensely like a scientist" and he..."remains a substantial Hollywood bogey-man, providing pleasant chills for the casual addicts to murder melodrama." She also liked the rest of the cast, "Miss Joan Wyndham, a provocative beauty, plays the leading supporting role, leading a cast of accomplished English actors which included Arthur Margetson and Miss Mona Goya." Oddly enough, one of the pressbook pictures of Boris Karloff and Mona Goya lists her name as Joan Wyndham. I wonder if this reviewer could have taken part of her information from that, since Mona Goya certainly "plays the leading supporting role" and Joan Wyndham, pretty as she is, could not really be called "a provocative beauty." William Boehnel in the *New York World Telegram* (July 15, 1937) was not as kind. To him, *Juggernaut* was a "feeble, fumbling English melodrama... crudely directed and acted, the film has little about it to recommend unless it is its courage in braving the competition that now exists along Broadway." An unidentified review from *The Sun* (July 15, 1937) was in the same vein. "The English, when they make bad pictures, do so even more thoroughly than Hollywood." This same review goes on to say, "The story is allegedly a thriller, concerned with the efforts at murder by the most bungling villains even the movies have concocted... They seemed, in fact, all three of them, to be quite as stupid as most criminals in real life. Nor are they entertaining about it. Boris Karloff plays the desperate doctor with his usual glum deadpan. The rest... all acted as though the cameras had alarmed them badly." Ditto in *The Motion Picture Herald* (October 17, 1936): "Boris Karloff is the shop-window asset of this very lurid melodrama... It is not a typical horror film, but Karloff's characterization of a doctor who murders in order to get money for medical research is a study of a warped and repellent type..."

R.B.F.'s review in the *Journal* (July 15, 1937) was something else altogether. "Karloff scores in a corking new film. Here's a whale of a story and its chief character is Karloff, but it contains less Karloff than it really should." (I couldn't argue with that!) "Capably directed, *Juggernaut* concludes itself in a manner befitting Boris Karloff..." *The Cinema* (September 16, 1936) reported, "Sympathetic work by Karloff in basically repellent role proves highlight... strong meat for the masses with stellar pull." Finally, the pressbook states, "That Karloff needs none of the fantastic masks and weird habiliments to create an atmosphere of terror, which usually have been an adjunct to his acting, was apparent. His performance was unforgettable, his piercing, fanatical eyes alone, being sufficient to titillate the spines of all his fascinated audience... Joan Wyndham plays the part of the scientist's assistant and registers splendidly in the emotional scenes. Arthur Margetson as the murdered man's son is more than adequate in a somewhat difficult role, while Mona Goya, as Lady Clifford, his stepmother, makes a most attractive villain." (It is comforting to think that none of these critics from 1936-1937 are remembered today, but Boris Karloff is. So it will be with today's critics. Time has a way of separating the wheat from the chaff.) I have been an avid Karloff fan since the age of eight and love *him* in everything he did. Some of the plots and supporting casts of his other films leave me cold, but I like *Juggernaut*. It is not his best, nor my own personal favorite (which will always be *The Black Room*), but it does not deserve its bad reputation.

As the film opens, a small skiff floating on a river slowly dissolves to an angry Dr. Sartorius tearing some documents and throwing them across the room. A colleague, Dr. Millet, is admitted by the somewhat mysterious Moroccan butler, Jacques. Inexplicably, though work is going very well, Sartorius' application for a grant to research cures for "certain types of flaccid paralysis" has been rejected. (It's interesting to note that all the biographies say ataxic instead of flaccid paralysis. The doctor is definitely saying flaccid and gives it a British pronunciation with a hard "c.") Rather than the "scowling facial expressions" that Mr. Nollen objects to, I see the character of Dr. Sartorius being *immediately* established as a man obsessed with one objective. When the means to achieve it are abruptly ended, he is despondent because it is his life's work and he is in poor health. He tells Millet, "I'd give 10 years of my life to get the money to enable me to carry on." Karloff's expressions and movements are strong and straight to the point. His delivery of, "They're far too occupied with other things to bother about the fate of future generations," as he raises one eyebrow and hurls a book across the room with a thud, is particularly good. This scene also, unfortunately, gives us our first glimmer of some strange dialogue that is sprinkled throughout the film. Dr. Millet accepts a drink from Jacques, and in the midst of listening sympathetically to Dr. Sartorius' woes, he says, "chin, chin." This casual toasting expression is glaringly out of place here. We next learn that Sartorius' friend, Dr. Bousquet, has offered him a practice on the French Riviera, which he has accepted.

Cut to a private gambling room in the Côte d'Azur. Lady Yvonne Clifford and her completely useless gentleman friend, Captain Arthur Halliday, are playing stud poker. They lose. Some rich, bored people milling about in the casino inform us that Lady Clifford is married to the "fabulously wealthy" cotton millionaire, Sir Charles Clifford, and so can afford to back Captain Halliday's extravagances. However, Yvonne informs Arthur that they have been spending a lot of money lately, that she is "hopelessly overdrawn" and that her latest check "won't be met." Arthur tells her that "something has to be done" and pettishly moves away from her when she tries to comfort him. Why can't this man get a job or ask his own family for money? Kudos to Antony Ireland! His portrayal of this unsavory man is amazing. He doesn't try to engage the audience's sympathies; not even once. It's a mystery why Lady Clifford who is beautiful, dynamic, rich, and a woman of action is so attracted to this gambling-addicted, brillantined, slothful casino lizard. Mona Goya's Lady Yvonne Clifford seems to personify *Juggernaut*'s faults to many people. Continuing his assault on the film, Scott Allen Nollen declares, "Worse than the nonexistent dramatic motivation, the lackluster direction, and Karloff's uninterested portrayal, the histrionic excess and childish outbursts of Mona Goya make *Juggernaut* a laughable viewing experience." Yet, her interpretation is incredibly correct. The woman is totally ruled by her passions. Common sense, decency, and loyalty have no place in her life. She is willing to do, and does do, whatever she thinks it will take to achieve her objective. Her acting gives us a vivid picture of this troubled, amoral woman. We wouldn't want to see Katharine Hepburn in this role.

  The next scene introduces us to Sir Charles Clifford and his sister, Mary (who, incidentally, gets my vote for one of the sweetest cinema aunts ever). Sir Charles does not like gambling or Captain Halliday and is unwilling to give Yvonne money for these purposes. Mary reminds him that the doctor has told him not to get excited. Sir Charles asks what the doctor knows, anyway, and his sister then suggests that he try Dr. Sartorius. Mary tells him that she "read somewhere that Dr. Sartorius is a great scientist." Immediate shift to the good doctor in his laboratory, peering through a beaker and jotting down notes; the transition is inane and obvious, but the actors can't be faulted for

Yvonne (Mona Goya) goes to Dr. Sartorius (Karloff) in hopes of striking a deal with him.

that. His servant, Jacques, tells him via speaking tube that Nurse Eve Rowe has arrived to interview for a job. Our first impressions of Eve are positive. She is personable, attractive, and seems capable. Joan Wyndham is instantly likable in this very sympathetic role. She does have one annoying habit; occasionally, while speaking to another character, she will slowly look away almost as if she is "cheating" out to the audience. A brief conversation settles that she will start working for the doctor at once. Gibb McLaughlin, as Jacques, is wonderfully oily and sycophantic. As he leads the nurse to the doctor's laboratory, his long, slightly swaybacked body undulates up the stairs with unbelievable fluidity. McLaughlin shades even the most routine expository dialogue with hidden meanings—such as, "You be here long, lady?" His timing is superb. In the Moroccan scene, he is wrangling over transportation costs for his employer, then is all civility the second he spies Dr. Millet. The first time I saw this film, I thought that Jacques would be important to the plot in some peculiarly sinister way. No such luck, but it's a lot of fun to see such a fully realized characterization in what could have been a throwaway supporting role.

    We next see Mary at home with her brother. Yvonne is at the mirror, preparing to go out. She treats her husband to some phony protestations of love and complains of having "so much to do that I don't know what to do first." Morton Setten as Sir Clifford gives a marvelous line reading when he says to Yvonne, "You mustn't keep your dressmaker waiting," with a meaningful pause before saying dressmaker.

    No one's favorite character, Captain Arthur Halliday, now tries to convince *Madame* (the actress is uncredited and the character is addressed by no other name) to give him some type of managerial position on one of her ranches. She laughingly informs him that he's a very good dancer but working on a ranch wouldn't be in his line. (So, Captain Halliday is a good dancer! This must be the secret of his elusive allure since there's nothing else to recommend him.) Our anti-heroine, Yvonne, dramatically enters and we discover that she was a cabaret entertainer in the past. She is, naturally, distraught that Arthur is speaking to Madame, even though the lady in question is anything but a *femme fatale*, and threatens to kill herself if she sees him talking to her again. They execute only a few tango steps before Captain Halliday pulls Lady Clifford off the dance floor. With shifty eyes and scornful sneer, he hints that a job on one of Madame's ranches is in the offing, but he hasn't promised to accept it. He nastily adds that he "can't live on air." These remarks push Yvonne to go to Dr. Sartorius in hopes of striking some sort of a deal with him. (She hesitates a moment before ringing the bell. This very subtle bit of business contradicts the comment about her "histrionic excess." She is not completely reconciled to what she has come to do.) Once again, Gibb McLaughlin as Jacques is a delight as he ushers her in and seems to know everything!

There are few false notes in the ensuing scene with Lady Clifford and Dr. Sartorius. The gravity of the discussion is enhanced by tight close-ups and constant interspersing of other short scenes. This technique heightens the suspense because we are not allowed to hear the entire conversation. Yvonne informs Dr. Sartorius that she read in the paper of his research funds being cut off. His clipped response, "Not many people interest themselves in my affairs, Lady Clifford," exposes all his bitter disappointment. It's unfortunate that the doctor has to tell Lady Clifford, almost as an aside, "I haven't very long to live, you know." This vital information about Dr. Sartorius should not be disclosed in a clumsy line that is impossible to deliver well. Dr. Sartorius cannot believe that this spoiled society woman could be so interested in science and, with a decidedly unwholesome glint in her eyes, she tells him, "It is my *husband* I'm interested in." Almost in awe, this dedicated scientist repeats Lady Clifford's offer, "20,000 pounds!" Only inches away from him, she urges, "Your opportunity, doctor, it may not come again." Angrily, Dr. Sartorius asks, "What brought you to me?" With serpentine skill, she flatters, "Your reputation and your great *need* to carry out your life's work." Worried that he will not accept her offer, she asks again. When he agrees to the Faustian bargain, her relief and tiny, satisfied smile are palpable.

After all is arranged, the doctor's household prepares for his trip to the Clifford villa. As Karloff slowly descends the stairs, one is reminded fleetingly of his character Janos Rukh in *The Invisible Ray*! When Eve asks him if he intends to concentrate on the one case, he replies, with a delightfully sinister brio, "Yes, it interests me—an unusual case—it interests me intensely." His friend, Dr. Bousquet, arrives to take over his practice and, as enacted by Victor Rietti, is totally credible as an outgoing, amicable professional. As Dr. Sartorius leaves, Dr. Bousquet remonstrates with him for working too hard. He answers, "I must!" Boris Karloff was always a master at speaking volumes, even when saying very little, and this scene is a prime illustration.

At the Clifford mansion, Yvonne asks the "resident physician" if there will "be any risk?" Dr. Sartorius dryly responds that, "if there is, talking about it is not going to lessen it." In Sir Charles' room, the millionaire is anxiously awaiting the arrival of Roger, his son from a previous marriage. When Roger comes, he greets his Aunt Mary affectionately and, upon meeting Eve, is immediately attracted to her. (Arthur Margetson was a perfect choice for this genial, honorable, and loyal son.) Roger, upon being taken to see his father, asks him what's going on and is told, "Goodness knows—I don't—and apparently no one else does either." Morton Setten is so touching and vulnerable here that it makes us forgive his former irascible crustiness. Sir Charles is worried about Yvonne's gambling and carrying on with Captain Halliday, so he has executed a power of attorney for Roger while he is still alive and has also made a new will so that Roger will become her sole trustee. Captain Halliday himself then arrives and declares that he has come to take Yvonne to dinner. (Aunt Mary is sweetly polite even to this questionable character. The woman seems not to have any ill-feeling toward anyone!) Halliday goes upstairs to wait for Yvonne, spies the doctor and says, offhandedly, "Oh hello, Sartorius." When he wonders if, perhaps, the doctor doesn't remember him, Dr. Sartorius, with delicious double-meaning, says, "No, I remember you. Your name is Halliday—a most interesting case." Halliday, taking him quite literally, replies, "I suppose these touch-and-go cases give you doctors no end of a thrill." As the disreputable pair leave arm-in-arm, Dr. Sartorius' expression plainly displays his distaste. Yvonne sees Roger downstairs, which allows Mona Goya to do one of the things she does best in this film—exhibit sham emotion. She expresses her "regret" that she must be out the first evening he is there, and pleads "a previous appointment" with a significant sideways look. Roger, barely controlling his disapproval of the man, sees that Halliday is "still knocking about these parts." In a revealing statement, Halliday replies, "As well here as anywhere else." Roger meets his father's new physician, which gives Boris Karloff another fine moment. Anxiously, Roger says, "Get him well, doctor. I'm sure he couldn't be in better hands." Dr. Sartorius' only response is an odd look and a chilly little bow, which should warn Roger that something is greatly amiss. Roger is puzzled, but dismisses any misgivings and goes into dinner with his Aunt Mary and Eve. While at dinner, he asks Eve to go out dancing with him and she accepts.

Joan Wyndham and Arthur Margetson are absolutely captivating romantic leads. They are not stereotypical for the period. She is too thin and not movie star glamorous; he is a bit too chubby and doesn't have a profile to die for. What a relief! These are real people who happen to like each other, with whom we can easily identify. They make a refreshing contrast to their annoying counterparts in *The Mask of Fu Manchu* and *The Raven*, to name two examples.

Yvonne sneaks Arthur into the house after everyone is asleep, or so she thinks, and they have a romantic interlude, which is interrupted by Roger who orders Captain Halliday out of the house. When Yvonne loudly protests, he says, "As long as you live under my father's roof, you'll observe the common decencies." This is spoken with exactly the right amount of strength and respectability. Yvonne, being the sort of woman she is, continues to complain about this treatment, which forces Roger to tell her about the new financial arrangements his father has made. She yells that she will never take orders from him. Then, in a frenzy, she rushes to Sir Charles' room, accuses him of treating her "cruelly," and shakes him. She is truly distasteful here, but as her character is not a sympathetic one, the interpretation is correct. The night nurse summons Dr. Sartorius to the sickroom and he hands Yvonne over to Roger with a little shove, demonstrating once again that he does not like this woman. Sir Charles, chin quivering, says, "I'm all right, doctor; I'm used to these scenes, you know." As Dr. Sartorius sends the night nurse to get a "stimulant," it is difficult not to want to warn the poor, trusting man of what is in store for him. Downstairs, Yvonne is unable to calm

Boris Karloff's Dr. Sartorius is *immediately* established as a man obsessed with one objective.

down and, when Roger tries to silence her by putting his hand over her mouth, she bites him! Aunt Mary then utters her only disapproving line in the whole film, "Yvonne, Yvonne how could you?" Roger Clifford is so much the gentleman that he seems to be more concerned about Yvonne's lowering herself than he is about his own wound. Dr. Sartorius administers the fatal "stimulant" to his patient and hands the syringe to Nurse Rowe. Aunt Mary bursts in and begs her to see to Roger's bleeding hand. Eve goes downstairs, carrying the syringe, and lays it in a magazine as she looks at the injury. She returns to Sir Charles' room and is reproved for unprofessional conduct and for misplacing the syringe. Naturally enough, Dr. Sartorius does not want the incriminating evidence to be found by anyone. As Sir Charles starts to slip away, Dr. Sartorius tells Nurse Rowe to call the family. Yvonne, when she is summoned, has a nice moment at her mirror as she rearranges her face to show appropriate grief. The scene closes on a reprehensible little note, as Dr. Sartorius, focusing on Yvonne just after her husband's death, sees her undisguised satisfaction.

Next morning, Lady Clifford, smoking and in a very good mood, asks Chalmers to bring Dr. Sartorius to her. The doctor himself, increasingly alarmed at the absence of the syringe, continues to question his nurse about it. Eve tells Roger that he should see the doctor about his hand since he is not feeling any better. Yvonne expansively tells Dr. Sartorius that she will have his check for him in a few days and he can stay on until

Boris Karloff's always expressive eyes and voice here telegraph this image of a man who has risked everything and is gradually losing control.

then. Roger asks Eve to bring him the magazine he was reading and to tell Chalmers to get him a brandy and soda. She says he should have Evian water, at least until the doctor examines his hand. On her way to find Roger's magazine, she encounters Dr. Sartorius, who by now is extremely worried and covers this emotion by exploding, "It's unprofessional. Find it! Find it!" Boris Karloff's always-expressive eyes and voice here telegraph this image of a man who has risked everything and is gradually losing control. Eve, of course, discovers the syringe in the magazine and keeps it because her suspicions are aroused. Cut to Yvonne screaming at Roger in furious disbelief about the terms of Sir Charles' new will. She rages that her late husband has treated her "like a child." Not missing a beat, Roger replies, "Perhaps he thought that would be the best way to treat you." Unable to contain herself, Yvonne runs to Dr. Sartorius and informs him that "Roger has control of everything." The doctor's response, "Then what I've done—I've done for nothing," uttered in total despair, proves once again how much this actor always has the power to move us, even when his character's actions are unconscionable. Dr. Sartorius swiftly decides that Yvonne must assist him in doing away with Roger. As she protests, he answers with a fierce intensity, "Everything I lived for is within my grasp and I'm not going to have it snatched away from me now." Lady Clifford and Dr. Sartorius change places in this scene. When the bargain was struck earlier, she had all the power. Now the doctor compels her to join him in his downward spiral. He has killed once; killing a second time will be easier. This scene convinces me absolutely that Boris Karloff would have made a magnificent Macbeth. Had he been as respected as Orson Welles and not been considered merely a genre actor, he would have been given the chance. In fact, the Macbeth parallels are strong throughout. Yvonne is the insidious Lady, urging Dr. Sartorius to murder for his own ends; more murders would have occurred if everything went according to plan, and neither protagonist survives.

Meanwhile, Eve has taken the syringe to the chemist, Duvall, to be analyzed and sent to her at the Clifford villa. Inconveniently, upon returning, Lady Clifford discharges her. Dr. Sartorius is now frantically looking for the syringe himself and casually tells Chalmers that, "It's of no consequence, but if you happen to find it, let me know." Dr. Sartorius searches for the syringe with increasing agitation. Smoking, he flings his still-lit cigarette away with a violent gesture. Duvall phones with the results of the analysis. Dr. Sartorius, already knowing what he will hear, takes the report anyway.

We next see Chalmers alarmed about Roger's condition as he's never known him to be ill "in all the years (he's) been with the family." J.H. Roberts, just as Gibb McLaughlin did with Jacques, gives us a completely fleshed-out portrayal of Chalmers. Never just a deadpan proper British butler, he convincingly shows affection for Aunt Mary, Eve, and Roger, respect for Dr. Sartorius, and disapproval of Yvonne.

Captain Halliday turns up at the Clifford residence just like a bad penny and Dr. Sartorius orders him to drive to the chemist's as, "This concerns you and Lady Clifford vitally!" When the doctor goes back inside for his hat, he overhears Eve on the phone exclaiming, "So it was poison." He grabs her from behind and takes her to his old laboratory. She wakes up, finds the door locked, resourcefully shoves a table beneath the skylight, and stacks a chair on top of it. Realizing that she will need a line to the ground from the roof, she tears down one of the curtains and uses that. While this is going on, Captain Arthur Halliday enacts what is, undeniably, *Juggernaut*'s most inadvertently humorous scene. He pours himself drink after drink and manages to get stinking drunk in a few minutes. He also puts a gun into his pocket, so I think the intention was to show him steeling himself to the decidedly unpleasant task of disposing of Nurse Rowe. However, this is not clear and conflicts with information that we receive from Nurse Rowe herself later in the film. Halliday breaks part of the door in with a chair only to see Eve escaping through the skylight.

Back at the mansion, Roger conveys his regard for Eve, in an inimitably British manner, as he asks Aunt Mary why his new friend left so abruptly, as they were "getting along pretty well together." Enter Dr. Sartorius, who prevents Roger from going out to search for Eve under the pretense that his patient is not well enough to do so.

Yvonne slips tremulously into Roger's study in order to tamper with his Evian water. Chalmers, hearing questionable sounds, enters the room himself and wrests the vial from her. In what is undoubtedly J. H. Roberts' best moment, he holds it up, looks at Mona Goya for a breathless minute, slowly nods, and says, "So this is why Mr. Roger is ill." Caught in the act and unable to face him down, Yvonne faints.

Dr. Sartorius examines Roger's hand, suspects it may be "septic" and recommends an injection. Quick cut to Eve driving up with Dr. Bousquet and wildly hurrying to the dining room where she surprises her former employer just as he is about to inject Roger with poison. Her pronouncement, "He's trying to murder you, just as he murdered your father," proves Joan Wyndham's impressive range as she leaps from being the calm young lady we have come to know to the outraged, desperate woman we see here. She tells Roger that Dr. Sartorius tried to kill her and if she "hadn't replaced the poison with water, he'd have succeeded." Earlier, we saw Arthur Hall-iday getting blotto so that he could shoot Eve and now discover that Dr. Sartorius himself tried to give her one of his "injections." We have the writers to thank for this confusion. Dr. Bousquet offers to analyze the contents of the syringe himself and a charmingly dignified Dr. Sartorius states, "But of course, my dear Bousquet—but wait"; injects himself and dies. Chalmers and a gendarme bring Yvonne in as her accomplice drops to the floor. In an affecting final shot, Roger comforts Eve after her ordeal. (Contrast this with *The Raven's* denouement!) *Juggernaut* closes with a stylish art deco clock whose sweeping hands display, "The End." (In the slightly longer version, which I have not seen, Dr. Sartorius, after poisoning himself, dictates a report on his symptoms before he dies.) It really is a shame that the 70-minute version is not readily available. Dr. Sartorius is far too interesting a character to have such an embarrassingly brief expiration and Yvonne, a major player in the rest of the film, is injected into the final scene almost as an afterthought. As a result, the ending appears haphazard and carelessly thrown together.

Unjustly maligned for far too long, this film has many intriguing elements that deserve mention here. The characters are worth comparing. First, there is the dark, passionate relationship between Yvonne and Arthur Halliday (although I strongly suspect that Halliday's passion is Yvonne's money and not Yvonne herself) and then the fond, unmistakably real regard that develops between Eve and Roger. Yvonne and Arthur are doomed from the beginning. They live for the moment, with as much money as they can lay their hands on. Yvonne does appear to feel more for Arthur than he does for her, but it's a safe bet that she is frequently involved in this kind of situation. Captain Arthur Halliday doesn't even have that excuse. The bounder truly believes that Yvonne should wheedle a constant supply of cash from her husband so that he can feed his gambling habit. He is dishonest, lazy, and purposeless. We can only hope that he is tried as an accessory to the murder. Eve and Roger unhesitatingly react to each other's generosity, sociability, and wit. Their dancing scene at the Splendide differs from similar scenes in other films in that it is never cloying and that we are not impatient for it to end so that we can return to the main action. We are comfortable with this couple, enjoy their lighthearted banter, and wish them well. They will probably have a happy marriage after the final reel.

Mary Clifford and Madame (sorry, no other name!) are both older, incredibly wealthy, apparently single women. Miss Clifford is completely devoted to her brother and her nephew and is unfailingly courteous and sweet to everyone. She goes out of her way to treat Nurse Rowe, who after all is hired help, as if she were family. She is an ideal aunt, sister, employer, and friend, although she is admittedly too trusting for her own good. Madame spends her time idling in the casinos, allowing herself to be doted on by obsequious twits who are only interested in her money and any advantage that her position might bring. We see one of them being sent from her table to make room for Captain Halliday, who is her particular favorite. She has no illusions about the scum around her, but certainly could do something more worthwhile with her time and resources.

Jacques and Chalmers are long-time servants. Jacques seems devoted enough, but spends a fair amount of time eavesdropping on Dr. Sartorius. He is insatiably curious and does not appear especially trustworthy. One gets the distinct impression that he could be bought. Chalmers is the perfect butler, unfailingly correct, accommodating and loyal. He never oversteps his bounds except when Roger's life is threatened.

Dr. Sartorius must be considered separately. It is the classic Karloff role, the high-minded doctor or scientist who commits an ignoble deed to achieve a noble end. *The Invisible Ray, Night Key, The Man They Could Not Hang, The Man With Nine Lives, Before I Hang, The Ape, The Devil Commands, Corridors of Blood*, and *The Sorcerers* are some other examples. This man pursues his dream of finding a cure for spinal paralysis with a selfless, single-minded fervor. He reasons, wrongly, that the death of one elderly man is justified in order to save many lives. It's a shame that the writers involved in *Juggernaut* didn't do a better job with the dialogue. Any insight

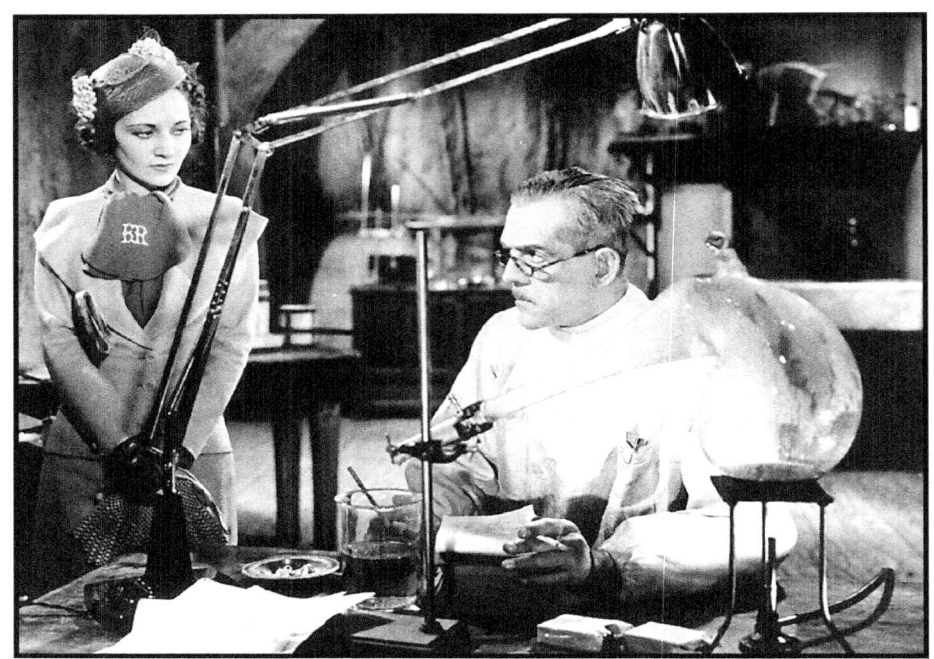

Juggernaut **will never be one of the top-ten classics, but it is an entertaining little film that boasts a wonderful Karloff presence.**

afforded into the soul of Dr. Sartorius is solely due to Boris Karloff's interpretation. The importance of his work is also unclear. "Certain types of flaccid paralysis," is far too ambiguous and leaves us (possibly) doubting the merit of his efforts. The brevity of the film doesn't help, either.

In the course of *Juggernaut*, doors play a pivotal role. There are 34 entrances and 21 exits. When one door closes, another opens—and vice versa. Thus, the doctor's application for a grant is denied, but Lady Clifford proffers 20,000 pounds in exchange for the murder of her husband. Sir Charles stops supplying unlimited cash, so his wife decides to solve the problem by arranging his premature death. Yvonne believes she has triumphed, yet soon discovers that her despised stepson has control of the estate. Dr. Sartorius thinks he has found the means, however base, of continuing his research, only to learn that Lady Clifford cannot pay him. Roger loses his father, but finds Eve. Windows figure into the plot only twice. Yvonne smuggles Arthur in through the window, following their dinner together. Hearkening back to the great silent movie heroines, Eve, the damsel in distress, rescues herself but exits through a window instead of the door.

The sets are suitably elegant and exotic. The Moroccan flavor of the first scene is enhanced by a small boat floating on a river, camels and donkeys milling about, men in Eastern headgear, and palm trees. Casino interiors look realistic and lavish. Dr. Sartorius' Victorian house is cozy and unpretentious. The Clifford villa is sumptuous, with crystal chandeliers and marble mantelpieces, but we could stand to see more of it.

Costumes, though uncredited, are effective. Mona Goya's are spectacular and she wears them with flair. A shimmering evening gown with matching coat and an Art Deco day dress with stylized belt buckle, white cowl collar sensationally draped in the back, and bell sleeves ending in white cuffs are two of the smartest. Joan Wyndham has a full range from practical suits and nurse's uniforms to demure dancing dress, complete with gauzy cape. Aunt Mary's gowns are stylish, but never flashy; I particularly like her black, fluttery mourning dress. Eastern headgear and apparel in the Moroccan scene look authentic. The men are dashing in suits and tuxedos. Antony Ireland is coolly caddish in his blazer and white slacks.

The acting is believable. Even the minor characters perform their parts with finesse. Dr. Millet, the sharper playing cards against Captain Halliday, the man and woman discussing Lady Clifford in the casino, Madame's fawning friend, the night nurse, and Duvall, the chemist, are all memorable. Director Henry Edwards deserves credit for orchestrating the ensemble so that they work together. My only complaint is that the Cliffords should have more servants as Chalmers is the only one we see.

Juggernaut's score is marvelously evocative. As the titles roll, we hear Dr. Sartorius' "fate" theme. Opening with a brass fanfare, the strings then introduce the theme. Fourths and minor seconds build to an octave leap that descends dramatically in a melodic minor scale. We hear it again at our first sight of Dr. Sartorius, as he prepares to leave Morocco. This music is grandly, tragically Verdi-esque. It is a wrenching picture of Sartorius' hopes, dreams, and ultimate end—an apt illustration of the definition of juggernaut, "A massive inexorable force or object that crushes whatever is in its path." It reappears, again and again, as we see Dr. Sartorius taking the steps that will lead to his own destruction. A pizzicato variation develops when Dr. Sartorius takes Duvall's report over the phone. Moroccan scenes are underscored with insistent woodwinds that are interrupted by the overpowering fate theme. Yvonne and Arthur have their own theme of swirling strings, Tchaikovskian in their melancholic despair. This same theme ends abruptly on three short notes when Roger interrupts them at the Clifford mansion. French cabaret tunes at the casino are followed by a sizzling tango as the couple dances. Yvonne slinks around the Clifford mansion, backed by ominous brass. When Nurse Rowe finds the syringe, the ugly truth slowly dawning on her, we hear, in contrast to the unresolved fate theme, the strongest possible harmonic closure: Dominant seventh resolving to its tonic. Only at the very end, with the death of Dr. Sartorius, does the fate theme have its own closure. Some musical transitions are poorly handled. One jarring example is when Roger asks the doctor to make his father well, which is instantly followed by Aunt Mary announcing dinner to the accompaniment of sprightly strings.

Juggernaut deserves a second chance. It will never be one of the top-10 classics, but it is an entertaining little film that boasts a wonderful Karloff presence, gripping storyline, terrific music, jazzy Art Deco look, and talented supporting players. I enjoy it each time I see it. Watch it again; you might change your mind!

WARNER-COLUMBIA FILM, S.N.C. présente stelt voor
CHARLTON HESTON
LE SURVIVANT
THE ΩMEGA MAN
A WALTER SELTZER PRODUCTION CO-STARRING ANTHONY ZERBE · ROSALIND CASH SCREENPLAY BY JOHN WILLIAM and JOYCE H. CORRINGTON
PRODUCED BY WALTER SELTZER · DIRECTED BY BORIS SAGAL · PANAVISION® · TECHNICOLOR® FROM WARNER BROS.
DE OVERLEVENDE

THE OMEGA MAN
by Jeff Hillegass

What is it that makes a film a guilty pleasure? I maintain that guilty pleasures are discovered retroactively. One day, you view a film that you hadn't watched for many years, and you suddenly realize that this wonder you used to love is, frankly, difficult to sit through. There is still a great deal you like about the film, but much of your pleasure derives from memories of your initial viewing, from a time when cinema was less sophisticated, and so were you. Seeing the movie again, you feel a nostalgic twinge, but realize you probably wouldn't think twice about the opus if this were your first viewing. More significantly, you hope that no friends or family members walk through and ask, "Why are you watching *this*?" If they do, you may mumble, "Oh, nothing, just some old film... I actually used to be quite a fan of this." All the while, you try not to let on the fact that you are still somehow enamored of this hoary old production. Your affections seem, on the surface, entirely indefensible.

Cult movies and guilty pleasures share this commonality of discovery. The difference is that a cult movie is embraced by a cross-section of people, while a guilty pleasure provides hidden and perplexing enjoyment for *one*. Cult movies are typically films that foundered on their initial release, but were rediscovered, either within the dying environment of repertory movie houses, on television, or, more commonly these days, on prerecorded videocassettes. Certain films attract a cult following in their initial release. For a film to truly qualify as a cult film, there should be an implicit acknowledgment by the audience that they've stumbled onto a real find, something far off the beaten path of worn multiplex carpeting. The concept of cult movies is really only a few decades old, dating to the advent of cinema studies programs in the 1960s and the concurrent rise of midnight screenings in college towns. Nothing is more offensive to a cult audience than a self-conscious cult film. Anything advertised as a "Cult Movie" prior to release is as suspect as the recent Disney marketing term, "Instant Classic." Usually, these marketing efforts are merely knockoffs of films that have successfully drawn cult approval; note the spate of neo-*Eraserhead* surrealistic endeavors, such as *Tales from the Gimli Hospital,* as examples.

Guilty pleasures, on the other hand, are often mainstream releases that may even have been heralded upon initial release. The test of time is brutal to these films, however, and many of them age as well as forgotten eggs in the back of a refrigerator. The film buff who has a guilty pleasure, and we all have one or two, is forced to admit that there is very little that redeems this particular work, and those few sterling elements are largely overshadowed by all the moments that make one cringe in embarrassment. The experience of a guilty pleasure is a highly emotional one. You are hard-pressed to explain yourself, but you take comfort in the reacquaintance with a cinematic old friend, although this "friend" is one you'd never want to meet in public.

Guilty pleasures are likely to stem from an era of restricted viewing. If certain viewing experiences are more difficult to come by, there is less chance they will be taken for granted. As one who was born in the sixties, I find myself drawn to the films of the late sixties and early seventies. While I have clear memories of being taken to theatrical showings of *Willie Wonka and the Chocolate Factory* and *The Great Gatsby* (yes, *The Great Gatsby*; my parents evidently tired of children's fare, and I can't thank them enough for giving me the social status of being the first 2nd grader to see PG-rated movies), my fondest recollections are of staying up to see the initial telecasts of films from the 1968-1972 era, which were broadcast in the mid-seventies. The 1968-1972 years were a wonderful time for movies, as boundaries were explored by productions such as *Midnight Cowboy*, *Planet of the Apes*, *Dirty Harry*, *A Clockwork Orange*, and *The Godfather*. New strides in storytelling, cinematography, editing, and music were evident in each new production.

Usually, I would be able to see only the first hour of the ABC Movie of the Week, as my bedtime would beckon. If the film was preceded by a parental discretion warning, I might have been denied access altogether, or finally allowed to watch the first hour after much protest, which, of course, fueled my fascination.

My first James Bond film was *Diamonds Are Forever*, and *Dracula Has Risen From the Grave* was the first Hammer film I had occasion to sample. Neither were particularly distinguished works, but they remain my favorites in each series because of their positions within my cinematic viewing chronology. Years of reading movie magazines and fanzines, countless discussions with other fans, and a formal education in cinema studies have taught me to identify characteristics that distinguish quality filmmaking. It is clear that, in the respective 007 and Hammer Dracula series, the shining lights are *Goldfinger* and *Horror of Dracula*. However, I saw those genre landmarks at a later date in my viewing career, so while I recognize their superiority, they fail to punch the same nostalgic buttons as *Diamonds Are Forever* and *Drac Has Risen*. It is amusing to note that both of these films mark the midpoints of successful series notorious for the irritability of their stars. An informed viewer can easily spot how weary Christopher Lee and Sean Connery had become of portraying the same one-dimensional characters yet again. None of this made an imprint on my adolescent brain. Both of these films now make me wince a bit, but I can quickly and easily defend my appreciation of them, and I wouldn't hesitate to screen them, albeit with a brief preface, for friends unfamiliar with the works. Therefore, films of this nature do not qualify for the "guilty pleasure" moniker.

In order to find a true guilty pleasure, I had to dig deep into the recesses of my filmic memories. Somewhere in there is a title that I would have difficulty redeeming. Cult films are not a valid option, as cult status indicates that a film has found a niche audience, and the accepted camp appeal of certain cult films legitimizes the work. No, my choice would have to be something that has significance in my memories, that I would consider, under duress, as one of the 10 films to bring to a desert island (assuming that my first 112 choices were unavailable), but one that would be so embarrassing, so indefensible, so guilt-inspiring, that I would have difficulty watching it, even by myself.

My guilty pleasure is *The Omega Man* (1971), starring Charlton Heston in a role similar to the fabled desert island dweller, his desert island being the entire planet Earth. Based loosely on Richard Matheson's *I Am Legend*, *The Omega Man* is actually the novel's second adaptation, the first being *The Last Man on Earth* (1964).

Richard Matheson's *I Am Legend* was first published in 1954. The narrative relates the tale of Richard Neville, an everyman who must deal with the living hell of being, as far as he can discern, the sole human survivor of a global plague. Neville tells his tale through first-person narrative, and the world we see through his eyes is dismal indeed. The year is 1976, and the remainder of the world's population has been infected with vampirism. It is this mentality of vampirism as disease that distinguishes Matheson's opus from countless formulaic vampire tales. *I Am Legend* is indeed blatantly revisionist; for instance, at one point, Neville consults Bram Stoker's *Dracula* for information, but dismisses the novel as a stodgy potboiler, full of misinformation. The majority of *I Am Legend* details Neville's attempts to protect his home against the nightly onslaught of vampires who inhabit his neighborhood. His worst nemesis is his former best friend and carpool buddy, Ben Cortmann, a point that resonates with the ubiquitous 1950s fantasy film theme of the "other" among us, a recurrent expression of the societal experience of McCarthyism.

The thematic complexity of *I Am Legend* is further enhanced by the descriptions of Neville's sexual repression. Alone for several years, he finds himself torn by his attraction to the female vampires who attempt to entice him to leave his fortress by posing provocatively on his front lawn. Although revolted by the idea of the undead, he has difficulty dealing with the sight of the opposite sex, which he has been damned to never again hold near.

Neville is a survivor. He rouses himself from his perpetual depression by focusing on determining the biological basis of vampirism, its causes, prevention, and cure. Through pages of deductive reasoning, he narrows down the list of situations that repel vampires, discarding those scenarios expressed in literature that he has found to be ineffective. For example, Neville decides that the sign of the cross would fail to work on an undead Jew. He investigates the function of the wooden stake, and discovers that the shape and composition of the stake are not significant; what matters is that the stake punctures a bodily seal on vampires, which instigates immediate decomposition. He finally settles on garlic as the one physical item that universally repels vampires, and breaks garlic into its key elements, arriving at an oil that he synthesizes into an anti-vampire vaccine.

In a poignant aside, Matheson devotes a chapter to Neville's pursuit of a stray dog, which he hopes will ease his loneliness. The dog is sick and scared, and Neville spends

Neville's (Charlton Heston) life is complicated by finding a healthy woman (Rosalind Cash).

several days painstakingly luring the dog into his home. Once inside, the dog hides under the bed and snaps at him. Neville tries to cure the dog, but to no avail. After all his efforts, the chapter ends with a single heartbreaking line, "One week later, the dog died."

Neville's life is next complicated by the daytime sighting of an apparently healthy woman. Doggedly pursuing her, Neville forces the woman back to his home for analysis. He suspects that she may be experiencing the early stages of vampirism, and tries to convince her to submit to testing and, if necessary, a cure regimen. She skillfully deflects his medical attention. It turns out that she is a member of a new society, a hybrid of human and vampire. Neville is captured by the group and informed of his imminent sacrifice. The members of the new order repulse Neville with their nonchalant violence. As they slaughter the vampires who had been taunting him throughout the story, Neville experiences great remorse. The cat and mouse game had become his life; he lived to outsmart his adversaries, and seeing them subject to wholesale slaughter dismays him greatly. As the last man on earth faces his own extinction and replacement, he ends his story with three words, "I am legend."

Richard Matheson's novel was immediately recognized as a landmark in horror literature. Shortly after its publication, the novel was optioned by Hammer Films, and Matheson was hired to adapt to his book into a screenplay entitled *The Night Creatures*. The production was ultimately nixed in preproduction by the British Board of Film Censors due to concern over the suitability of its gruesome scenario for mass consumption. The first filmed version of *I Am Legend* appeared in 1964 in the Italian-American co-production, *The Last Man on Earth*, starring box-office draw Vincent Price. Horror genre fans have argued for the superiority of *Last Man* over *Omega Man*, but I must admit that I don't understand the appeal of the Price flick. Its predominant virtue is the fact that it is a reasonably faithful adaptation of *I Am Legend*. This is not at all surprising, given that the screenplay was a doctored version of Matheson's *Night Creatures* script. However, Matheson was displeased enough to replace his name in the credits with the pseudonym "Logan Swanson." The picture is flat and devoid of style, and its 84 minutes drag by interminably.

While fans of novels always cry for decent adaptations, the truth is that many stories work far better in print than on the screen. In most cases, some form of artistic license must be taken in order for the story to play visually. How do you tell the story of an incredibly introspective man who has no peers left for conversation? This is a dilemma faced by screenwriters who adapt any source that is laden with internal monologues. For this reason, so many Stephen King novels have been transformed less than successfully into motion pictures. *The Last Man on Earth* addresses this issue by having Vincent Price speak volumes of dialogue in voice-over, a tired device that is rarely effective when employed ad infinitum. In fact, instead of empathizing with this poor loner as I did while reading the novel, my reaction to Price's Neville was, "Won't this guy ever shut up?"

I Am Legend devotes pages of text to descriptions of Neville carrying out his daily routine. On paper, the descriptions form a powerful metaphor; our protagonist has been forced by his environment to make survival his only goal, so he goes about hanging garlic and sharpening stakes with the purposeful detachment of one performing domestic chores, such as vacuuming and yard work. The translation of the chores to imagery is terribly unsuccessful. Seeing Vincent Price spend minutes going through these protective measures, while droning on in the voice-over about his weariness, makes for an extremely dull viewing experience.

The concept of being kept prisoner in your house each and every night is terrifying, but *The Last Man on Earth* is simply not a scary film. The story calls for an air of paranoia, such as that found in Roman Polanski's films of the period, like *Repulsion* and *Rosemary's Baby*. After a recent re-viewing of *Last Man*, I was tempted to ascribe its lack of tension to its low production values, until I realized that a famous shoestring-budgeted production covered similar ground to tremendous effect.

The finest adaptation of *I Am Legend* was the unofficial one, *Night of the Living Dead* (1968). Although the George Romero film comes from an original screenplay, it is easy to draw parallels with its obvious influence. *Night* concentrates on the action within and around a house under attack by the undead, zombies rather than vampires in this case, whose existence is accounted for via a questionable scientific explanation. The humans inside the house devote their energies to shoring up their defenses and rationalizing their predicament, all the while bickering with each other. It is a social version of the Matheson story, a veritable *We Are Legend*.

Three years after *Night* saw the release of the major-studio-backed *The Omega Man*. When a project like this is backed by a major studio such as Warner Bros., it can benefit from opulent production values. Unfortunately, the studio's need to recoup investments can lead to the casting of bankable stars who may not be appropriate for their parts. The role of Richard Neville requires a strong actor who must appear tor-

We are never really sure just *what* the zombies of *The Omega Man* want from Neville. To make him "one of them" surely, but what does that entail?

tured yet resilient, never backing down from the incredible adversity thrown his way. However, the viewer should never be allowed to lose sight of the fact that Neville is not a super-hero, but an ordinary man facing extraordinary circumstances. Answering that challenge, *The Omega Man* offers Charlton Heston in one of the most hamfisted performances of his career. Heston is best known to the general public as Moses in *The Ten Commandments*, and to fantasy genre enthusiasts as the hapless astronaut in *Planet of the Apes*. Heston was successful in both of these roles, because they properly channeled his essential pomposity. Neville, as envisioned by Richard Matheson, could not afford the luxury of self-aggrandizement. Neville's overriding concern is making it through each night of his horrible existence, an inarguably humbling experience. Heston expresses emotions by alternating between whispering through clenched teeth and screaming through clenched teeth. His acting range is suited only to characters who are larger than life, so he need only appear as an icon; he must not be required to act in order to paint a complete characterization.

The Omega Man was also artistically handicapped by an ugly style of cinematography that was all the rage in the early 1970s. By 1971, the glorious process of color cinematography had progressed from the infantile stages of the two-strip Technicolor process, through the classic three-strip Technicolor look of the 1950s, into the revisionist approach of the muddy, low-contrast Kodak stock used in the lensing of *M*A*S*H* and *The French Connection*. The *cinema verité* style popularized within the prior decade mandated the inclusion of hand-held shots and ambient lighting conditions for some exterior night scenes, resulting occasionally in murky, impenetrable images. Much of *The Omega Man*'s action occurs at night, thus much of the film is difficult to watch. The film was shot in Panavision, the anamorphic wide-screen process in which the image is squeezed to fit on standard 35mm stock, then unsqueezed via a lens on the projector. The hard-edged urban dramas of the early seventies shared this washed-out widescreen look, which blended the Hollywood excess of widescreen technology with the frugal atmosphere of independent efforts shot on non-Technicolor stock. In fact, *Pulp Fiction* (1994) commandeered this look for a film that, barring a few stray props and references, could very well have been shot in 1970, with Dustin Hoffman and Richard Roundtree essaying the parts acted by John Travolta and Samuel L. Jackson, and Charles Bronson in the Bruce Willis role. As a child, many of the films I viewed on TV were shot in widescreen and panned-and-scanned (if the telecine operator monitoring the transfer were vigilant, or simply cropped [more frequently the case]). With the release of Warner Home Video's letterboxed laserdisc of *The Omega Man*, I've finally been able to view some elements I had never before seen, such as the true sense of desolation in the opening images of the abandoned city. Prior to this, I had been ignorant of the composition of images.

Now, accepting that the lead actor is a card-carrying scenery chewer and that the cinematography is of the ugly style of the era, the most glaring problems with *The Omega Man* are rooted in the liberties it takes with its source material. Most significantly, the vampires of *I Am Legend* are now eloquent zombies, an oxymoron if ever I've heard one. Somehow, the global plague turns the afflicted into pale-skinned, well-spoken zombies who manage to find matching hooded cloaks and mirrored sunglasses for all of their converts. Showing all of Neville's tormentors in the same outfit is designed to evoke the horror of cults and of mob mentality; they are portrayed as members of a coven and call themselves "The Family." The result is silly, and made me wonder where they managed to get all those matching sunglasses. Surely, one of them would be forced to find a different pair of shades to shield their blown retinas; the local pharmacy couldn't have *that* many Foster Grants.

Deleting the concept of vampirism was a silly move, one likely predicated by the notion that vampires are passé, or possibly, ironically, by an attempt to cash in on the success of *Night of the Living Dead*. This alteration defeats the purpose of Matheson's book, which was to breathe new unlife into the vampire mythos. The concept of a house surrounded by vampires is terrifying, if you really stop and consider the possible consequences. We are never really sure just *what* the zombies of *The Omega Man* want from Neville. To make him "one of them" surely, but what does that entail? What benefit would the brotherhood derive from another member? How is the physical transformation enacted? In a vampire story, the answers to these questions are apparent, as the trappings of vampire mythology have been passed down through generations of stories. Change vampires into cultish zombies, and motivation is inescapably weakened.

Another problem I have with this adaptation of *I Am Legend* is the character of Ben Cortmann. One of the repeated elements of vampire literature is the protagonist's shock at discovering relatives and trusted friends returning as the undead. In the book, we discover midway through that the vampire leader Ben Cortmann was Richard Neville's carpool buddy. Vampirism strikes suburbia, a chilling notion, bringing the myth out of the realm of Gothic literature and into the subdivision. Anthony Zerbe, the actor who

The Omega Man affords Charlton Heston one of his most hamfisted performances.

plays Cortmann in *The Omega Man*, bears a laughably close physical resemblance to Paul Williams, hardly a figure to strike terror into the hearts of audiences. Furthermore, Neville's tormentor has been renamed with the pretentious name "Matthias," and any notion of a prior relationship between the two is left for the audience to infer. It is here that *The Last Man on Earth* holds an edge over *The Omega Man*. *Last Man* had a brief but creepy flashback of Cortmann arriving at the Neville household in the bucolic days before the plague.

So, here I am, two thirds through my analysis, and all I've managed to do is damn my choice, explaining why it is a poor movie and a crummy adaptation. You see, guilty pleasures work this way. The analytical approach will yield negative results. It is very easy to tabulate the reasons a film such as this is unsuccessful; you need only write down all the thoughts that occur to you as you watch it. Each gaffe and miscalculation makes you shudder, as you attempt to convince yourself that you couldn't possibly enjoy the film anymore. What is far more difficult is determining why some buried emotional part of you is still enamored with this hunk of celluloid junk. This is a daunting task, but now that I've cleared the air concerning the many evident failings of *The Omega Man*, it is time for me to try to pinpoint why I still felt it worthy of a $34.95 laserdisc purchase (although, admittedly, I hadn't included it in my collection until the writing of this article made it a mandatory research investment).

A screening of the disc revealed to me that *The Omega Man*'s strengths lie in its expository sequences, but once the basic scenario is established, the film falters. *The Omega Man* opens with Heston cruising the deserted streets of Los Angeles, enjoying an easy listening tape in his car's 8-track system. This joyride is interrupted when he notices silhouetted human movement in an office window. He stops the car, whips out a semi-automatic assault weapon, and unleashes a spray of bullets at the building's

*The Omega Ma*n—celluloid junk at its best.

inhabitants. Satisfied, he returns to his drive, and the Lalo Schifrin-esque strains of Ron Grainer's score are heard under the main titles, which are superimposed over the action.

Heston then bumps a curb, puncturing a tire in the process. He goes "car shopping" at a nearby dealer, which is frozen in time from the moment of the apocalypse. Choosing a sporty new convertible, Heston drives out through the showroom window. With all the time in the world to kill, he ambles into a neighborhood theater and runs *Woodstock*, quipping, "Held over for the third straight year." After lip-synching all the dialogue and music throughout the picture, he emerges from the theater to discover that he lost track of time, and dusk is fast approaching. He rushes home, but he must run a gauntlet of Family members who invade his garage with Molotov cocktails. He manages this successfully, and retreats to the confines of his "honky paradise," as a formerly black Family member puts it: "Those are words from the old days, Brother," cautions another. Heston's lair is a hybrid of comfort and science, with opulent furniture battling for space with laboratory equipment. A large screen television overlooks a chess set on which Heston plays "against" a bust of Caesar while lounging in foppish Edwardian gear, all the while comparing his chess strategies to the more serious game he plays with the Family each day.

Heston's Neville is tortured by memories of the past, which are cinematically encapsulated in imagery of the world's population falling prey to the ravages of the plague.

There are apocalyptic scenes of people watching TV and listening to radio broadcasts warning of the plague, with the camera widening to reveal that it is too late for

Heston is captured by the Family and held on trial in a cultish tribunal meeting.

the listeners; they are dead in their plush living rooms. We discover that Matthias had previously been a newscaster who reported the grim updates of international war and plague, but we don't know if he had been an associate of Neville's or just a recognizable media figure. This variation from the book steals a powerful irony. Having the undead led by Neville's neighbor is chilling, but having them led by a guy he knew from watching the news is silly. Despite this flaw, the opening scenes are the finest in the film. The entire scenario up to this point is fast-paced and thought-provoking. Just what would the last man on earth do with his spare time? Imagine a world where money and the quest for it are entirely irrelevant; all that matters is survival. How could one survive without human contact? How could a mind cope with the concept of always being another's potential prey?

Things turn downhill from here, as much of the remainder of the film is routine and hokey. As the flashbacks continue, we learn that Heston was a military researcher who had access to a test vaccine, thus he became immune to the plague. Coming out of flashbacks, we follow Heston on another of his daily rounds of Family decimation. In one refreshingly creepy scene, a brief shining moment in the middle of the film, he investigates a luxury hotel that could double for the Overlook Hotel in *The Shining*, but all he finds is a couple in bed in the advanced stages of decomposition. He devotes his energies to uncovering the Family's hive. Although his violent methods are effective, he recognizes that the plague is killing off the Family and that by using his blood as a serum, he could restore them to humanity.

In a moment of inattention, Heston is captured by the Family and held on trial in a cultish tribunal meeting, evocative of *Island of Lost Souls* and *Planet of the Apes*. The Family opposes the use of weapons and electricity, as they were tools that contributed to the final World War. Heston is outcast as the last normal man. The Family is convinced they have been chosen to cleanse the Earth and cancel civilization. Heston serves as their final reminder of the old world.

Heston is rescued by Lisa, another living human, who temporarily blinds the nocturnal Family by switching on floodlights. Lisa takes a shocked Heston to an outpost of survivors, who explain that they are in the very early stages of the plague. As Lisa explains to Heston, "Between the Family at night and you shooting at everything that moves during the day, Baby, we had to stay low."

Lisa's brother Richie is in the secondary stages of plague, as Heston determines by examining his off-white irises. An apparent goof is visible here; while Heston pulls open the delirious Richie's eyelids to check his eye color, the special effect contact lenses move on Richie's eyes, temporarily revealing the brown eyes beneath.

Heston tests his blood/serum hypothesis on Richie and successfully brings him back from the plague. Richie seeks out the Family to tell them that a cure is now available. Matthias scolds Richie, informing him that the Family is not interested in returning to the forms of the past. The Family kills Richie.

Lisa inexplicably turns into one of the Family instantaneously. This makes no sense, as Richie's illness showed that the plague is a gradual process. However, logic be damned, one moment Lisa is alive and vibrant, the next she's a glassy-eyed zombie, sporting one of the Family's trademark hooded robes. Lisa leads the Family to Heston, who is speared by Matthias.

This recent viewing of the film showed me that there is a specific moment, early in the film, at which my appreciation turns to scorn. However, the contempt in which I hold the majority of *The Omega Man* in no way diminishes the regard I have for the film's strong opening sequence. In my mind, while watching this opening, I create an entirely new scenario, different from both the remainder of the film and the novel's source material. Having established the power struggle between Neville and Matthias, I want the film to continue in this vein (pun only mildly intended). I want to see a game of wits unfold, matching the intellects of the former doctor and the former journalist, but accounting for the fact that their intellects have been warped by tremendous situational stress. I don't want to see any other survivors, and I want the other Family members to fade into the background. I basically want to see the horror movie equivalent of *Sleuth*, an intelligently scripted battle of wits with supernatural overtones. As I type these words, I realize that such a film has already been made; it was called *The Wicker Man*.

Thus, I recognize that my affection for *The Omega Man* is based largely on the strength of the first 20 minutes of the film. These are the moments that are the most insightful, best produced, most nostalgic for me, and least likely to make me crawl for cover if anyone catches me watching them. Of course, tied in with my earlier comments regarding guilty pleasures as films initially viewed in an atmosphere of naiveté, it may be possible that I only got to see the first reel of *The Omega Man* as a child before being whisked off to bed. That would explain the greater resonances for me in the initial scenes than in the rest of the film. In any case, my accolades for *The Omega Man* are complex and peppered with caveats, as befit any guilty pleasure. Therefore, let it be known: I heartily recommend the first reel of *The Omega Man* as a wonderful, unappreciated short film, but if anyone asks who told you this, be warned, I'm liable to deny any connection with the picture and leave you fending for yourself.

Cheryl is a lovely girl...
But to George, she's a living doll.
PRIVATE PARTS
Original screenplay by PHILIP KEARNEY and LES RENDELSTEIN · Produced by GENE CORMAN · Directed by PAUL BARTEL
R RESTRICTED
METROCOLOR

PRIVATE PARTS
by Gary J. Svehla

In this era of kinky cinema which thrives upon perversity and pushing all the buttons to the limit, 1972 certainly seemed like tamer times. David Lynch's *Eraserhead* was still five years away, by God. Yet the decade of the 1970s was the decade in which boundaries continued to be broken both in the arena of sex and violence and in the rapidly changing American value system. In fact, 1970s cinema was "untamed" in every sense of the word.

This was the era when the independent filmmaker was flourishing, with theaters booking all array of deviant and cutting-edge movies. B movies played the neighborhood houses and the drive-in theaters alike throughout America, and such product attracted a curious, youthful viewing market. Even the mainstream studios upset the sensibilities of the moviegoing public by producing innovative movies crossing all genres: science fiction (*Alien*), neo-noir (*Taxi Driver*), Western (*The Wild Bunch*), war (*Apocalypse Now*), and horror (*The Exorcist*).

But I was not quite prepared for the subtle perversity and off-hand sense of humor which permeated an almost forgotten player in the theaters of 1972. Who would think that a Hollywood major, MGM, would release theatrically an odd little gem called *Private Parts*, directed by first-timer Paul Bartel (who would carry on, becoming a staple in both B character acting and directing for decades to come).

Director Paul Bartel is most known for his New World futuristic science fiction gem *Death Race 2000,* which introduced a then-unknown Sylvester Stallone to theater audiences. Produced for Roger Corman, the movie featured a car race involving participants who earned points for hit-and-running down everyone from babies and children to senior citizens. The movie was a delightful guilty pleasure of its own. Then, in 1982, Bartel directed (and starred in) his generally considered masterpiece, *Eating Raoul*, a satirical look at cannibalism which once again featured Bartel's slightly askew sense of humor.

Actor Paul Bartel, appearing at first in Corman's New World Productions, later appearing in all sorts of B movies and even television (*Amazing Stories* and the revamped *Alfred Hitchcock Presents*), is remembered for his appearances as director Erich Von Leppe in *Hollywood Boulevard* (1976), Dumont in *Piranha* (1978), Mr. McGree in *Rock 'n' Roll High School* (1979), which highlighted The Ramones, Paul Bland in both *Eating Raoul* (1982) and *Chopping Mall* (1986), Mr. Walab in Tim Burton's short *Frankenweenie* (1984), and the theater manager in *Gremlins 2: The New Batch* (1990). And this only covers the tip of the iceberg of character roles which Bartel has enacted over the years.

But back in 1972 Paul Bartel was directing his first feature film for MGM (produced by Roger's brother, Gene Corman), a twisted and often entertaining taste of awakening female sexuality in a modern, mythic updating of *Little Red Riding Hood* where young innocence is attracted to and ultimately stained by the evil which becomes all consuming.

Odd, exotic actress Ayn Ruymen portrays our Red Riding Hood character, runaway Cheryl Stratton, who escapes to the big city with roommate Judy (Ann Gibbs), who just

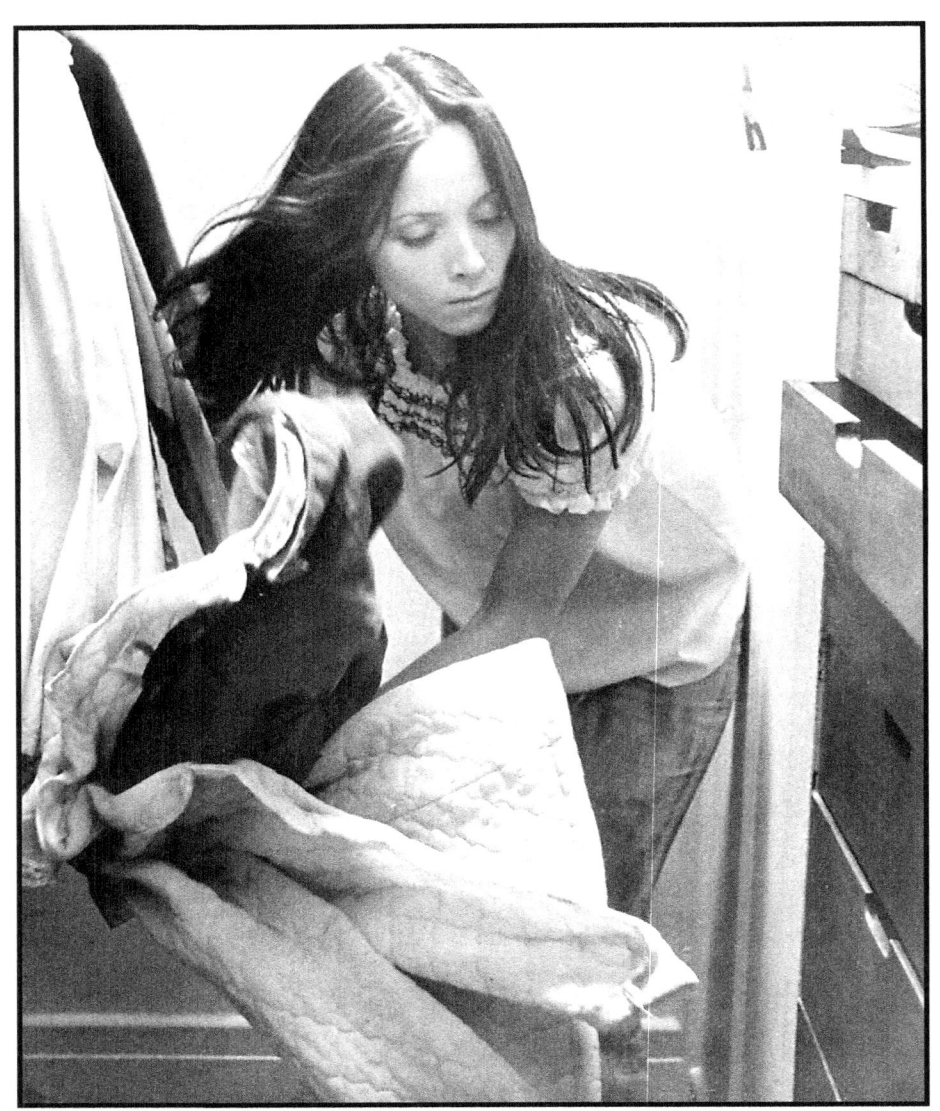

Odd, exotic actress Ayn Ruymen portrays our Red Riding Hood character, runaway Cheryl Stratton, who flees her apartment after being terrified by her roommate's boyfriend.

happens to have a real boyfriend Mike (Len Travis). Two-years-younger Cheryl curiously spies on the sexually indulgent lovers (through a Norman Bates-style peephole, no less) and is immediately caught. The more brazen Judy invites Mike to strip Cheryl proclaiming that the interloper can't "get any action." "She's too young," Judy remarks. As the terrified and unhinged Cheryl grabs her things to escape, Judy yells out, "Baby mustn't forget her teddy!"

Taking refuge at the King Edward Hotel, managed by her never-before-seen aunt Martha Atwood (Lucile Benson), young Cheryl asks Aunt Martha (more the grandmotherly type) if she can stay at the hotel for a few days until she can find a job and a

Taking refuge at the King Edward Hotel, managed by her never-before-seen aunt Martha Atwood (Lucile Benson), young Cheryl asks if she can stay at the hotel for a few days.

place of her own. Martha agrees on the condition that Cheryl stay to herself and not wander around the decidedly unsavory locale.

Cheryl Stratton is a wildly inventive character, and with the exception of one or two sequences, actress Ruymen does a fine job of portraying Cheryl's duality, one of the themes of the movie. Here we have an enthusiastic young woman, barely out of her teens (if that old), who is both repelled by and attracted to her emerging womanhood with all its inherent sexual baggage. She is curious about what goes on beyond closed bedroom doors, yet she is embarrassed and shocked when she finds out.

The communal bathroom of the King Edward Hotel becomes a pivotal image for Cheryl's emerging sexuality. The first time she enters the facility (room 225, two rooms down from her room 223), she is armed wearing a bathrobe and carrying a towel. She always politely knocks on the door before entering (almost apologetically intruding). She nervously looks down at the stained tub and tentatively begins to run the water. She gazes at herself in a mildly distorting full-length mirror. But before she can disrobe, a pounding knock threatens to bring down the locked door as an irritated male voice bemoans, whenever the room is occupied "I wanna take a piss." Cheryl, deciding that a bath is not worth the hassle, grabs her towel and rushes back to her room.

But the young female is not so innocent after all. That evening, Cheryl stays awake in bed reading a book, *First Time I Saw Him Undressed*, which reflects her healthy interest in sex. However, her reading pleasure is interrupted as she hears people walking down the corridor, water plopping from the drain, and squeaks and other minor disturbing sounds. Another evening we see a *Secret Romance* comic on a dresser in Cheryl's room as she is once again reading erotic literature in bed, but this time she

The obvious message-writer and male object of attention is professional photographer George (John Ventantonio), who operates a darkroom in the cellar of the hotel.

hears the real (or imaginary?) sounds of a couple making love as she turns the page of the book and finds a slip of paper which has a hand-written message: "How do you like it so far, Cheryl?"

The obvious message-writer and male object of attention is professional photographer George (John Ventantonio), who operates a darkroom in the cellar of the hotel. "Good looking but kinda strange," Cheryl says, but she is obviously interested in getting closer to the curly-haired young man. In fact, the first time she confronts George, he beams, "You're becoming one of the regulars around here... How do you like it so far?" echoing the note that he placed in her book. Things get interesting when George leaves a package containing a skimpy, sexy black dress and masquerade face-mask in her room. A simple message accompanies the package, "Wear them for me." Cheryl takes this gift as a sign that George desires her to "model" for him. But her fertile imagination is soon cooking up even more interesting recipes.

Unknown to Cheryl, George has stolen a photo of her and has blown up the face to life-size proportions. In the privacy of his studio apartment, he has placed the photo of Cheryl overtop the face of his clear plastic blowup doll (which he inflates with warm water). Dressing the doll in exotic lingerie, the deviant George makes love to the Cheryl-faced doll in a very unusual manner. He takes out his hypodermic needle, draws blood from his arm, and during the moment of climax, injects his own blood into the doll with the cascading streams of blood flowing throughout the formerly clear party doll as George collapses in utter exhaustion.

One day while Aunt Martha is at a funeral (Martha takes a camera to try to capture the exact moment when the spirit leaves the body, or so she claims), Cheryl uses a broom handle to free an electrically protected hook on which hangs the hotel's master keys and decides to go exploring around the hotel (but this Goldilocks will *never* find a bed or porridge that feels or tastes "just right"). She investigates the empty room that sits between her room and the bathroom and discovers a small peephole allowing voyeuristic thrills for anyone spying upon occupants of the bathroom.

Later, when George returns home, Aunt Martha scolds him: "Leave that child alone. If I'd known she would get you all upset, I wouldn't have let her stay... She's like all the women in this family—can't wait to wiggle her little body to get men worked up. That's the way women are... weakness of the flesh. It can be overcome—I overcame it!"

Aunt Martha discovers a photo of Cheryl that has been blown up and placed overtop the face of George's clear plastic blowup doll.

Aunt Martha knows more about George than previously thought. George, who speaks of his loneliness and shame about his "dolls," is countered by Martha: "George, you can't hurt them, and they can't hurt you... You don't want another Alice, do you, George?" George pitifully responds, "I'm a human being and I need human contact now."

Cheryl has plans of her own. Returning to the pivotal setpiece, the hotel bathroom, Cheryl wears George's sexy black dress and dons the facial mask and goes to the bathroom knowing that George will be "peeping" at her. In fact we soon see his eye in close-up as he stares through the hole in the wall. Cheryl suggestively undresses and slowly climbs into a soapy bubblebath (still wearing the mask). After bathing, Cheryl walks to the mirror where the peephole is located, drops her towel and mask, and slowly dresses, pretending that she is totally alone. Before she returns to her room, she cracks an all-knowing smile.

After giving George her private show, Cheryl is later confronted by George who asks her how she likes the clothes he gave her. The shy girl states, "I don't know exactly

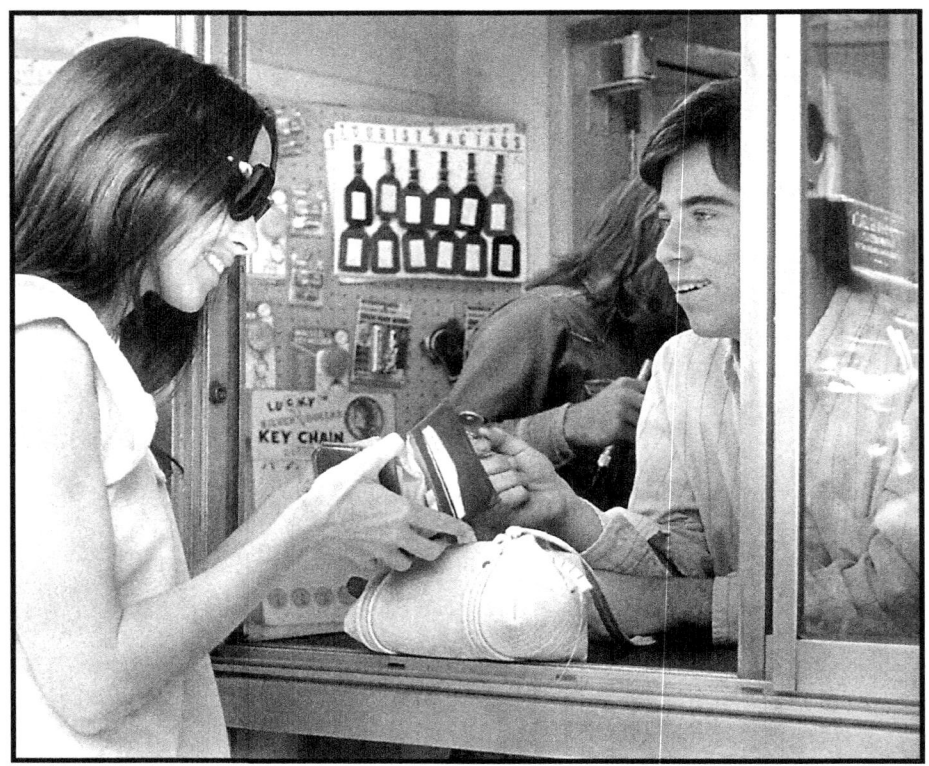

Hoping to have a duplicate master key made, Cheryl goes to a shop and makes goo-goo eyes with whitebread heartthrob Stanley Livingston.

what you want. You think of me as a *woman.* Wouldn't you *really* like to get together. I'd *love* to pose for you! I'd wear the things you gave me... tonight at 10 o'clock?"

Unfortunately, Cheryl's Prince Charming is actually the big, bad wolf in *another*'s clothing. And what a surprise this will be when we discover *whose* clothing!

This primary plot is interwoven with kinky diversions and subplots. First of all, one of the occupants of the hotel, Reverend Moon (Laurie Main), decorates his living quarters as a gaudy memorial to Christianity that makes it sinister and perverse. Lying amid the religious paraphernalia is a deck of erotic playing cards and a beef-cake photo of a sexy male model.

Also lurking about the seedy apartment complex is Mr. Lovejoy, a perennial alcoholic, who passes out amid the utter filth of his apartment, and an old senile woman who always mistakes Cheryl for George's former "girlfriend," Alice.

Hoping to have a duplicate master key made, Cheryl goes to a shop and makes goo-goo eyes with whitebread heart-throb Jeff (Stanley Livingston) who used to date model Alice before she suddenly disappeared from the King Edward Hotel. And Jeff wants to investigate.

Both former roommates of Cheryl's, Judy and Mike, individually come to the King Edward Hotel to try to find the girl, but each one is brutally murdered. First Mike is beheaded as he walks down an unoccupied corridor, and then Judy is led by Aunt

Martha down to George's darkroom where Judy is stalked by an unknown fiend who murders the screaming victim. In other words, director Bartel has to insert gratuitous scenes of murder and violence performed by a mysterious fiend to justify the film's marketing as a horror film.

And throughout all, the not-so-sweet Aunt Martha fills the soundtrack with her quirky behavior and moral instructions to Cheryl. "Wash that paint off your face before coming to dinner!" Further speaking of funerals and spirits, Aunt Martha states, "You'll realize, when you're older, that the body is a prison that traps and bends the natural spirit to its will. It makes us weak or sick or ugly. It makes us into men or women or *whatever* it likes, whether we like it or not." Aunt Martha claims to be protecting Cheryl from becoming like "all the other women in this family." At one point Cheryl asks about Martha's husband Orville and their daughter. Martha mentions that Orville passed on, but that when it came to having children, we "went to a doctor and worked it out another way... *didn't need Orville.*" And Martha is vague about the fate of their daughter, simply stating, "You can say she's in the Lord's hands."

Private Parts **is filled with weirdness and perversity.**

In the film's climax, all is revealed in a rather sleazy manner. George plays an audiotape of the late Alice speaking about posing "practically naked" for him when suddenly she pleads, "For God's sake, what are you doing with that needle!" Alice's former beau Jeff enters, has a bottle smashed against his head, and is left unconscious in the darkroom. Later returning to his room, George finds the ever-willing Cheryl dressed down in her sexy black best, replacing his former plastic lover beneath the sheets, purring: "Would you like to take some pictures?" Thinking this is what becoming a woman means, Cheryl is shocked when George produces his hypodermic needle, and she accidentally kills him by knocking over one of the photographic lamps, which strikes him in his head. Aunt Martha, in shock, comes to his rescue, screaming that "he cannot rape you," ripping back George's clothes to reveal well-developed female breasts. Yes, George is Martha's long-lost daughter. Thus, Martha is forcing her daughter to suppress her femininity and assume a male disguise living alone in the hotel as George the photographer. Martha painfully discovering that he/she is dead, declares, "His spirit is free of the body at last. You can take his place—stay here and *be my son!*" Deciding that Cheryl would not make a good son, she instead bares a butcher's knife and attempts to "liberate" the corrupting female flesh. When the police investigate later, they find the bloodied corpse of Aunt Martha wearing the sexy black dress which George gave Cheryl. Truly, this is the most perverse shot in a film which contains more than enough perversity.

MGM Presents
"PRIVATE PARTS"
METROCOLOR

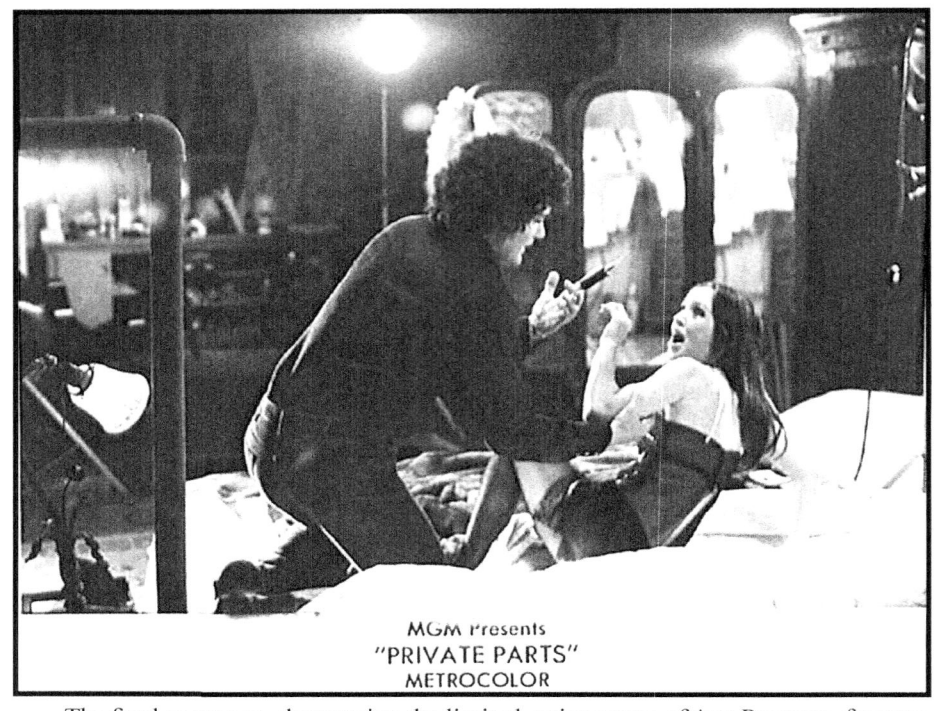

The final sequence, showcasing the limited acting range of Ayn Ruymen, features the young actress wearing Aunt Martha's clothes, walking down the main hotel staircase as an older woman might, mimicking the lines frequently echoed by Aunt Martha: "I'm sorry, I have no vacancies... This is one of the last respectable hotels in the city. We have to be selective about our clientele." Unfortunately, Ruymen's performance comes off as more of a poor spin-off of Gloria Swanson's inspired overacting in *Sunset Boulevard*. In fact, she resembles a sitcom variation of Shelley Duvall from *Fairy Tale Theater*. Unfortunately, her embarrassing inability to effectively portray age closes the film and thus ends the movie on a less than satisfying note.

Yet *Private Parts* is truly a guilty pleasure for all time. Its perversion of *Little Red Riding Hood* is clearly framed. While the fairy tale stressed only the duality of the wolf (his feminine disguise and facade of friendliness vs. his true predatory nature), here we have a Red Riding Hood who performs a hot striptease for the wolf to prove her womanly nature. Poor Cheryl, shocked and embarrassed by Judy and Mike's lovemaking, still enjoys some cheap voyeuristic thrills from watching them perform. But she sings a different tune when she is caught in the act and thus her sexual curiosity is revealed and shames her.

Traveling to the "woods" of urban hell, she takes refuge in the seedy King Edward (such a majestic name too) Hotel with her never-before-seen Aunt Martha who wants Cheryl to retain her virginity and keen moral sense of purity. However, the squeaky-clean virgin loves to read erotically-charged books lulling her to dreamland and she fantasizes about having a real, adult relationship with the big, bad George (the wolf in male's clothing). However, in this relationship, Red Riding Hood becomes the wolf ready to gobble up the true virgin, the sexually confused George (who cannot rape anyone). While the young, innocent Cheryl loves to entice and perform her frisky strip for George, George's duality is just as frustrating and confusing. George, in actuality a she, becomes the dutiful "son" to obey the moral cleansing lifestyle of her mother, going against all laws of nature and her own sexuality to become the good "boy" mother wishes her to be. True, she gets her kinky climaxes from playing with dolls (a very "girl" thing to do), but as mother says, dolls don't hurt you and you don't hurt them. Just when her sexually safe appetites are confusingly transferred to actual female flesh— Alice and then Cheryl (both of whom pose provocatively for her and thus are negative, seductive forces that she finds impossible to ignore)—only then does her repressed lust turn to harmful violence. Aunt Martha's duality forms the third perverse interwoven thread: She is the nurturing, protective female presence (the titular grandmother figure who is also the wolf in disguise) yet at the same time she is a true female-hater who would rather see her daughter as a male than act out her natural role as a corrupted Eve from the Garden of Eden. Martha would kill the female spirit in all the world—and for a second think—was George *ever* the murderer or did Aunt Martha kill Alice when Martha observed the seductive influence she held over her daughter? Did Martha kill Judy and Mike because they came snooping around the hotel? Perhaps the "impotent" George killed no one.

And finally, Cheryl, already displaying the duality between innocent virgin and sexually ripe vixen, finally becomes Aunt Martha, killing both George and Martha (two women remember) and assuming the matron's position at the head desk of the King Edward Hotel, carrying on her legacy to make the world pure and safe by denying her own female sexuality. Remember, Aunt Martha becomes the movie's main predator, typically a male role, and she kills with a large knife, here a phallic symbol of male strength which is *usually* directed against females.

Back in those more innocent days of 1972, Paul Bartel with Gene Corman's financial backing produced one of the most misogynistic movies in the history of the horror film. As a 22-year-old single male, I was enthralled by the film back then, but when viewed today, *Private Parts* seems more insidious, manipulative, and mean-spirited than ever before. Truly, as I stated before, it is a guilty pleasure for all time!

MOON MONSTERS LAUNCH ATTACK AGAINST EARTH!
HOW CAN SCIENCE MEET THE MENACE of ASTRAL ASSASSINS? New SCIENCE-FICTION THRILLS!
3D
ADVENTURES INTO THE FUTURE in New TRU-3 DIMENSION!
ROBOT MONSTER
with GEORGE NADER
CLAUDIA BARRETT
Produced by AL ZIMBALIST
RELEASED THRU ASTOR PICTURES CORP.

ROBOT MONSTER
by Dennis Fischer

The parameters of an art form are created by its best and its worst examples. Just as there are apexes of achievement, it follows that there are depths of ineptitude. Any fantasy film fan worth his or her salt has sat through dozens of bad films so horrendously awful that they completely reorient a filmgoer's standard of badness. In comparison, films others typically refer to as bad come off as merely disappointing.

It's no great sin to make a bad movie, though it's no great honor either. The greatest sin most of these types of films make is to waste the viewer's time and bore one's pants off. However, there are those special few films, usually of ambitious intent, which aim to achieve and fall so far from the mark that they create a whole new field of entertainment. Dubbed by Michael and Harry Medved as "Golden Turkeys," those films are so entertainingly bad that they can be considered enjoyable. These films have a certain magic where even the simplest filmic efforts become botched, adding a patina of delightful incompetence destined to sink the hard work and efforts of even the most dedicated filmmaker.

One of those special films is Phil Tucker's notorious epic *Robot Monster*. While it certainly ranks among the worst science fiction films ever made, it is far more entertaining than many comparable films such as *Fire Maidens of Outer Space,* any of W. Lee Wilder's science fiction films, or any of the other truly awful films from Astor Pictures (*Frankenstein's Daughter, Giant From the Unknown, Missile to the Moon, She Demons*).

Castle of Frankenstein dubbed it "among the finest terrible movies ever made.... This early 3-D effort has attained legendary (and richly deserved) status as one of the most laughable of all poverty row quickies...." Charles Beesley, in *The Psychotronic Encyclopedia of Film,* describes it as "Belly laughs meet stark terror as the last six 'hu-mans' in existence are caught in a death struggle with the dreaded Ro-man...."

Famed horror writer Stephen King reported in *Danse Macabre*, "I made a grave mistake concerning *Robot Monster*... about 10 years ago. It came on the Saturday night Creature Features, and I prepared for the occasion by smoking some pretty good reefer. I don't smoke dope often, because when stoned *everything* strikes me as funny. That night I almost laughed myself into a hernia. Tears were rolling down my cheeks and I was literally on the floor for most of the movie. Luckily, the movie only runs 63 minutes; another 20 minutes of watching Ro-Man tune his war surplus shortwave/bubble machine in 'one of the more familiar Hollywood caves' and I think I would have laughed myself to death."

Whether *Robot Monster* was actually filmed in 3-D has become the subject of debate. Years ago, Bill Warren, author of the excellent *Keep Watching the Skies!*, told me he had learned that the filmmakers assumed that if you took two prints of a film and projected them through polaroid lenses, that the film would come out in 3-D. They little realized that the visual information sent to each eye should fuse two slightly different perspectives. This meant that when viewed in "3-D," this film still looked flat. It is also well known that the film incorporated sequences from other films that were shot flat.

Hence, when Rhino Video released *Robot Monster* on video in 3-D, (the most commonly available version of the film), I was interested in checking out if it indeed had true 3-D. The answer, like most things associated with the film, proves more complicated than it ought to be. The print offered is a Medallion TV print with occasional 3-D sequences, indicating that at least some of the sequences were shot in 3-D. (Rhino's print of *Cat-Women of the Moon* also varies between images that are flat and those that are in even worse 3-D, often giving the lead characters four eyes and two noses.)

However, Rhino's print of *Robot Monster* has been mucked about with to some extent. It overdubs a couple lines of snide commentary not in the original film (apparently from when the film was given a *What's Up, Tiger Lily?*-type treatment from a cable broadcast), dubs sounds of a balloon being rubbed when George Nader caresses Claudia Barrett's arms, slows down the film speed during a love scene, adds a "censored" box over Barrett's breasts when Ro-Man undoes her halter top (suggesting nudity which does *not* appear in the original), and trims the final "The End" credit. The best copy of the film I've seen is the now out-of-print Image laserdisc version which also includes the trailer for this Astor-released epic.

The trailer to the film, which includes a reference to monsters from the moon (something the film itself never asserts), promises, "*Robot Monster* brings you an actual preview of the devastating forces of our future! Unsuspected revelations of incredible horrors that will terrify you with their brutal reality!" Yeah, I'll bet. Over scenes from the film, the following promises are superimposed: "See... Prehistoric Monsters Return to Earth! See... Sultry Beauty in the Clutches of a Half-Crazed Monster! See... The World Battle for Survival! Overwhelming! Electrifying! Baffling!"

The only promise it fully delivers on is that last one. In many ways, this unusual film is indeed quite baffling, but also a lot of fun. It's easy to champion a quality product such as the horror thrillers of Val Lewton, but when it comes to schlock cinema, *Robot Monster* is one of the most entertaining examples ever made.

Robot Monster begins with a credit sequence superimposed on a potpourri of garish comic book covers. We may suppose that these are the inspiration for the story that follows, qualifying *Robot Monster* as one of the very first films to warn against the potentially pernicious influence of the media.

The film was mainly the work of a lanky Westerner, Phil Tucker, who, after serving stints in the Marines and as a dishwasher, wrote for some of the more obscure science fiction pulps. After exhibiting low-budget burlesque films in Fairbanks, Alaska, Tucker decided to try his hand at making some quickie sexploitation pictures himself.

He made several films in the "After Midnight" series, the titles of which include *Paris After Midnight, Hollywood After Midnight, New York After Midnight, London After Midnight* (no relation to the lost Tod Browning film), and *Tijuana After Midnight*. He also made a now-lost science fiction effort entitled *Space Jockey*, which he described as "a real piece of shit. In fact, [Tucker claims] it's probably the worst film ever made" (*The Golden Turkey Awards*). (Whether it was a film or simply an unsold television pilot has still not been established.)

Originally Tucker wanted to star a robot in *Robot Monster*, but he could not find a robot costume that he could rent cheaply. "I originally envisioned the monster as a kind of robot," he recalled in *The Fifty Worst Films of All Time*. "I talked to several guys that I knew who had robot suits, but it was just out-of-the-way, money-wise. I thought, 'Okay, I know George Barrows.' George's occupation was gorilla-suit man. When they needed a gorilla in a picture they called George, because he owned his own suit and got like forty bucks a day. I thought, 'I know George will work for me for nothing. I'll get a diving helmet, put it on him, and it'll work!'"

Needless to say, it doesn't really, unless the intention was to create one of the most laughable menaces ever created. The film is rife with shots of the overweight Barrows suffering for his art by puffing up a hillside in the undoubtedly unbearably hot Ro-Man costume, which help to pad out the film but provide no palpable menace or thrills. However, a silly-looking monster is not the only criterion by which a film should be judged. After all, subpar acting and unintentionally hilarious dialogue should count for something.

Nevertheless, there are many larger-budgeted features that have less on their minds than *Robot Monster* does. Part of what is endearing about the film is that on its meager budget, it tries to say something about global relations, about individuality and the core of humanity, about women's roles in society while spinning a passably engaging tale.

The Robot Monster is one of the most laughable menaces ever!

The main characters, set up at the outset, are a charmless lad named Johnny (Gregory Moffett), his mother Martha (Selena Royle), and his sisters Carla (Pamela Paulson) and Alice (Claudia Barrett), who are on a picnic. Johnny is wearing a plastic space helmet and playing with a toy raygun that shoots bubbles when he sees two men in a nearby cave. He tells the more elderly of the two, "Spaceman, you must die!"

The men are Roy (George Nader), an assistant to a genial, German-accented professor (John Mylong) who responds, "Wouldn't it be nicer if we could live at peace with each other?" This is the first of many platitudinous speeches in this often all too sanctimonious movie.

Johnny responds, "OK, I'll be from a friendly planet," indicating that the choice of peace is ours. The men are archaeologists, and Johnny is excited at the prospect of their being scientists. Johnny invites the men to meet his mother and sisters. He is a lonely little boy whose father is dead and who lives in the fantasy world suggested by the lurid pulps featured under the main title. He wishes for a new father who would be a big scientist and make rocketships. The core of the film is simply his dream, much like the one in *Invaders from Mars,* where a small boy's hopes and fears are brought into play (e.g., his parents might not be his parents; army generals listen seriously to his tales of alien invasion, etc.) In this case, Johnny dreams of being one of the few heroic survivors of an alien invasion with the professor for his father and his annoying sister eventually killed by one of the invaders.

When Johnny apparently wakes up from his nap, he heads back to Bronson Caverns, the site of most of the film and one of the most frequently employed film locations in Hollywood, used in virtually hundreds of films and television series. It is featured in such diverse works as *Attack of the Crab Monsters, The Cyclops, Dreamscape,* the original *Invasion of the Body Snatchers, It Conquered the World, Killers From Space, King Dinosaur, Star Trek VI: The Undiscovered Country, Unknown World, V* (miniseries), and numerous Westerns. Tucker himself returned to that location for *The Cape Canaveral Monsters.*

In the best Edward D. Wood tradition, footage of lightning, lizards dressed up as dinosaurs fighting, and animated dinosaurs are inexplicably inserted, perhaps suggesting that the world has now gone topsy turvy. (Later the aliens will release a ray to revive prehistoric reptiles, but that takes place at the end of the film, making the "dinosaurs" initial appearance rather puzzling.)

There in the cave, which symbolizes the "pit of man's fears," is Ro-Man (apparently short for Robot-Man) and his infamous bubble machine, which adds a curious touch of surrealism to the film. Perhaps Tucker felt that bubbles drifting out toward the audience would look terrific in 3-D, but instead it simply suggests a low-budget Lawrence Welk program gone mad. Additionally, positive and negative footage have been interspersed along with crackling sounds to suggest powerful forces at work.

Ro-Man is contacted on his viewscreen by the Great Guidance, also referred to as the Great One, who looks almost identical to Ro-Man, indicating the rigid regimentation and comformity of their society which makes no allowances for individuality. Ro-Man is referred to as Extension Ro-Man XJ2, and has a round disk on his transparent faceplate (sometimes revealing the face of George Barrows with a stocking over his head) and a knob at the bottom-center portion of his helmet, while the Great Guidance has a dark, opaque faceplate and no knobs or discs.

After reporting that he was delayed because Earth's gravity is .7652 higher than on their planet, Ro-Man reports, "Hu-Mans know about atomic energy but had not mastered the cosmic ray. Wherever I directed the

150   Son of Guilty Pleasures

There in the cave, which symbolizes the "pit of man's fears," is Ro-Man (apparently short for Robot-Man) and his infamous bubble machine.

calcinator ray their cities crumbled. At first the fools thought it came from among their many nations and began destroying each other with hydrogen bombs. I announced myself to keep them from wiping out cities which will give our people much amusement. Too late they banded against me. Their resistance pattern showed some intelligence. All are gone now. The way is clear for our people."

Aside from the scientific ignorance of thinking there is only one "cosmic ray," this speech does reflect the concerns of many during the Cold War that paranoid leaders would begin employing hydrogen bombs against an imagined enemy, destroying much of the Earth in the process. Obviously, international conflicts make these conquerors' job easier and, in its own way, the speech is a plea for people to work together and not react without thinking.

However, Guidance is upset and obsessed with details. "I want facts, not words!" he insists, pointing out that there is an error of 16 millionths, meaning that eight people are left on Earth. One of the big mysteries of the film is why the Ro-Men are concerned about a pitiful handful of survivors and delay their invasion until all are destroyed. Nevertheless, Ro-Man is instructed to find them and destroy them.

The tin-eared script for the film was written by Wyott Ordung, who the following year directed *Monster From the Ocean Floor*, the film that has the distinction of being Roger Corman's first foray into fantastic cinema, though perhaps fantastic is a less than accurate description for this turkey which gives *Robot Monster* a run for its

There is a clear suggestion that Ro-Man (George Barrows) is sexually attracted to Alice (Claudia Barrett).

money in the bad movie department, but lacks the humorous qualities which redeem *Robot Monster* as an entertainment experience. While the dialogue in *Robot Monster* may be risible and extremely overblown, it's not dull. A gorilla in a deep-sea helmet with antennæ attached may make for a cheap monster, but at least it's amusing, unlike Ordung's awful creature in *Monster,* which is merely an octopus marionette adorned with lights and an obvious light bulb sticking out of its head.

Throughout Ordung makes an attempt to suggest that the Ro-Man is part machine, hence his emphasis on calculations, and that he is unused to speaking English. Ro-Man, for example, appears before the family on a viewscreen and announces, "Hu-Mans, listen to me. Due to an error in calculation, there are still a few of you left. You escaped destruction because I did not know you existed. Now I know. I see five of you are watching that have not been destroyed. Show yourselves and I promise you a painless death." At another point he offers "a choice between a painless surrender death and the horror of resistance death." Who could resist choices like those?

Regardless of his presumed mechanical origin, Ro-Man proves quite fallible. Despite the Great Guidance telling him there are eight people left, Ro-Man assumes there are five because that's all he can see in his viewscreen; later Alice appears as the beauty who attracts the beast and awakens his latent lustful longings.

I wonder whether Ro-Man might not have been intended as a symbol for the Soviet Union, who was seen as swallowing up smaller countries and destroying ideologies other than its own. Russians were frequently characterized as calculating, soul-less

Poor Alice is the beauty to Ro-Man's beast.

beings who worked with each other with mechanical precision, i.e. robot people. They were also seen as intent on conquest and big on oppression, whereas a subsequent mock "marriage" of Alice and Roy indicates that the surviving Americans are all good, Christian people concerned about their community.

Of course, some of the utterances by the humans prove just as strange. The Professor, who with Ray has developed an antibiotic that blocks the killing power of Ro-Man's ray, recontacts Ro-Man, who assumes they are surrendering, and bravely asserts they have fought him to a standstill. The Professor tells Johnny, "If Ro-Man wants us, he should calculate us," which truly makes us question the old man's sanity.

Alice says: "We want peace, Ro-Man, but peace with honor," leaving one to wonder if President Nixon ever saw this film and recalled it when he wanted to describe U.S. relations with Vietnam. When Alice accuses her boyfriend Ray of being "bossy," he counters with one of the film's funniest retorts, "I'm bossy? You're so bossy you ought to be milked before you come home at night." Nor is the mammary association in this retort accidental.

For a fifties film, *Robot Monster* is refreshingly obvious in its sexual undertones. There is a clear suggestion that Ro-Man is sexually attracted to Alice (though the voice-over on the Rhino version about dating her wasn't part of the original film and is obviously a different voice). "I will talk with the girl," promises Ro-Man to the Great One. "It is not in the Plan, but although I cannot verify it, I feel she will understand." Poor Ro-Man, denied feelings and sexual outlet by his own culture, he comes to Earth simply looking for a little understanding (and a little nookie).

Consider the following sexual roles called into play: Despite the Professor insisting he is the head of the family unit and therefore should make the decisions, Alice agrees to meet with the marauding menace. "Is Alice going to have a date with Ro-Man?"

asks Carla in wide-eyed wonder, one of her few lines where Johnny's pesky sister is not asking her brother to play house with her and which again emphasizes the underlying sexual element.

The sexual tension is apparent from Alice's subsequent, seemingly inspirational lines when the men object to her intentions: "You mean there are certain things nice girls don't do? Even if it means that man's millions of years of struggle up from the sea, the slime, to fight, to breathe air, to stand erect, to think, to conquer nature, you mean all this is to stop cold by a jealous father and a doting suitor?" Alice presents herself as a fearless feminist who won't be restrained by an outmoded patriarchy in her attempts to save mankind while the men try to dictate what should be her standard of virtue. (That she is virginal is pointed up after she and Roy finally get some time alone to make out, when she quickly puts a stop to their necking and insists that the Professor marry them first.)

Alice has trouble with Roy because he "wouldn't admit I was good in my field," though what that field is is never specified. Roy is consistently condescending toward her, telling her things such as "You're either too beautiful to be so smart, or too smart to be so beautiful," as if beauty and intelligence were mutually contradictory and frankly someone as good-looking as she is should stop trying to be intelligent. Strangely, Alice falls into the party line by responding, "I guess we do get along all right at that. Let's work together now—we can play later," apparently interpreting Roy's male chauvinist assertions as flirtatious.

Mention should also be made of the film's special *defects* which it has in place of special *effects*. Rather than add two more cast members and actually build an interior set (the entire film was shot outdoors to keep the budget down), the other two surviving members of humanity are depicted as unseen passengers on a toy rocket with a lit sparkler in the back making its way to a space platform through what appears to be dense smoke (thick clouds in the upper atmosphere?). Ro-Man destroys the ship with a mighty blast which also destroys what's left of the illusion by revealing a gloved hand rotating the ship on a stick.

Many of the effects in the film, credited to Jack Rabin and David Commons, were lifted from other sources. There are out-takes of meteors from *Flight to Mars*, and much of the dinosaur and disaster footage is lifted from *One Million B.C.* Shots of the destruction of civilization seem to come from *Invasion U.S.A.* Rabin could be a quite capable effects artist, supplying effects for *Rocketship X-M, Unknown World, Invaders from Mars,* and *Kronos* among others, but his work could also be uneven and obviously the budget here was minimal.

That human emotion is superior to alien intellect is a cliché that appears in seemingly almost every science fiction film. It's a way to assure the audience that no matter how superior some alien species may seem, humanity is still better than they are because we have feelings. (I'm not certain I buy this concept. For example, I know a man who is regularly rude to people but assuages his conscience because he feels bad about it in private afterward. He may have feelings, but it certainly doesn't make him act any better toward other people.)

However, this seems to be the central theme of the film—that humans are sentimental idiots and that's a good thing. The drama of Alice's willingness to sacrifice her virginity to Ro-Man for the sake of what's left of humanity, however, isn't accorded serious consideration. "I don't believe that any human being should degrade himself in order to survive," says Roy.

When Alice responds, "You mean you'd rather have us go out of business, is that it? Never return, no forwarding address. Can't you see you're being sentimental idiots letting your emotions run away with you?" The Professor chides her, "Perhaps that is the quality of being human—the very thing that makes us different from Ro-Man, the very thing we are trying to preserve." If the criterion for preserving people is their being sentimental idiots who let their emotions run away, then Ro-Man also qualifies for perservation.

The biggest shock in the film is when Ro-Man kills Johnny's sister Carla (when her mother makes a reference to it all being over, indicating that humanity has come to an end, Carla assumes she can then go to "Janie's house and borrow her dolls," a moment meant to be poignant but which instead makes Carla come off as moronic, as do her cries of "My daddy won't let you hurt me," just before Ro-Man strangles her). The lives of little kids were usually sacrosanct in fifties films, though in this case much of the audience is glad to see her go. However, when Ro-Man has a similar opportunity earlier with her whiny sibling Johnny, who stupidly spills the beans about the serum that protects the survivors, instead of killing the annoying tyke, Ro-Man makes a speech about humanity "getting too intelligent. We couldn't wait until you were strong enough to attack us, we had to attack you first." Some intelligence.

Ro-Man, having fallen for Alice, succumbs to unfamiliar emotions and reports to the Great Guidance, requesting that the "plan should include one living human for reference in case of unforeseen contingencies." (The Great One is not amused and insists that all be destroyed). Ro-Man is enraged by the sight of the now married couple necking, and attacks Roy. While Alice batters at the beast ineffectually, Ro-Man strangles him and tosses him over the edge of a precipice (Ro-Man is so distracted by Alice that he lets Roy live long enough for him to return and tell the others what has happened). The amorous robot ape picks Alice up in his arms and carries the struggling bride away, pausing only to tell her, "I am ordered to kill you. I must do it with my hands."

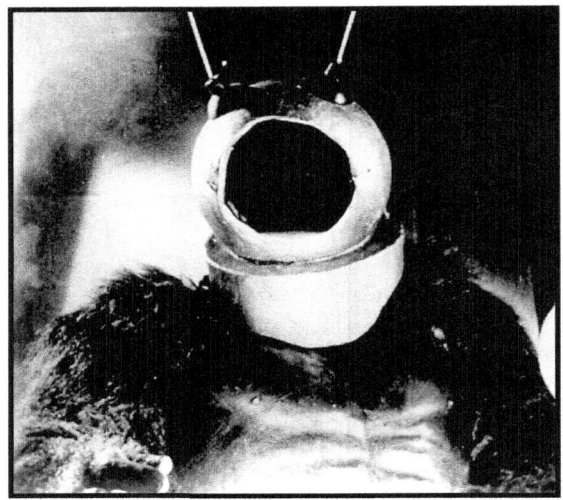

"How is it you are so strong?" asks Alice, alertly searching for a weakness. "It seems impossible." Though a typical victim, Alice does show pluck and cunning.

"We Ro-Mans obtain our strength from the planet Ro-Man, relayed to our individual energizers," explains the enamored alien, confirming his energizer is in the cave. This is clear proof that Ro-man has fallen for Alice's feminine wiles as he tells her exactly what she wants to know, thereby sealing his fate, although this information is subsequently ignored in the rapid climax that concludes the film.

Johnny, ever the hero in his dream, concocts a final plan, where the Professor tells Ro-Man that they plan to surrender to an easy death as a ruse to rescue Alice. However, Ro-Man is more intent on making moves on Alice. "Suppose I were human, would you treat me like a man?" he says while putting his hirsute arms around her as she tries to discover the whereabouts of the energizer. His intentions are clear from his removing the back of her halter top, but he is interrupted first by the Professor's surrender call ("Why do you call me at this time?" Ro-Man asks peevishly before agreeing to a delayed meeting) and then by another call from the Great Guidance.

"You wish to change the plan?" the annoyed Great One asks. "To think for yourself is to be like the Hu-Man."

"Yes," responds Ro-Man in his big, emotional moment, "to be like the Hu-Man. To *laugh, feel, want*. Why are these things not in the plan?"

Ordered to kill the girl, Ro-Man becomes an outer-space Hamlet: "I cannot, yet I must. How do you calculate that? At what point on the graph do must and cannot meet? Yet I *must*, but I *cannot*." Indeed, it is one of the most memorable speeches I've heard in any science fiction film, and one which aids *Robot Monster* in joining the screen immortals.

The Professor gives a gun to Johnny who becomes the diversion, yelling out, "Here I am, Ro-Man!" Ro-Man ignores his leader's instruction to kill the girl first, explaining, "Great Guidance, I cannot kill the girl, but I will kill the boy (a move most of the audience can easily understand). Alice, do not hate me. I must!"

With that, the apish invader approaches and strangles the boy; however, Guidance has had enough. "You wish to be a Hu-Man. Good. You can die a Hu-Man," he intones

Martha (Selena Royle), Alice, and the Professor (John Mylong) wonder what will happen next.

before pointing his fingers at the screen from which emanates scratches on the celluloid, suggestive of lightning that shoots out and kills his Earthly representative.

The Great One then unleashes his final plan. "I shall release our cosmic Q-rays which shall release prehistoric reptiles to devour whatever remains of life," he soliloquizes as stop-motion dinosaur footage and battling lizards are shown onscreen. This is followed by his avowal that "Psychotronic vibrations will smash the Earth out of the Universe," which makes one wonder why he bothered unleashing those dinosaurs except that it gives the filmmakers an excuse to include the footage.

But the final twist/cheat is yet to come. As the Earth splits apart, Johnny wakes up with a bruise on his head to find himself being carried in Roy's arms. Martha invites the archaeologists to dinner. When Carla asks Johnny to play house, he reluctantly agrees, having learned to treasure his sister, but promising to watch out for Ro-Men.

"Really, Johnny," responds Alice, "you're overdoing the spaceman act. There simply aren't such things." After all, this is the stuff of comic books whose garish and suggestive covers were the inspiration for Johnny's obviously fevered imagination.

But Tucker has one more trick up his sleeve. They leave—while out from the cave a series of Ro-Men (actually the same double-exposed shot repeated three times) emerge and head menacingly toward the camera as Bernstein's overbearing Ro-Man theme gets its last work-out. (A black curtain is clearly apparent behind Ro-Man in the double- exposed footage.)

There are some odd continuity errors in the film. When Roy goes out to neck with Alice, he has blood dripping from his right ear for no apparent reason. Yet, shortly afterward when he marries Alice, the blood is gone. Later, Ro-Man will start to tie up Alice but is interrupted by a call. When he is finished, someone has finished tying Alice up, but who? Surely not Alice herself.

As noted above, the composer-conductor for the film was a neophyte Elmer Bernstein, who also scored *Cat-Women of the Moon* the same year. His work here is overemphatic and repetitive but by no means incompetent. Bernstein would go on to write truly great scores for *The Magnificent Seven* and *The Great Escape*, and would also compose the scores for such projects as *An American Werewolf in London, Heavy Metal, The Ten Commandments, To Kill a Mockingbird,* and *True Grit.* He did a marvelous job reorchestrating Bernard Herrmann's original score for *Cape Fear* for Martin Scorsese's remake.

It's hard to believe but *Robot Monster* has permeated our culture.

The editor credited on the film is Merrill White A.C.E., whose credits include the classics *Love Me Tonight, The Red House,* and *The Fly* (1958), though many sources award credit solely to associate editor Bruce Schoengarth. Why this should be remains another *Robot Monster* mystery.

Executive producer Al Zimbalist kept up his association with bad filmmaking and was later associated with other classic bad films such as *Cat-Women of the Moon* and its even worse remake, *Missile to the Moon* (for which he is given story credit), *Monster from Green Hell,* and *Valley of the Dragons.*

Tucker defended *Robot Monster*, saying, "I still do not believe there is a soul alive who could have done as well for as little money as I was able to do.... For the budget, and for the time, I felt I had achieved greatness." (*The Golden Turkey Awards.*) It's certainly true that with a larger budget and more time, some of the film's problems could have been fixed, though it would then lack the charm which makes it a guilty pleasure. The budget for *Robot Monster* was, according to Tucker, as little as $16,000 plus lab rentals, and the shooting schedule was a mere four days. He believes that the film collected rentals of over a million dollars, but his partners left him without a penny. "They personally made money on that picture by stealing from me. I didn't get anything from that picture. At one time, I was going to sue but I couldn't find a lawyer who would help." (*The Fifty Worst Films of All Time.*)

Tucker was not even allowed an advance peek at his own film by his backers after it was completed, forcing him to buy a ticket to see it. Following the wretched reception the film received, Tucker was plunged into depression and even attempted suicide, winding up in the psychiatric ward of a Veterans Administration Hospital. The film later showed up on television under the title *Monsters from the Moon*.

He struck up a friendship with Lenny Bruce and together they produced *Dance Hall Racket* (1954), which featured Bruce in what was then his natural environment, assisting strippers in strip joints. Tucker also made a drag-strip drama called *Pachuco* (1956), which is his favorite among his own films.

He later returned to science fiction with *The Cape Canaveral Monsters* (1960), which he both wrote and directed. In it, aliens, represented by big white dots sprinkled liberally on the film footage, come to Earth to sabotage our space program. The film is as bad as *Robot Monster*, but not nearly as enjoyable. It is another in a long line of films where aliens take over human bodies or corpses, so that for most of the film, the aliens are portrayed by Jason Johnson and Katherine Victor. The most clever aspect of the film is the fact that even though the corpses that the aliens inhabit are decaying, it doesn't cut down on their sex drive at all.

In the book *Scream Queens*, Victor recalled the erstwhile director: "Tucker knew what he wanted and didn't hestitate to fulfill his responsibilities as a director. This, plus a two-week shooting schedule, enough money to enable him to shoot several takes per shot if something went wrong, and the added attraction of color, all made the project seem promising. The color was the first thing to go. Last minute budget cuts restricted it to black and white. Then, as film days went by, the cost of necessary special effects ate away at the money reserve. Scenes were shortened, changed, or compromised. When the film was finally screened, it proved a disappointment to everyone involved."

Abandoning his film directorial career, Tucker worked as an associate producer on several television shows and documentaries. He later found a niche as a post-production supervisor for fellow schlockmeister Dino de Laurentiis, working on *King Kong* (1976) and the equally laughable *Orca, the Killer Whale*. He also served as editor of the notorious bombs *The Nude Bomb* and *Charlie Chan and the Curse of the Dragon Queen*.

Robot Monster however remains his main claim to fame. Formed out of the sweat and toil of its ill-compensated participants, it continues to live on in the hearts and minds of those who have experienced it. Perhaps the best tribute to it was paid in Ken Shapiro's one-time cult film *The Groove Tube*, a filmic series of shaggy-dog sketches in which the image of a gorilla with a television for a head was featured prominently in ads for the film and as the climax to its *2001* parody. Anyone who had seen Tucker's film knew instantly where Shapiro had gotten the idea for it.

Robot Monster has permeated our culture. I've seen Ro-Man at Hollywood Halloween parties and in Drew and Josh Alan Friedman drawings. He is a true clockwork orange, a mechanical being with a simian shape, tortured by the same conflicts and feelings that affect all of us. He has become a symbol of technology run rampant and of inspiration out of desperation, a representative of wonked-out, low-budget filmmaking, of blighted aspirations and of tormenting dilemmas. You can't fear or respect him, but you must see the movie. The pleasure will be yours.

SSSSSSS
by John E. Parnum

Let's face it, I'm a ssssucker for sssnake flickssss. Like 'em even more than dinosaur movies (see *Guilty Pleasures of the Horror Film*). My passion for serpents extends to real life also. I've owned a python named Monty for four years, although I just found out last month that Monty is a girl.

When it comes to snake movies, especially the scariest ones ever filmed, the general populace will vote for *Raiders of the Lost Ark* (1981), with Indiana Jones (Harrison Ford) and his lady of the moment (Karen Allen) trapped in the Well of Lost Souls, trying to avoid thousands of reptiles placed there courtesy of director Steven Spielberg. But this film doesn't count in my book since the slitherers are on the screen for less than 10 minutes. I did have great hopes for *Anaconda* (1997), but the totally preposterous myths perpetrated about this illusive inhabitant of the Amazon basin and the highly exaggerated, computer-generated animated movements were unrealistic and diluted the scare quotient for me. The most memorable moment in *Anaconda* was that wink Jon Voight gave Jennifer Lopez after being regurgitated by the title creature.

There have been innumerable snake movies of every conceivable kind: snakes on a rampage *(Rattlers*—1976 and *Venom*—1982); giant snakes (the 1976 *King Kong* and *Conan the Barbarian*—1982); snakes as a method of murder (*Stanley* and *Killer Snakes*—both in 1972); witchcraft and Satanism (*Jaws of Satan*—1984 and *The*

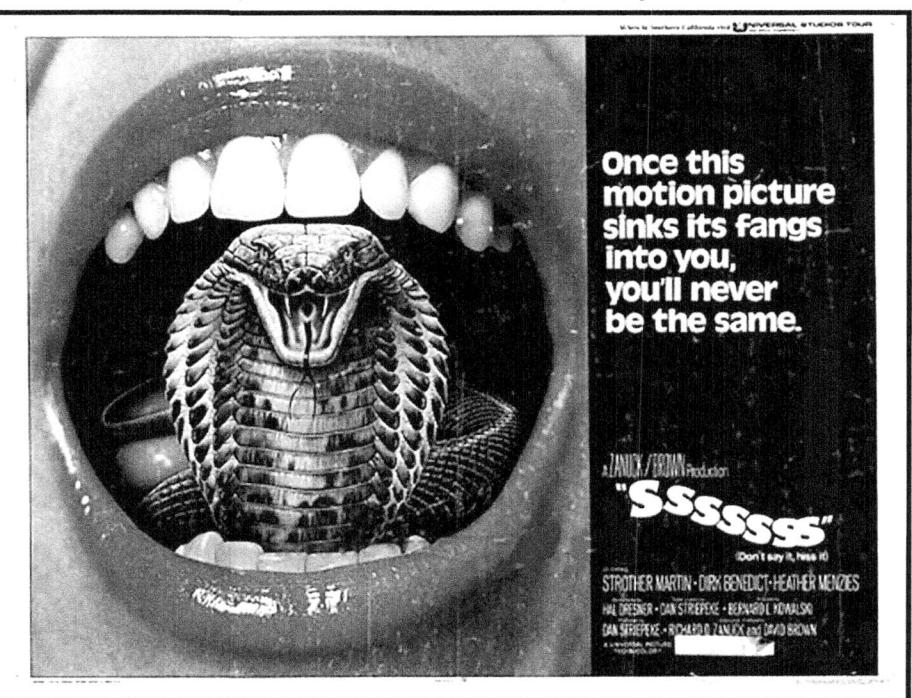

Strother Martin as Doctor Carl Stoner gives a performance reminiscent of Boris Karloff in one of his early forties Columbia mad doctor forays.

Craft—1996); films about Medusa, in which the Gorgon's hair is laced with serpents (mostly portrayed sloppily by mechanical prostheses, such as in *The Gorgon* and *Seven Faces of Dr. Lao*—both in 1964); and, of course, the were-snake film where a person is transformed into a serpent (this sub-genre first being filmed in France in 1910 as *The Snake Man,* in which a visitor to a zoo takes lessons on how to become a snake so he can join a circus freak show).

Production values range from the ludicrous to the repulsively graphic to the extremely realistic. In *Hard Ticket to Hawaii* (1987), the giant cancer-ridden serpent is an immobile model pulled along by very visible wires. With its floppy tongue in a perpetually open mouth, it makes its initial entrance by exploding out of a toilet, causing the hero to quip, "Just when you thought it was safe to take a pee!" Audiences watching *Curse 2: The Bite* (1989) might, themselves, start throwing up as snake man J. Eddie Peck vomits real pythons that slither after girlfriend Jill Schoelen in a sea of mud. And contrary to my comment about the rubber reptiles used for Medusa movies, actress Rosemarie Gil in the 1976 Philippine production *Devil Woman* had an actual nest of serpents woven into her hair. This process was effectively repeated in *Bram Stoker's Dracula* (1992) when Florina Kendrick, as one of the vampire brides, submitted to having 15 king snakes ensnared in her locks, calling the dangling serpents writhing hypnotically about her neck "symbols of sensuality."

It is Heather Menzies as Kristina that is the icing on top of my guilty pleasure cake.

So to make a snake movie truly believable, you've got to have real serpents. Which brings us to *Ssssssss*, a guilty pleasure of mine that possesses a lot of special qualities which upgrade it so that I actually don't feel that guilty about watching it over and over again. This flick contains an incredibly hokey premise concerning a mad doctor (Strother Martin) who transforms his assistants into king cobras since he believes that after man has annihilated himself through pollution and famine it will be the reptile that inherits the earth. And the best part of all is that the actual co-stars of *Ssssssss* were serpents from the Hermosa Reptile and Wild Animal Farm, although in a preface thanking the cast and crew for their courage (actors are actually bitten on camera), it was added that the king cobras were imported from Bangkok and the python from Singapore.

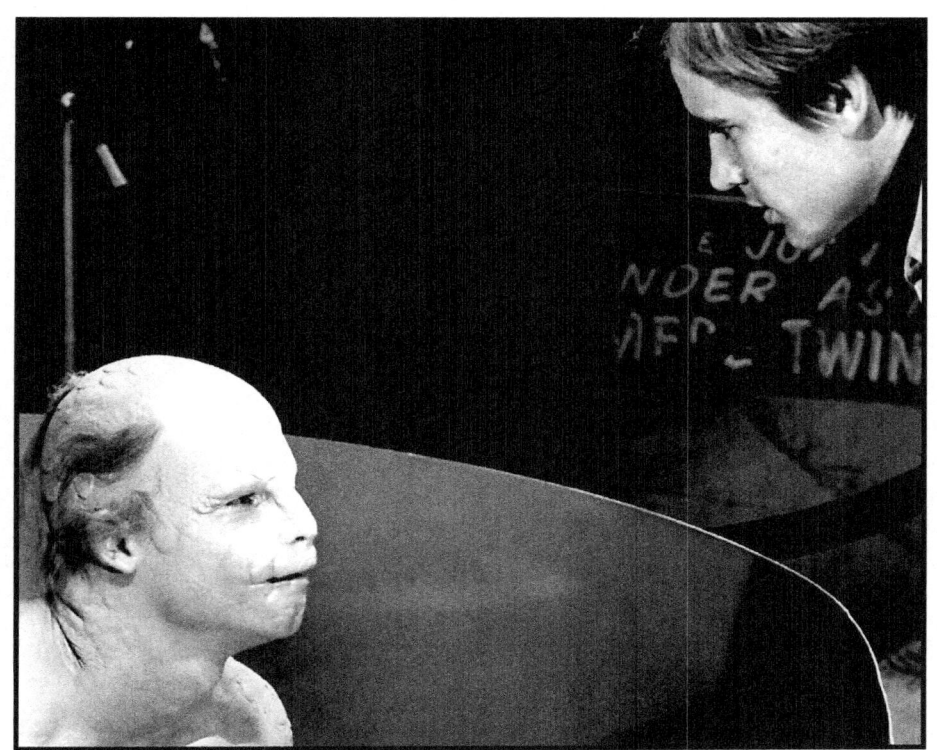

At a carnival sideshow, David (Dirk Benedict) checks out the Snake Man (Noble Craig), not realizing that he is destined for a similar fate.

Strother Martin as Doctor Carl Stoner gives a performance reminiscent of Boris Karloff in one of his early forties Columbia mad doctor forays, only Martin infuses a great deal more humor as Stoner. Like Karloff, he believes that his unpopular experiments are for the good of mankind. He truly loves his myopic daughter Kristina (Heather Menzies) who assists him in his reptile demonstrations for passing tourists. For recreation he enjoys the company of his alcoholic red-tailed boa, Harry, to whom he reads Walt Whitman and plies with booze. "Look sober now, Harry, or else Kristina will make us blow in a balloon," he tells the inebriated snake. Kristina is always having to settle Harry's hangovers the next morning by slipping Alka Seltzer in his water bowl.

But it is Heather Menzies as Kristina that is the icing on top of my guilty pleasure cake. I have always had a thing for this lovely but unsophisticated Toronto native who followed *Sssssss* with a heroine role in Joe Dante's 1978 *Piranha* and was cast as a regular (Jessica) in the TV series *Logan's Run* (1977-78). Ms. Menzies had worked as a young teenager with Julie Andrews in both *Hawaii* and *The Sound of Music*, portraying one of the older Von Trapp children in the latter, who, being relegated to the singing formation's far end of the Cinamascope screen, sometimes gets chopped off when the musical runs on television. *Sssssss*, however, is Heather's leading-lady debut, and her discreet nude swim with lab assistant David Blake (Dirk Benedict), filmed in soft-focus with strategically placed leaves and plants, unleashed fantasies in me that I *really do* feel guilty about. Thinking I'd discovered an unearthed treasure, my daydreams were dashed when Ms. Menzies appeared nude in *Playboy*, baring a bit of heather for all the world to see in the August 1973 issue.

Released in 1973 by Universal on a double bill with *The Boy Who Cried Werewolf*, *Sssssss* was the initial collaboration of executive producers Richard D. Zanuck and David Brown who hired Twentieth Century-Fox's head make-up chief, Dan Striepeke, to produce their first venture. Striepeke had worked with John Chambers on the unique simian make-up for the *Planet of the Apes* series at Fox, and was actually thinking about filming a man-into-snake movie at the time. While the problem of such a transformation seemed unfilmable (witness fully-clothed Faith Domergue's metamorphosis carelessly superimposed over a dead snake at the climax of the 1955 *Cult of the Cobra*), Striepeke hired screenwriter Hal Dresner to concoct a scary story with plenty of comedy relief, and then persuaded Chambers, along with Nick Marcellino, to provide a believable method of turning Benedict into a king cobra. Dresner's original title for his script was *King Cobra*, but that really didn't do anything for Striepeke, who came up with *Sssssss* when one of the hundred inhabitants recruited as supporting players from Hermosa's hissed at him. All agreed that the unmistakable and universally feared sound was an appropriate title. "Don't say it, hiss it," became the imaginative promotional campaign.

As directed by Bernard Kowalski (his early flicks included American International's *Night of the Blood Beast* and *Attack of the Giant Leeches*), the film begins with an air of mystery as sleazy carnival owner Kogen (Tim O'Conner) gives $800 to Doctor Stoner for something that whines pitifully from within a crate. "It'll settle down in time," assures Stoner. "He'll get to meet a lot of interesting people," remarks Kogen; "You're a real gentleman, Doc, and a genius besides—first one I ever met." Stoner is not flattered but replies, "It's rare to be appreciated for one's failures."

The sign of a successful book is when the author can "grab" us in the first paragraph, making us want to continue to read. So, too, with a film, and the opening scene of *Sssssss* intrigues us: What is the "it" within the crate? Why is "it" Doctor Stoner's "failure"? What does "it" look like? Not only are we puzzled, but we see Stoner's persona as basically good, certainly more noble than some of the lesser characters in *Sssssss*. Toward the end of the film, a disagreeable Kogen harasses Kristina when she visits the carnival after hours and recognizes the freakish snake man as her father's missing assistant, Tim.

There's a nasty garage mechanic who pours gasoline on Tim's replacement, David, and gets "wrapped up" in Harry's coils. But even more reprehensible is patronizing fellow scientist, Doctor Ken Daniels (Richard B. Shull), a lecherous professor at the local university from whom Stoner asks for an extension of his grant and a recommendation for the new assistant. Later, Daniels takes particular joy in rejecting Stoner's application. Snooping around Stoner's laboratory grounds he is shocked to see David in the early stages of snake transformation. Stoner chains Daniels in a shed and tests his herpetological knowledge by telling him that there are identical keys to his shackles in two aquariums, each confining a snake: one reptile is the harmless western hog-nose and the other a venomous hog-nose pit viper. Daniels has earlier given a lecture on the difference between the docile Florida king and the poisonous coral who have similar red, black, and yellow markings, except that the coral can be identified by remembering "red touch yellow; kill a fellow." Daniels makes the correct choice, but gets his

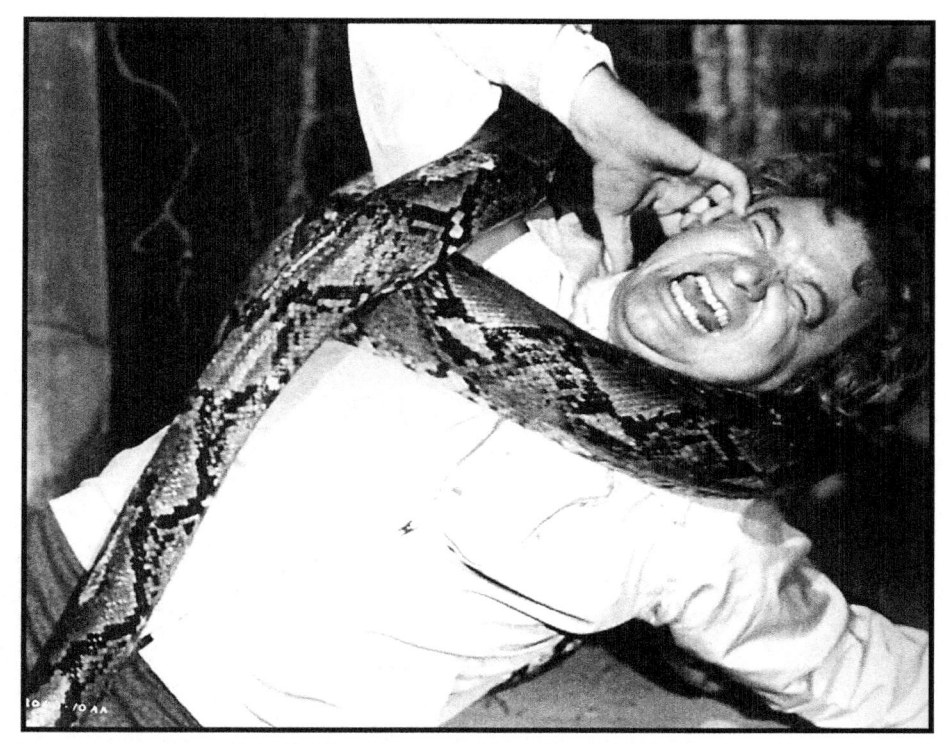

Dr. Ken Daniels (Richard B. Shull) learns the fate of those who snoop around Dr. Stoner's laboratory, as a 30-foot reticulated python drops in on him.

just deserts when, to the accompaniment of crunching bones, he is gobbled up by an ailing 30-foot reticulated python, shown graphically by a foot disappearing down the creature's throat.

Another unpleasant fellow is bully football hero Steve Randall (Reb Brown), who takes particular delight in taunting David and provoking him into a fight in which David "strikes" at Steve several times, biting him on the neck. This is a particularly impressive bit of action on actor Benedict's part, and is his first aggressive snake attribute. So angry is Steve that he later visits the Stoner residence, climbing into Kristina's bedroom window, but is attacked by the pet boa. With the snake wrapped around his arm, Steve bludgeons Harry to death on the ground. Big mistake. That night Stoner slips into Steve's dorm room and, while the jock is showering, drops a deadly black mamba into the stall. Steve is bitten is slow motion and his demise is somewhat reminiscent of Janet Leigh's watery death in *Psycho*. In a humorous bit, Steve's girlfriend Kitty (Kathleen King) sobs hysterically to the local sheriff (Jack Ging) that she killed Steve because the coach had warned him that while he was in training he couldn't have sex more than twice a night. "I loved him too much," she sobs to the sheriff. "How much did you love him?" asks the curious sheriff. "Three times!" Kitty confesses.

Like Karloff's mad doctors, good-intentioned Stoner disposes of his detractors only when they become a threat to his research in experiments he feels are ultimately for the benefit of humanity. Theorizing that food consumption, at the present rate, will result

Kristina Stoner shows off her two-headed snake to her father's new laboratory assistant.

in world-wide shortages in less than 50 years, he injects David with cobra venom on the pretext of immunization. Stoner informs David that cobra venom is one of nature's strongest hallucinogens, and that night David experiences wild dreams in a montage of abstract visuals that include smoke, lava, Lucifer standing over the pits of Hell, fallen angels, Brueghelesque demons, and naked bodies on a sea of tranquility. The first signs of his physical change occur when David begins to shed his skin (Stoner explains that peeling is just a natural allergic reaction to the shots). Soon David's body temperature drops two degrees a day until it finally stabilizes at 80. Next, the boy's eyelids begin to recede and his nostrils flatten. When Stoner notices scales developing on David's arm and his voice changing to a higher pitch, he sends Kristina away for a few days on a ruse to await the shipment of the rare aruba snake. It is on this trip away from home that Kristina recognizes her father's former assistant, Tim (played movingly by quadriplegic Noble Craig), in the sideshow tent. Limbless, covered with scales, and looking more like a turtle than a snake, the creature sheds tears from his blue eyes, the last remaining sign of his lost humanity. Fred Blau, who was one of nine make-up artists to "tattoo" Rod Steiger in *The Illustrated Man* and who worked with John Chambers on the *Apes* series, was brought in to help with the snake-man creation. At this point, Kristina realizes with horror what her father is doing to David, and rushes home.

With his insides feeling like they've been rearranged, David is already in the final stages of transformation into a king cobra. It is a visualizingly hypnotic transforma-

Dr. Carl Stoner approaches a deadly king cobra to extract venom from its fangs at a tourist demonstration.

tion that utilizes make-up, models, and photographic dissolves, all accompanied by an irritating violin score by Pat Williams. "You are the future, David," Stoner consoles a pain-wracked David lying naked, glabrous, and covered with scales, while pitiful moans issue from his reptilian mouth. "Just as Adam was the first man, you are the first creature of the next evolution. You will survive pollution, the holocaust, the famines, the plagues that will make man extinct. You will survive and multiply."

It is interesting to think what might have been going through Strother Martin's mind as he recited these lines. Martin claimed that this was the kind of role he'd "been looking for over many years.... Except for the misuse of science," he related in the pressbook; "this man is closer to my real self than any character I've portrayed in motion pictures. I'm an ecology buff and I love nature. It bothers me when I see how we're destroying the very foundation of our life and inventing destructive forces that could blow up the world." Even Stoner's daughter has that famous poster originating from the Vietnam war hanging on her bedroom wall: "War is not healthy for children and other living things."

While Kristina's poster, her dutiful daily exercises, and other environmental reminders are nostalgically interesting and seem almost as pertinent today as they did 25 years ago, the most fascinating aspects of *Sssssss* are the wealth of factual tidbits scattered throughout the movie. Stoner and his daughter run a country reptile farm and give demonstrations to passing tourists in order to raise money for the doctor's venom research. There's Sam, Kristina's pet albino turtle from Malaysia, and a two-headed snake named Aaron and Aaron the Second, which Kristina explains is not an unusual phenomenon but that only one in a million survives. Similar "Aarons" made an appearance as a roadside tourist attraction in the 1980 film *Resurrection*. In another bit of enlightenment, Stoner informs David that the black mamba is the fastest snake in the world and secretes enough venom to kill 10 men. The neurotoxic poison inhibits breathing and constricts the Vagus nerve, causing the heart to beat rapidly. The victim usually succumbs within an hour in what appears to be a heart attack. He tells David that sometimes when the mamba won't eat, it must be force-fed, and demonstrates by shoving a tube into the snake's mouth and squirting a solution of milk, eggs, bone meal, vitamins, liver, gelatin, and chicken blood ("for flavor") down its throat. Actor Martin actually allows himself to be bitten on camera during a later sequence involving this snake.

As he continues to show David around the laboratory, he explains, "The fear that most people have of snakes is based on the misunderstanding that they have about any other minority group. If they're told that one member is harmful, then they generalize and believe they're all dangerous." Stoner demonstrates the docile nature of some snakes by prodding the hog-nose and commenting that it cannot be induced to bite. Too bad he didn't follow up on this by informing his assistant that, when disturbed, this snake will roll on its back and pretend to be dead, and even after the "corpse" is turned over, it will flip onto its back again until the danger has passed.

Most impressive of all, however, is the king cobra that the Stoners keep as the feature attraction for the tourist trade. Stoner goes head-to-head with the serpent, makes a few passes to mesmerize it, then seizes it behind the head and milks the venom from its fangs as Kristina describes the creature's habits to their audience. She explains that a single bite of the king cobra can kill 30 men and that, unlike most snakes, the cobra will continuously chew its victim. "Being of royal heritage, the king rarely attacks unless annoyed," she reassures the crowd. Then adds: "Unfortunately, almost everything annoys the king." Kristina cautions them not to take pictures during the demonstration, and, of course, one tourist thoughtlessly sets off a flash, causing a near fatality. Stoner later explains to David that the king cobra is "the most cunning, most vicious, most insolent of all God's creatures. Six years, and he still doesn't like me. Why should he? I'm just a common human; he's the king." The only thing the cobra fears is a mongoose, which Stoner just happens to keep in a nearby cage, and which becomes more and more agitated as David starts taking on his own cobra features.

With David's transformation complete, Stoner unleashes the real king cobra, challenging it with, "Your majesty, I regret to inform you there is a pretender to the throne. A king with the power of a cobra, but the intelligence of man." This really "hisses off" the snake and it strikes the doctor, killing him, and then slithers into the lab to seek its usurper. Kristina returns and discovers her dead dad as the challenged cobra prepares to lunge at her. The sheriff and deputy arrive in time to shoot the serpent, and the three rush into the lab where the escaped mongoose is tearing away at the David-cobra. Kristina screams and the scene is frozen in an unfulfilling and unsatisfactory ending.

Ssssss is truly an innovative film, providing both fun and fright for the audience. Only a few hardened viewers will not jump when a hissing, open-mouthed, fanged

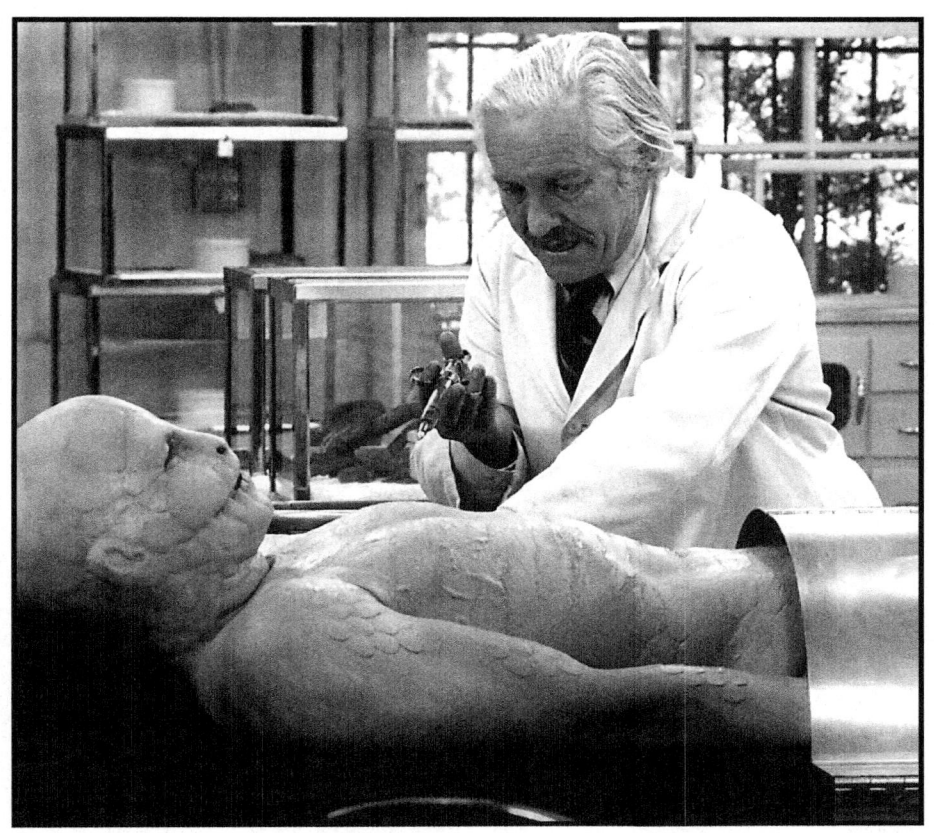

Dr. Stoner administers a shot to his laboratory assistant, David, now in the final stages before transforming into a king cobra.

serpent lunges at them on the screen. Never before had so many actual reptiles been used in a motion picture (remember, this was eight years before *Raiders*). I thought the Chambers/Marcellino transformation of David into a cobra impressive for its time, certainly smoother than those Lon Chaney, Jr./Wolf Man dissolves from the 1940s. (In a February 1998 *Starlog* interview with Mark Phillips, Benedict relates how it took four makeup artists seven hours to paint and apply the textured scales to his shaved body.) Suspense is maintained throughout, especially when David, closer to reptile than human, slithers across the floor trying to reach a ringing phone for help before Stoner can answer it. Heather Menzies, as I mentioned before, charmed me more than any other actress with her infectious smile and coy expressions. At first, especially when lecturing before the tourists, her attitude might be deemed a bit condescending. But all is forgotten when she shyly agrees to the nude swim and teasingly admonishes David for peeking, then admits guiltily that her scolding stemmed from not being able to see his naked body without her glasses. One fault that bothers me, outside of why the Stoners would keep a mongoose on the premises, is the python swallowing Doctor Daniels: Factually, that species of snake would not dine on an adult of that size, no matter how hungry the creature was; and technically, there would be a huge bulge (Daniels) in the neck behind the python's mouth when we see it wolfing down the doctor's foot. One final problem: While all the factual material is certainly more accurate than that perpetrated in *Anaconda*, the Brazilian aruba that Kristina expects at the post office is so rare that I could find no reference to it in any reptile encyclopedia.

The film did not do well at the box office, but critics, for the most part, were kind to the production, and perhaps for this reason *Sssssss* might not really be classified as a guilty pleasure. Murf in the July 18, 1973 issue of *Variety* (page 14) had the following comments: "The film's relaxed tone almost invites an audience to gasp, then chuckle at their own momentary outburst.... Reb Brown is good as a brutish football player who learns that a black mamba is not some new Afro dance.... (Strother Martin) has a

The film did not do well at the box office, but critics, for the most part, were kind.

major opportunity to depart from the crotchety-character rut, and he is very effective in conveying underplayed, paradoxical terror." Bhob Stewart in *Cinefantastique* (Volume 3/Number 2, Spring 1974, page 20) found the transformation scene "particularly disappointing" but, in summing up concluded: "Highly praised by Howard Thompson of *The New York Times*, the film's assets are its emphasis on research, realism, characterization, and fine acting, achieved mainly by the casting of good character actors in important roles. Strother Martin, a familiar face from many Westerns, seems to understand the value of a sense of humor and the mechanics of low-key acting that Karloff knew so well."

Many critics, however, agreed that the contrived ending was too abrupt and left the plot dangling. Did the mongoose really kill off the David-cobra? If not, does the mongoose kill off the sheriff and deputy? Do Kristina and the David-cobra live happily ever after, raising lots of squiggly serpents together? There's a scene midpoint during the film before David exhibits obvious changes in which he and Kristina make love. Stoner returns home earlier than expected and sees the cast-off clothing strewn about the living room floor. He is angry and fearful for his daughter. He chastises her that "one drop of..." He pauses. Is he about to say "semen"? He finishes "...David's blood could affect the inoculations; there's a period where venom could have a damaging effect on his nervous system." Then, recall Stoner's promise to David: "You will survive and multiply." Could it be that Producer Striepeke had a sequel in mind? *Sssson of Sssssss*? Now that would be a real guilty pleasure!

HYPNOTIZED!
Reincarnated as a Monster from Hell!
THE SHE-CREATURE
IT CAN AND DID HAPPEN!
Based on authentic FACTS you've been reading about!
CHESTER MORRIS · MARLA ENGLISH · TOM CONWAY
CATHY DOWNS · LANCE FULLER · RON RANDELL · Freida Inescort A GOLDEN STATE Production

THE SHE-CREATURE
by Randy Palmer

In September 1956, American International Pictures released a low-budget monster movie called *The She-Creature* in support of Roger Corman's *It Conquered the World*. This unimposing $106,000 black-and-white quickie ended up becoming one of the company's most popular fifties films, though it took nearly 20 years to earn a reputation as something special in the eyes of fantasy film fans.

AIP was carving a niche in Hollywood as the only film company unafraid to make films aimed at youngsters instead of adults. Sandwiched in between its other monster pictures, *The She-Creature* must have seemed like just one more in a long line of undistinguished chillers. Roger Corman and Alex Gordon were making them hard and fast in those days, and much of the time the films suffered from their low budgets and short shooting schedules. Paul Blaisdell, who created the title monsters for many science-fiction and horror productions of the time, often complained sarcastically of the "rush-rush" nature of AIP's particular brand of budget-conscious filmmaking: "Move it in! Move it out! There's no time! There's no money! Blah, blah, blah!" Though Blaisdell had ample opportunity to bring his own special brand of macabre magic to the movies, more often than not the creature costumes and monster make-ups he designed were given short shrift, because time was at a premium and the production schedules of these pictures just didn't allow for much innovation.

The She-Creature was a committee film. The rhyming title was originated by Jerry Zigmond, who offered it to AIP president Jim Nicholson at a party hosted by one of the company's sub-distributors, Red Jacobs. (Jacobs went on to become the president of Crown International Pictures.) Zigmond hadn't any story to go along with his title, but Nicholson promised to credit him with the idea for the film anyway.

In actuality Nicholson and AIP vice-president Sam Arkoff had been interested in getting something onto the screen that would take advantage of the public's fascination with the famous Bridey Murphy case, and Zigmond's title seemed to fit. In the early 1950s, a businessman by the name of Morey Bernstein hypnotized a Pueblo, Colorado, housewife, Ruth Simmons, who claimed to be the 20th-century reincarnation of an 18th-century Irishwoman named Bridey Murphy. Bernstein wrote a book about his experiments, *The Search for Bridey Murphy*, in 1956. Nicholson and Arkoff were hoping to make a picture based on the book and get it into theaters before public interest in the subject waned. Unfortunately this would mean forfeiting a sizable chunk of money just to secure the rights to the property—definitely a no-no at this stage in the company's history.

A brainstorming session with Alex Gordon, producer of one of the earliest AIP pictures, *Day the World Ended*, led to the construction of a story outline that incorporated the most exploitable elements of the Murphy case without naming names. Nicholson called in screenwriter Lou Rusoff, a brother-in-law of Arkoff's, to discuss the idea further. He wanted Rusoff to come up with a straightforward monster scenario that combined elements of hypnotism and reincarnation, two of the major themes in Bernstein's book. In fact, Rusoff ended up incorporating not just the themes Nicholson and Arkoff had re-

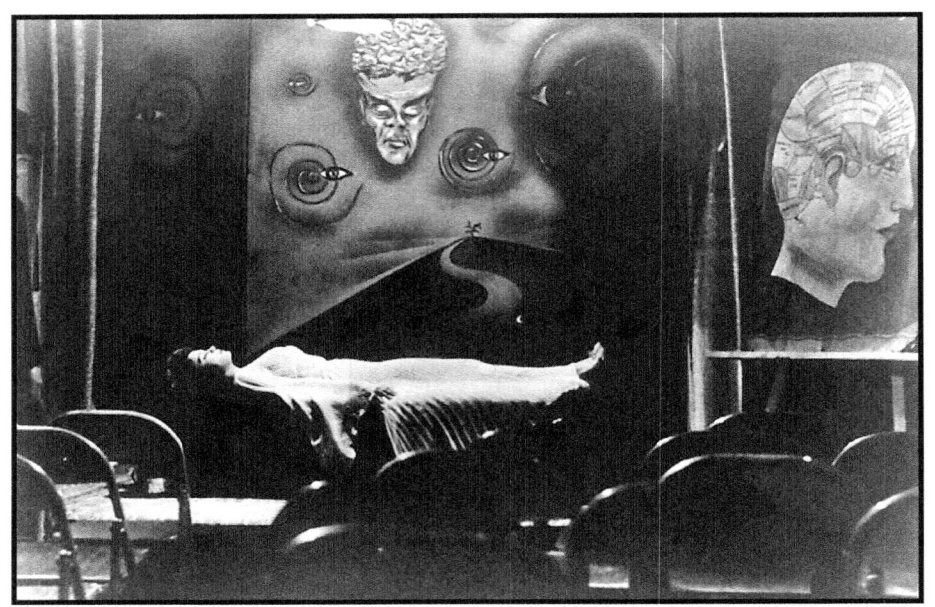

For years Lombardi has kept a carnival-follower named Andrea (Marla English) under his Svengali-like spell.

quested, but also elements of spiritualism, age regression, soul transference, extrasensory perception, prediction theory, fictionalized prehistoric monsters, blackmail, and murder-for-profit to boot. The amazing thing was, Rusoff was able to pull these disparate ingredients together into an intelligent and cohesive whole without ever losing sight of the major plot thread. The final script would appeal to adults as well as youngsters. For the youthful members of the audience there would be the title monster, of course; for the teenaged element there was the titillation of the creature's human counterpart, so well portrayed by newcomer Marla English (AIP's answer to Elizabeth Taylor, according to some critics); and for adults there would be the mysterious world of the evil mystic, the references to contemporary themes like the Bridey Murphy case, high-society money-making scams, and down-and-dirty murder-for-profit/status/fame schemes by the denizens of society's underbelly. The final advertising campaign made only indirect references to the Bridey Murphy phenomenon: "It can and did happen!" screamed the one-sheet poster. "Based on authentic facts you've been reading about!" With Bernstein's book on the bestseller list, there was no doubt to whom AIP was referring.

Once the property was assigned to a producer, Nicholson turned his attention to monster-maker Paul Blaisdell, who was contracted to supply the film's monster. Blaisdell liked the script, and in meetings with Nicholson, Arkoff, Alex Gordon, and director Edward L. Cahn, he took the opportunity to discuss not only the visual appearance of the creature, but potential problems as well. Blaisdell's main concern was the script's description of the monster as an amphibious being. If this meant he would have to creep around in the surf in full monster regalia, some method of photographic "cheating" was going to have to be employed, because foam rubber monster costumes were not designed to be submerged underwater. The year before, while filming Roger Corman's *Day the*

World Ended, Blaisdell had almost passed out inside his rubber monster hide when the film crew soaked his Mutant costume with a mixture of "rainfall" and special effects "fog." He was not keen to repeat the experience. Finally it was decided that rather than having the monster emerge from beneath breaking waves at California's Paradise Cove (where most of the location shooting was to take place), Blaisdell could just get his monstrous feet wet, walking through water that was merely an inch or two deep. For a similar sequence that came earlier in the story, a simple superimposition of the monster and the churning ocean waters would suffice.

When that was settled, everyone wanted to get in their two cents' worth about the look of the creature. The script dictated action that dared Blaisdell to craft something unusually lifelike, that could stand up to some fairly strenuous wear and tear. Heretofore AIP's monsters had been either partially immobile (*It Conquered the World*), perched high above activity on the ground (*The Beast with a Million Eyes*), or were required to do not much more than carry off the leading lady (*Day the World Ended*). This time the title monster was going to be doing much more.

Blaisdell began preliminary sketches of the creature, keeping in mind that it needed to be as feminine in appearance as possible. At the same time, any suggestion of femininity could not sacrifice the creature's inherent fierceness. All told, over a hundred drawings of the costume were made before a final design was decided on that incorporated many elements that had come out of the "Meeting of the Minds." Alex Gordon and Jim Nicholson, in particular, were excited about the film, and had plenty of suggestions for

Chester Morris (with Marla English) is outstanding as Dr. Lombardi.

Paul: "Give her a face like a cat," "give her an enormous tail," "make her swim out of the ocean," "make her a prehistoric, reptilian kind of creature." Blaisdell, who felt that there was too much input coming from too many individuals at the same time, put his foot down. "Look, it's going to have a little bit of what each of you wants, but you're going to have to leave it up to me and my imagination," he demanded. "If you do that, it's going to be the best one I've ever done." He wasn't kidding.

Alex Gordon recognized the potential of the production and was determined to enlist a cast of veterans that would do the story justice. He was especially keen to sign Peter Lorre for the role of Dr. Lombardi and he wanted Edward Arnold for the role of entrepreneur Timothy Chappel, because he thought the two actors worked so well together in their 1935 classic, *Crime and Punishment*. In fact the Jaffe Agency, Lorre's representatives, committed him to *The She-Creature* shortly after Gordon approached them. However, once Lorre got an opportunity to read the script he dismissed it as so much tripe and fired his agent for getting him involved in the first place! Gordon then tried to interest John Carradine in the role, but Carradine was on a high, having momentarily escaped the chains and manacles of horrordom by landing a prestigious role in *The Ten Commandments*. He told Gordon he was swearing off horror movies for good. (Of course, inside of a year he'd be hamming it up once more in turkeys like *The Black Sleep* and *The Unearthly*.)

As it turned out, Gordon was having difficulty getting Edward Arnold involved, too, so he turned to Eddie Cahn for help. Cahn and Arnold had worked together in the 1944 MGM film, *Main Street After Dark*. Sure enough, Cahn had no problem getting Arnold to sign on for a flat fee of $3,000.

But Edward Arnold then had the audacity to die, and Gordon freaked. *The She-Creature* was booked for studio time in two days, and it was impossible to do any

Director Eddie Cahn strongly objected to the monster's abdominal "teeth." Blaisdell corrected Cahn, noting that they were the monster's "lunch hooks."

rescheduling. In a flurry of phone calls, Gordon managed to locate Chester Morris in New York and asked if he would be interested in taking over the Edward Arnold role. Morris agreed to fly out to Los Angeles to spend a week shooting the picture, but by the time he arrived Gordon had decided to "bump up" the available actors a notch, leaving a gap lower in the roll call that would have to be filled by whoever was available. Now Morris would be playing evil Dr. Lombardi rather than shifty Timothy Chappel. Tom Conway, who was flying in from England to play the police detective, then found out he had been bumped into the Chappel role. This left the role of the detective unresolved. Gordon managed to do some fast talking to get Ron Randell to take the part without his even having seen the script. The twists and turns of the casting fiasco undoubtedly compromised the film, but at least Gordon was assured of getting a few decent performances out of Morris, Conway, and Randell. Gordon was particularly pleased with himself for getting commitments from a handful of his old-time favorites, including El Brendel, Luana Walters, and Jack Mulhall, all featured in secondary roles.

The casting dust had only just settled when another minor glitch turned up the day Paul Blaisdell arrived at the AIP offices to show off his new monster suit. Nicholson loved the creature (he was a Blaisdell fan anyway), but director Eddie Cahn strongly objected to the monster's abdominal "teeth." Blaisdell corrected Cahn, noting that they

The creature attacks Johnny (Paul Dubov). Note Dubov's hand, poised to grip the side of the tilting bedframe for safety.

were the monster's "lunch hooks." Actually the opening allowed Blaisdell to get some much-needed ventilation through the costume, but he had built it in such a way that by exercising his stomach muscles the hooks could be made to squeeze inward. The effect was weird, and when one stopped to think about it, it was downright grotesque because this was how Blaisdell thought the She-Creature should kill its victims: with someone in her clutches, the lunch hooks would rip them wide open. Of course, *that* would have to be left to the viewer's imagination, but a couple of close-ups of the clenching lunch hooks followed by a long shot of the monster grabbing its victim in a bear hug and a nicely timed scream from the victim would be enough to test viewers' sensibilities. But Cahn vetoed the idea instantly. "Paul, we can't use that, it's *too* horrible," Blaisdell recalled the director complaining. Instead, it was decided the monster would kill its victims with a simple claw-swipe. It was neat and clean: no fuss, no muss. (Never mind that audiences would be left wondering just what the heck the lunch-hooks were supposed to be. As a youngster I thought the lunch-hooks were merely decorative, like the creature's nonfunctional shoulder fins. A friend of mine who was a remarkable guesser, it turns out, felt that it must be "an extra mouth." Another friend lied about seeing a "complete" version of the film in theaters and claimed the monster actually used the hooks to trap *fish* while swimming underwater!)

    The She-Creature turned out to be a success despite Eddie Cahn's indifference to the material. Much of the credit must go to Rusoff, whose script combined new elements with old in such fashion that the result was refreshingly original. The monster scenes were minimal (par for the course for the 1950s, when most filmmakers kept their titular terrors well offscreen until the climax), and monsters in dark corners were nothing new, certainly; but Rusoff's method of unleashing the darkness of another world and another time through the mental power of a sociopathic hypnotist struck a chord with fantasy fans anxious for something a little more novel and daring than radioactive giants, mutant insects, and invaders from outer space.

The story, along with the visualization of the unique title monster, remains the film's strong suit. After a haunting opening theme by composer Ronald Stein there is an ominous voice-over by Dr. Carlo Lombardi (a phonetic anagram of another Alex Gordon favorite, Carole Lombard; I wonder if this was intentional?). Dapper in top hat, cane, and black cloak, and strangely, almost surreally out of place, Lombardi stands on a lonesome stretch of beach during a summer night, studying a wispy, ethereal shape gliding over the moonlit sea. The creamy-white form is too indistinct to identify, and in a moment it is gone entirely, vanished into the breaking waves, to return to another time, another place....

Lombardi (beautifully played by a perpetually sneering Chester Morris) is a hypnotist of extraordinary talent. Stuck in a nickel-and-dime amusement park sideshow, Lombardi harbors a strange and terrifying secret: He alone among men can call forth from the depths of time and space the primordial life form of a person living today. For years he has kept a carnival-follower named Andrea (Marla English) under his Svengali-like spell for just this purpose. By predicting a series of gruesome murders and using Andrea's prehistoric alter-ego as the mechanism to fulfill his prophecies, Lombardi figures to gain international recognition.

Entrepreneur Timothy Chappel (Tom Conway) latches on to Lombardi as a business investment, building him up until he becomes a national figure. But the mystic's predictions remain prophetic: The beachside murders continue. Chappel eventually becomes convinced of the reality of Lombardi's power and tries to cut their bond, but Lombardi calls up the She-Creature and sends it out to murder Chappel as well as a nosy police lieutenant (Ron Randell). With the creature at his command, Lombardi figures to dispose of one more person in his way, but Andrea's alter-ego manages to turn the tables on her psychic jailer....

The film shoot went smoothly. Eddie Cahn's years of film experience helped accelerate production, and the crew was able to get through an astonishing number of setups—as many as 40 in a single day. Cahn, being the demonstrative sort, enjoyed showing off how fast he could work. Paul Blaisdell recalled, "We would hardly be finished with one scene when Eddie would jump up from his chair and point to another spot on the ground and say, 'there.' That was where he wanted the camera to go next. So the crew would scurry over and begin setting up for the next shot."

Although there are only two major and a few minor monster scenes in *The She-Creature*, Blaisdell was on call for five of the film's seven shooting days. One of the earliest shots filmed was for the opening of the picture, when the monster's ghostly form swims through the ocean as Lombardi watches from the beach. All that was required for the shot was a simple superimposition, so Blaisdell was photographed in the studio lying face-down on a black-draped mattress, mimicking the motions of a swimmer. The image was later married to a long-shot of the ocean, but the two viewpoints were

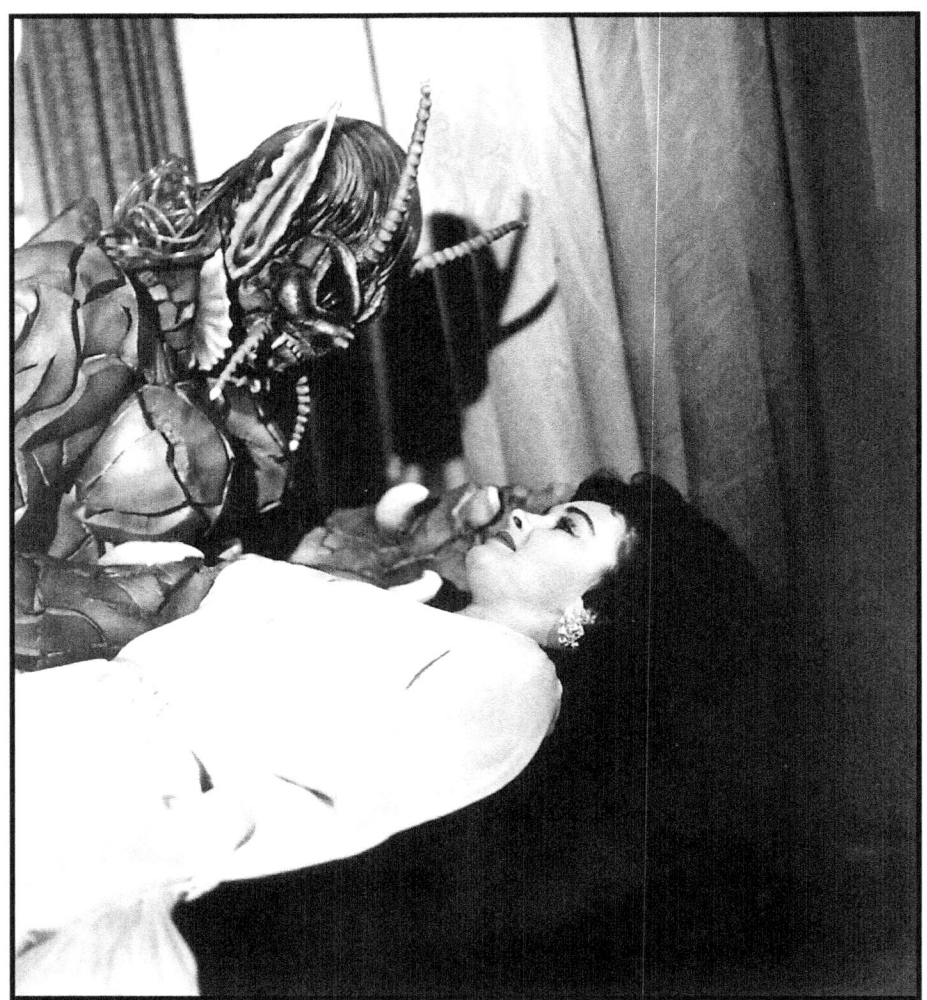

Marla English was more than adequate as the raven-haired *femme fatale* whose alter-ego was portrayed by Blaisdell.

improperly lined up, with the result that the creature seemed to be drifting *above* the water rather than swimming *in* it.

Another superimposition was utilized for the scene in which the creature materializes in the seawater beneath a pier. In this instance Blaisdell crouched down against a black studio floor covering while the camera was rigged overhead. On the director's cue Blaisdell stood up and flailed his arms. The shot was superimposed over footage of bubbling seawater created with an underwater agitator.

In the creature's first major appearance it smashes through an apartment door. The crew prepared a specially scored door made of balsa wood that would break apart easily. The only problem was, it was so delicately fitted together the whole thing would come tumbling down at the drop of a hat. To protect the breakaway prop it was reinforced with plywood from the opposite side.

When it was time for Blaisdell to knock hell out of the door, no one remembered to remove the reinforcements. Cahn had two cameras running so the action could be caught from both front and rear angles. When Blaisdell smashed at the door his rubber-coated costume just bounced off. In fact, Blaisdell hit the door with such force he was knocked backward and fell on his own creature's tail. There was so much foam in the tail it almost bounced Paul back up.

Finally someone remembered to take down the reinforcements and the cameras were cranked up again. This time Blaisdell easily smashed through the door, but tripped over a piece of splintered wood and fell forward. But because the door had splintered so nicely, Cahn decided just to trim off the end of the sequence and save the rest.

The climactic appearance of the monster was filmed on location at Paradise Cove near Los Angeles. "Get out in the water, Paul," Cahn instructed Blaisdell. "*Way* out."

Blaisdell tiptoed into the surf and turned around.

"Farther!" Cahn yelled.

Blaisdell backed up a few paces.

"No, no! Get really far out! Get out up to your *waist!*"

By the time Blaisdell had reached the designated spot he had become a mere blur in the camera lens. Everything was set up as a wide-angle shot, but Blaisdell didn't know that, and besides, he had other things to worry about: His costume was acting like a giant sponge, soaking up so much cold seawater he could hardly move.

When Cahn called "Action!" Blaisdell pushed forward, but the outgoing surf pushed him right back. Cahn called out, "Move faster, Paul, move faster!"

"*Sure*, Eddie, I'll be right with you," Blaisdell shot back sarcastically.

As it turned out, Blaisdell suffered through the oceanic acrobatics all for naught. The image of the monster lumbering out of the ocean had been shot from so far away, nobody could tell what it was, and most of the footage ended up on the cutting-room floor.

The She-Creature came and went without much fanfare during the summer of 1956, and Blaisdell hung the costume out to dry. Little did he dream that he would end up inside that unforgettable "72-pound suit of armor" not once but *twice* more for two different films, and loan the headpiece to AIP for yet a third production. Not only that, but clips of the lumbering monster were incorporated into Roger Corman's 1958 picture, *Teenage Caveman*, so the costume was actually on display in a total of five different movies.

Obviously this modest AIP production can't boast the kind of quality that makes genre offerings like *Forbidden Planet* and *Curse of the Demon* such gems of the genre, but *The She-Creature* possesses enough pizzazz to give fifties fans a fair size bang for their buck. Project the film side by side with other low-budget shockers of the time and it's evident that more thought (if not care) went into the construction of this film.

Unlike some other titles of the era that purported to generate chills and thrills, *The She-Creature* is actually a pretty spooky picture. Frederick West's sharp black-and-white photography (which unfortunately is printed too dark in television copies) occasionally conjures a *noir* mood, but West was also good at capturing the elusive, murky grays that seem to settle in so many northeastern coastal towns, and that turns up here as part of the ongoing amusement pier lifestyle. There is a slight problem with some day-for-night photography, which naturally never looks like anything photographed at night, but it's not so obtrusive as to sabotage the film entirely. On the other hand, some of the amusement pier footage has an appropriately rain-fogged look, and most of the shots of the She-Creature itself are staged with foreboding shadows and sharp-edged blacks and grays. (There is an especially nice extreme close-up of the monster's face which shows off some of the detail of Paul Blaisdell's handiwork.)

The music score by Ronald Stein is beautifully eerie and other-worldly, just right for this particular story. Following the opening theme behind the film credits, Stein's music fades as a foghorn bellows from somewhere in the immense blackness that hovers above the night ocean. This eerily imaginative opening sets a tone that the rest of the picture sometimes succeeds in emulating. When Chester Morris as Dr. Lombardi recites in sepulchral tones, "She is here, and with her coming the world will never be as it was," there is a finality in his voice that conjures bleak images of quiet desolation, a future slate wiped clear of modern culture. Just what is it that this man knows that could possibly be so far-reaching that the world will be forever changed? Lombardi's braggadocio hints at an overblown evaluation of self-worth, but at the same time it's a warning we would be foolhardy to ignore.

Though it's never so openly stated, Lombardi's plan is nothing so much as a megalomaniacal twist on the careers of monsters like Mussolini and Hitler. But unless this madman intends to use threats to get what he wants, it will take a long time indeed to make the world over as he sees fit. Of course, Lombardi is not stupid; he must realize that it would be virtually impossible to make over the Earth with a single She-Creature at his command, no matter how powerful his prehistoric pet may be. According to the other characters, the monster is "huge and indestructible," "tall like a building," and has "arms like a piledriver." None of this is true; such remarks are exaggerations or outright lies, but the characters in the film are apparently caught up in Lombardi's mind-twisting rhetoric.

Lombardi is proud of his role as the creature's puppeteer. He announces to Lt. James (Ron Randell), "I am the force that gives her life." Playing a game of cat-and-mouse with the detective, Lombardi sees this battle of wills as a cerebral volley, nothing more. To him, it is a game to be played for the diversion it affords. As the police eventually come to realize, it's impossible to threaten someone who won't take them seriously, which effectively makes Lombardi an even more formidable adversary. Toward the end of the picture Lt. James admits, "[Lombardi's] a murderer, yet I can't touch him!" In fact, Lombardi is never brought to justice by authoritarians; it takes a twist on the *Frankenstein* legend to do him in properly. Whether intentional or not, this prolongs AIP's penchant for minimizing the effectiveness of adult morals and societal laws, which continued apace in subsequent pictures like *I Was a Teenage Werewolf* and *Invasion of the Saucer Men*.

Chester Morris is outstanding as Lombardi. In other hands the role could have degenerated into a one-dimensional cardboard cutout, but Morris seems to be having fun. Thankfully he never breaks out the ham or charges forward with his tongue jammed in his cheek. It's difficult to imagine how Peter Lorre would have played the character. By 1956 Lorre had lost much of the sinister bravado that had made him such a chilling persona in the hands of directors like Fritz Lang and Alfred Hitchcock. His rather silly turns in AIP's *Tales of Terror* and *A Comedy of Terrors* were not far off, so

Tom Conway, who played The Falcon for years after his brother, George Sanders, abandoned the role, appears as the weasely Timothy Chappel.

it's probably for the best that he trashed his copy of *The She-Creature* script without a second thought.

Tom Conway, who played The Falcon for years after his brother, George Sanders, abandoned the role, is quite good as the weasely Timothy Chappel. He was generally at his best in those classic portrayals of not-quite-above-board characters in the Val Lewton pictures of the previous decade (Dr. Judd in Jacques Tourneur's *Cat People* and Mark Robson's *The Seventh Victim*). Chappel was another sleazy character, but Conway had lost some of his gentlemanly charm since the Lewton days (probably due to his heavy drinking), so Chappel was sleazier than usual. Conway would probably have made a decent Lt. James (the part he was originally supposed to play), but I suspect he was more suited to the Chappel role anyway.

The Lt. James character was picked up by Ron Randell as a favor to Alex Gordon. Since Randell had to be in Australia only a week after signing on to *The She-Creature*, he really had to cram to pull off this characterization. Randell, however, is a little bit like Jack Nicholson: He generally plays himself, usually talking out the side of his mouth with an expression of mild bemusement. Randell's performances in other genre work (*Most Dangerous Man Alive*, "The Duplicate Man" on TV's *The Outer Limits*) are very similar.

Marla English, who was crowned "Miss Science Fiction of 1951" at a San Diego sci-fi convention when she was just 15, made a few pictures for AIP and retired from the limelight. Paul Blaisdell said Marla preferred the quiet and solitude of a domesticated

The She-Creature's attributes are its originality, an innovative script, and Paul Blaisdell's imaginative monster. Note the strands of "hair" which unraveled during filming.

home life; she was simply not interested in becoming a "star." Blaisdell said Marla worked exceptionally hard rehearsing her lines for *The She-Creature* and was continually concerned that she just wasn't getting the hang of it. Truly, she was more than adequate as the raven-haired *femme fatale* whose alter-ego was portrayed by Blaisdell. More believable here than as the bad girl from the wrong side of the tracks in the 1957 follow-up *Voodoo Woman*, her character's background remains tantalizingly obscure. There are a couple of questionable remarks from other characters that suggest Andrea may have been more worldly than most people suspected. "I knew [Andrea] long before you did, doc," Boardwalk Johnny reminds Lombardi. "I knew her when she was a carnival follower." Lombardi objects, "I've asked you to forget that," as if trying to erase a painful memory. Is Andrea a reformed "carnival groupie?" If not, what is it about Johnny's remark that Lombardi finds troublesome? Whatever it was, Lombardi found it objectionable enough to conjure up the She-Creature and make Johnny sorry he ever opened his mouth in the first place.

As Andrea's love interest, Lance Fuller leaves a lot to be desired. (He played opposite Marla in *Voodoo Woman*, too, and was almost as bad.) Fuller seemed to have difficulty keeping his eyes in their sockets; he continually looks as if he's rehearsing for some kind of showdown with Peter Lorre. (Alex Gordon must've forgotten to tell him Lorre wasn't coming.) Funny facial expressions aside, Fuller at least could memorize lines; he just couldn't recite them with conviction. His best scenes were those he shared with actors who happened to have more dialogue than him. Fuller was fine as a white-smocked, pipe-smoking lab boy, checking statistics charts while chatting with Ron Randell; admittedly, not a very memorable moment—but prop him up next to Tom Conway or Marla English, give him a page or so of dialogue, and he stiffened right up. I get the feeling he was camera-shy, and may have felt uncomfortable whenever he knew the camera would be pointing its cyclopean eye his way. Too bad he was on camera so long. At least he got killed off halfway through *Voodoo Woman*.

Several other members of the cast are worth spotlighting. Freida Inescort, who played Mrs. Chappel, was a Scottish-born actress who had started in films in 1921. Mostly she had appeared in standard melodramas and film noir roles, often as society gals with something to hide. She's merely decorative here; her roles in her two other genre credits, *The Alligator People* (1959) and *The Return of the Vampire* (1943), were more significant. She made *The She-Creature* as a favor to Alex Gordon. Inescort died in 1976, a victim of multiple sclerosis.

El (short for Elmer) Brendel was basically a comic performer who appeared in second-string roles in a variety of films from 1926 on. He often spoke with a broken Scandinavian accent—as he does here—although he was actually born in Philadelphia. Brendel died in 1964. *The She-Creature* was one of his last films after appearing in genre entries such as *Just Imagine* (1930), *The Spider* (1931), and *House of Fear* (1939).

As it stands, blemishes and all, *The She-Creature* is a remarkably effective little film. If nothing else, it is deserving of critical accolades for offering a storyline that eschews standard fifties bugaboos like atomic radiation and cosmic rays for something more original. Among the general public hypnotism was a mysterious and ill-understood "force" in 1956, and most lay people thought of it as a "mystical" implement employed by a favored few, probably for unimaginably nefarious purposes. (Of course, pictures like this one, and *Horrors of the Black Museum* and *The Hypnotic Eye,* certainly didn't help educate anybody.) Perhaps it wasn't too great a stretch of the imagination to think that someone as ornery and misanthropic as Carlo Lombardi might use this strange power to conjure from the unplumbed blackness of time and space something cold and slimy to do his grisly bidding.

The theory of age-regression had become part of popular culture by the time *The She-Creature* was released. Combining it with other exotic subjects like hypnotism and touching on religious beliefs about reincarnation made for some contemporary and relatively effective storytelling. Assigning Lou Rusoff's script to director Edward L. Cahn was chancy, but he probably didn't damage the film any more than Roger Corman or Bernard Kowalski would have. Cahn's work on *The She-Creature* doesn't appear particularly rushed, though there is a paucity of inventive photographic angles and tracking shots. Most of the footage is composed of medium- and long-shots, with relatively few close-ups, though here and there are some rather surprising compositions. For example, when Andrea first meets Erickson, Cahn has Marla English pause directly in front of the lens for a dramatic close-up, with Lance Fuller staring at her

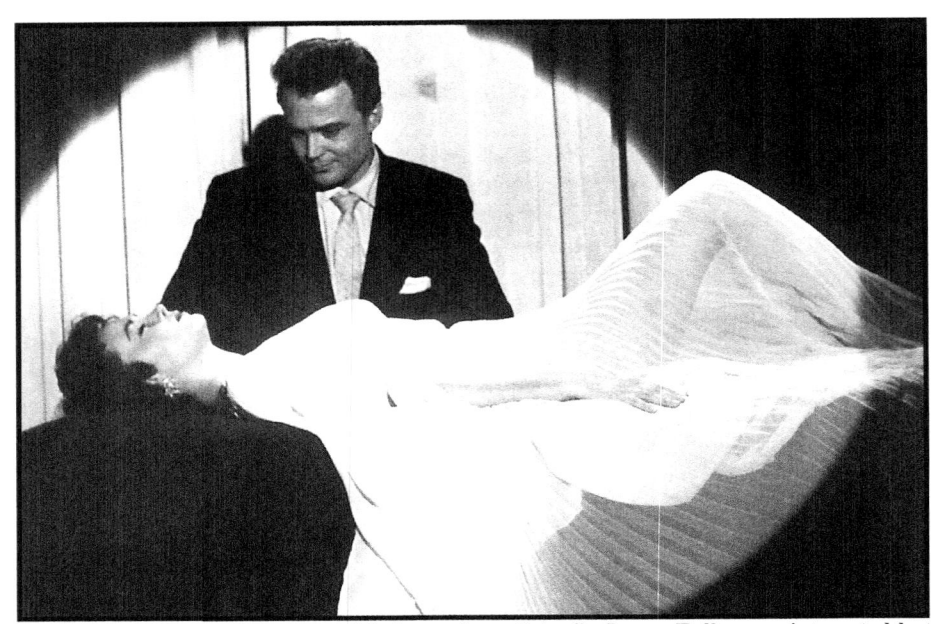

Marla English was not interested in becoming a "star." Lance Fuller was interested but lacked dramatic talent.

from the background, while a menacing shot of Chester Morris' eyes is superimposed over them. After a beat of silence Andrea mutters, "I can't go with you!" and runs off, a befuddled Erickson staring uncomprehendingly after her. It's the kind of setup one does not normally expect to see in an AIP film, especially one directed by "Fast Eddie."

Several other sequences deserve mention. In the final third of the picture, as Andrea and Erickson stroll along the beach, Lombardi (somewhat incongruously still decked out in his stage apparel, cape, and top hat; doesn't this guy have a change of clothes?) apparently hypnotizes the dog, King, commanding, "Kill him." The mutt floors Erickson, but Andrea's presence spooks the beast, and it scurries away, whining. A quick shot of Marla English advancing on the dog is effectively framed, her jet black hair billowing backward moodily. Her dark eyes are downcast as an eerie, sepulchral whisper escapes her lips: "Get away... get away...." Here again, a scene which could have been routinely executed is bolstered by effective placement of the actors within the frame.

The origin of the She-Creature (she dwells in the ocean and comes from the primal sludge at the dawn of time) is Rusoff's nod to Darwinism. Paul Blaisdell used the amphibious nature of the beast as a jumping-off point for his design of the creature costume, but not much is ever made of the creature's ability to live and/or breathe underwater.

Rusoff incorporated a few other esoteric touches into his script, which unfortunately did not translate well to the finished film. For example, much is made of the monster's footprints, which always double back on themselves, indicating that the creature follows her own prints back to the ocean to return to the point of origin after each materialization. Lt. James remarks to Erickson, "Whenever there are footprints coming out of the ocean, they always go back—in exactly the same spot." The idea is repeated again during the film's climax, when the detective (Frank Jenks) tells a patrolman, "[Lt. James] said to put a circle around all those prints, and whatever killed him will be back, and we'll set fire to it." In fact, the police do exactly this, but to no good effect. Dr. Erickson, who arrives on the beach only moments after Lombardi has been killed and the She-Creature is returning to the sea, points at the trail of footprints and instructs the cops to blast away. But they can't see anything. (And neither can we. The monster has dematerialized itself, and is in its "ectoplasm" form.) Does Erickson actually see something in the ring of fire? Or is he only guessing? ("Fire where I'm pointing at!" he shouts. "Hurry up!" Sure sounds like he can see something. A moment later one of the cops asks him, "You still see something?" Erickson softly replies, "No. I was mistaken.") And what has the ring of fire to do with all this, anyway? Is the She-Creature supposed to be afraid of fire? And why does Erickson want to kill the creature when it has just been proved that this is Andrea's own ancient life form? If he managed to destroy it, wouldn't her present-day live body perish as well? And if that happened, *then* where would we be? Not in the 1950s, certainly; that kind of downbeat ending didn't come into vogue until years later.

The most important question of all, however, is this: Is *The She-Creature* a great film? Of course not. But, it is better than most run-of-the-mill monster movies produced by AIP and others in the 1950s and sixties. Its attributes are its originality, its innovative script, and its incredible Paul Blaisdell monster. On the downside, the film suffers from a couple of lackluster performances, mediocre lighting, and pedestrian direction. Still, there's one thing nobody can deny: *The She-Creature* is a fun picture, full of innocent, childlike wonder. And it does enough things right that even some adults can appreciate it.

Son of Guilty Pleasures

THE STRANGE DOOR
by Nathalie Yafet

The Strange Door starts with a smokily evocative scene (which *Corridors of Blood* would use later to better effect) as Sire Alan de Maletroit joins some of his henchmen at The Red Lion tavern to find an unsuitable husband for his niece, Blanche. They point out their prize candidate (whom they have been watching for several days), young Denis de Beaulieu, who is drinking and wenching. One of the thugs picks a fight with Denis, fakes his death, a hue and cry instantly ensues, and our hero runs away. He winds up at de Maletroit's castle and is warmly welcomed by the Sire who wants posthumous vengeance on Blanche's mother for marrying his brother instead of him. This widowed brother, Edmond, is locked up in the dungeon, feigning madness with only the faithful Voltan to serve him.

Blanche and Denis do marry and, instead of loathing each other, fall in love. Denis meets up with an old family friend, Count Grassin, who promises to help the couple escape. The Sire's henchmen murder the Count, rout the escape, shoot Voltan, and return Blanche and Denis to de Maletroit's chambers. An increasingly unhinged de Maletroit then locks the two young people in with his brother and sets the gears going which will eventually cause the walls to come together à la *The Raven*. A wounded Voltan kills the Sire and manages to get the key to the imprisoned trio nanoseconds before the walls close in. Cut to Edmond, more well-groomed than he's been in years, who tells the young man that he is free to leave if he wishes. The redeemed-by-love Denis (of course) chooses to stay.

This film is not in my top five or even my top 25 Karloff films. Then why is it a guilty pleasure? It's entertaining, has some great lines, if you take the trouble to listen to the dialogue, and allows my hero to be a hero. *The Strange Door* should have been terrific. After all, it has Charles Laughton, Boris Karloff, Alan Napier, henchmen with acting ability, and is based on a Robert Louis Stevenson story. Unfortunately, there are many missed opportunities here.

The director, Joseph Pevney, loses control over Charles Laughton before the film is half over and allows his star to overact and mug outrageously. This really is a shame because Laughton's opening scenes are nicely done. He tells Denis, "Your impertinence is very entertaining," and, "You'll find me a gracious host if you don't try my patience," (very effectively said in a slightly sotto voce semi-snarl). And later, when asked about the prospective bridegroom's reaction to the marriage, "The usual reaction of a rabbit in a trap; he fought a little, what else could he do? What would you do under the circumstances? It would quite spoil the game if there were not a struggle in it," spoken while lolling backward on a desk with a beautifully subtle hint of something distinctly nasty behind his eyeballs. There's another fine moment much later on, after the wedding reception when he sees a supposedly besotted Denis, leans over him in a confidential, mockingly affectionate manner, and says, "Get to your feet, you drunken sot (draws out the sibilant "s" sound), arouse yourself. It's time you joined your bride" (extends the long "i" sound in bride). Laughton makes this line very uncomfortable for the audience as we are left free to imagine the implications. He also tends to separate his scenes into mini-vignettes where we have to guess who he's imitating now. For example,

The Strange Door should have been terrific. After all, it has Charles Laughton (right) and Boris Karloff (left).

after Blanche and Denis' failed escape, leaning on the mantel, de Maletroit greets them with, "So the honeymooners return, reluctantly, I gather. You ran away, why? Why, why, why do you want to desert me so soon?" The craft here is admirable, especially the multiple why's, but is more suited to Oscar Wilde than *The Strange Door*. And his reactions to the curtained portrait of Blanche's mother (which he looks at whenever he wants to make himself feel even worse) make him a failed Clifton Webb (in *Laura*) wanna-be. It's my guess that this actor's actor was impossible to reign in and the poor director never had a chance. In fact, the entire movie has the feel of being directed by someone who threw up his hands in despair/disgust, sat back and told his actors, "all right, go to it!"

Romantic leads in horror films are seldom endearing, often annoying, and occasionally unbearable. Surprisingly enough, this duo (although I would not go so far as to call them endearing) do grow on you after a while. Their initial scenes when Blanche appears in Denis' room after dark to warn him of his danger and later when they are formally introduced by de Maletroit are executed with verve. Sally Forrest is particularly good and manages to somewhat belie her doll-like blonde prettiness. (No small feat for a romantic female lead in a fifties programmer!) She makes one noticeable gaffe when she mispronounces Grassin immediately after Denis pronounces it correctly! Richard Stapley makes a good-enough hero for this type of film, at his best when he's mocking or sarcastic, rather than when he's attempting to be heroic or romantic. He also has a distinct tendency to mince down the stairs. The screenwriter must take the blame for the ludicrous speed with which the heretofore unrepentant wastrel, Denis, falls in love with the pure woman, Blanche.

Michael Pate as Talon and William Cottrell as Corbeau both contribute finely etched character portraits within the painfully obvious strictures of the confused mess of a screenplay. Contrasted with Morgan Farley's eternally grinning Rinville, they are even more impressive.

Talon is mocking and watchful in all his scenes with de Maletroit and amusingly amoral in his scene with Denis. When the young hero shows no gratitude for Talon's offerings of fresh clothing, food, and drink, he tells him, "...if you want to keep blood in your veins, you'd better change your tune." The clipped enunciation of "change your tune" is exactly right and is a good contrast with the rest of the sentence. And when Denis asks what they call him, Talon replies, "Anything from pig to dog through the whole animal kingdom." This line has the same flavor of amused detachment, but the actor's subtle subtext reveals his anger and hurt which is further developed in a mutton eating scene where he is the only one not partaking. (de Maletroit does toss him a chop, but only after he himself has taken a bite out of it!) Denis also foolishly asks Talon to help him escape, at first vaguely appealing to his sense of justice and then hinting at some kind of payoff. The response is, "I know nothing about justice; bribery's different. What have you to offer?" Michael Pate's business-like manner here gives us a distinct picture of a less-than-faithful servant.

Corbeau, although also in league with de Maletroit, is an atypical villain. He asks his master, who is bemoaning the lack of loyalty in his henchmen, "Tell me, could you tolerate an honest man in this house?" His straightforward line reading creates the perfect setup for the Sire's answer, "That's right, Corbeau, in my secluded dominion, villainy binds men together." In fact, throughout the film, William Cottrell seems to be one of those actors who help fellow actors along rather than just staking out their own moments. He saves a later scene when Laughton spouts off the unbelievable line, "I'm in the mood for relaxation, let's visit the dungeon" by his moving response, "Forgive me, I'd rather not. It depresses me. When I think of what he was and what he's become now," revealing a fine person spoiled by circumstance. And yet, he is fully capable of being a conventional villain also, as he proves in his scene with Denis and Blanche as they attempt to escape with Count Grassin's help. The young couple discover they've gone nowhere when Corbeau mockingly offers his hand to help them out of the carriage. Denis turns on Grassin angrily, saying, "And you call yourself a friend!" Corbeau almost spits out his reply, "You'll have to speak louder, Denis, much louder." A little later when de Maletroit swings Edmond's cell key, gleefully preparing to take Blanche and Denis to the dungeon, Corbeau mimics the action by rotating the barrel of his revolver. Touché! We have yet to see the best. The evil Sire has just set the mechanism in motion that causes the walls of Edmond's cell to come together and has locked Blanche and Denis in with his brother. He joins Corbeau on the parapet overlooking the moat and says, "It will not be long." Corbeau answers with a controlled flood of pent-up feeling, "I wonder if you really hate her so much... Love and hate are often confused; they are not dissimilar and she is like her mother." Cottrell's masterful line reading is rudely interrupted by an excessive, inappropriate emotional outburst

Once again, Boris Karloff transcends hackneyed role and material to present us with yet another endearing persona.

from Charles Laughton as he shouts, "You go too far, Corbeau," and buries his head in his hands. However, the mood is quickly reestablished as Corbeau continues with, "Well now we can speak truthfully. My life has always been empty. I was born without purpose and I'll die that way, but I envied you because you knew the passion of both love and hate and that's what made you my superior... I'm only telling you this lest you regret what you're doing." Laughton once again breaks the tension when he says, "...I know no pangs of conscience. My way is clear." The delivery is fairly restrained, but his body language is absurd—flouncing toward the wall and folding his arms across his chest. The other actor rallies with a nicely leveled, "I was wrong. You'd carry your hatred to the grave. I am still your servant." Not one to leave well enough alone (or to be outdone), Charles Laughton puts his final stamp on the scene with an inane smile. This relationship, explored earlier in the film and more skillfully, would have been a real boon.

Alan Napier, always an asset although criminally wasted in this small part, sparkles with his repartee at the wedding reception. Teasingly, he tells Denis that he once knew some de Beaulieus, calling them, "...rather an impetuous lot," and mentions that the son was disinherited. His obnoxious snuff taking, right before he asks Denis if he is related to those particular de Beaulieus, is hilarious. He is also completely believable later when we discover that he has been putting on an act to throw de Maletroit off the scent. His role could have been expanded or he would have made an intriguing Edmond.

The director, Joseph Pevney, loses control over Charles Laughton before the film is half over and allows his star to overact and mug outrageously.

(Paul Cavanagh's portrayal is decent but lacks originality. He never engages our sympathy.) Why was this actor never given roles worthy of his considerable (underrated) abilities?

And then, there's Voltan. Once again, Boris Karloff transcends hackneyed role and material to present us with yet another endearing persona. But, make no mistake, this Voltan is no cuddly pushover. Murder is one of his many jobs and he does it well and often. In one of his responses to the Sire, "Voltan knows a way, a very good way," he flashes his amazing eyebrows menacingly and curls his lip with a decidedly mean twinkle. But this guy definitely has a soft side as his touching loyalty to the unfortunate Edmond shows. When Edmond tells him that he must find the courage to do a special job for him, Voltan repeats, "Courage? I'm too afraid of him," with a half-voiced, almost childlike sound that nearly breaks our hearts as he looks behind him to see if anyone is listening. In spite of his fear, the faithful servant promises his master that he will do away with Denis before he can marry Blanche. Creating a Lewton-like ambiance, Voltan sneaks along the dimly lit hallway leading to Denis' room, hugging the walls as he does so, measures the strength of his fist, knocks out the night watchman (Talon), and helps himself to the key to Denis' room. He raises his knife, ready to use it on the intended bridegroom, when Blanche enters. Voltan hastily hides the knife and doesn't really lie when he says, "I came to warn him; he's in danger." Denis then ungallantly utters the film's most infamous line, "Who is this nightmare?" Blanche graciously chides, "You mustn't say that. He's my friend, Voltan." Her friend, Voltan responds to this comment

Boris Karloff's expressive body language and facial expressions more than compensate for his limited lines as we see his silent-film training put to good use.

with a smile that would melt ice in Alaska. Blanche then asks Voltan to help Denis escape. Boris' expression here is priceless, almost as if his subtext were, "Oh great, where's the script?" The crafty servant decides to carry out Edmond's request, rather than Blanche's, as he leads Denis into the dungeon ostensibly to show him the way out but really just waiting for a good opportunity to do him in. Denis makes a sound that alerts the guards and he and Voltan polish them both off after a brief skirmish. One of the dead guards is the man that Denis supposedly shot in the opening tavern scene. The young man decides to stay and help Blanche. Voltan decides at this point to let him live. Boris Karloff's expressive body language and facial expressions more than

Romantic leads in horror films are seldom endearing. Surprisingly enough, this duo (Sally Forrest and Richard Stapley) do grow on you after a while.

compensate for his limited lines as we see his silent-film training put to good use. (The dialogue that follows the murder of the two dungeon guards [and general utility men] is a keeper. de Maletroit: "Two of my men were slain last night." Denis: "Oh, and were they right again?" de Maletroit: "What do you mean by that?" Denis: "Your men are so hardy. Like cats, they have nine lives.")

Surprise, surprise—Voltan is the real hero of *The Strange Door*. He appears in the graveyard, miraculously, just as one of de Maletroit's men is threatening Blanche and strangles him. Corbeau takes instant action and shoots him. Staggering, he collapses on a headstone (in a quaint homage to *Bride of Frankenstein*). Still persevering, Voltan crawls/falls slowly across the graveyard, swims the moat, drags himself up the castle wall, and sneaks up on Corbeau who shoots him again. He strangles Corbeau and tosses him in the moat. de Maletroit returns the favor, by sneaking up on Voltan and stabbing him in the back. Voltan pays him back in spades and throws him from the parapet down into the moat, after helping himself to the key which will open Edmond's cell. Mortally wounded, he agonizingly nearly falls down the stairs to the dungeon, appears at the door, and gleefully announces that he has the key. Almost dead, he collapses, inches along face downward on the dank floor, and moves slowly toward the cell. At this point the trio inside the cell are all understandably nervous and keep urging him on. His last breath shoves the key toward Denis' outstretched hand. It's an incredible rescue scene and Boris' skill, pluck, and heart make it shine.

Denis (Richard Stapley) decides to stay and help Blanche. Voltan decides at this point to let him live.

Background music is recycled from *The Wolf Man*, *House of Frankenstein*, *The Ghost of Frankenstein*, and other films we know and love. Oddly enough, rather than being irritating, it gives us a very cozy, down-home feeling. For example, as our hapless hero, on foot, flees pursuing horsemen, he is accompanied by some familiar strains from luckless Larry Talbot's prowling scenes. But the real prize is the scene where Denis admits to Blanche what a waste his life was before he met her and she also confesses her love. We hear our beloved Ilonka's Gypsy love music—wildly inappropriate for 18th-century France, but stirring anyway! Less successful is a selection from *Abbott and Costello Meet Frankenstein* during Blanche and Denis' aborted escape. The slightly goofy music gives the scene an odd cartoonish flavor.

Sets, probably also recycled, are correct for the period with an especially impressive dungeon, moat, and mill wheel. Costumes are variable. Silk vests, frilly shirts, tri-cornered hats, and frock coats for the upper-class men look polished and Voltan's rude blouse, smock, large leather belt, and boots are just right. However, the ladies attending the wedding reception look confusing in omni-period gowns. Blanche's dresses are much better, especially her exquisite velvet hooded cape, but would a sheltered, shy 18th-century miss really flash obviously bare legs as she runs down the stairs?

Camerawork is pedestrian. No artsy touches here. In fact, numerous tight close-ups on Edmond and Voltan on either side of the bars make me want to scream, "Enough, already, I get the point. We are all prisoners!"

The screenwriter, Jerry Sackheim, is the real villain in this film. He shows no concern for clarity or continuity, lazily preferring to let us drift along snatching explanations, character development, or plot wherever we can. In fact, the Sire de Maletroit's excellent line, "Life hangs by a slender thread," could easily refer to the plot as well. Either he was overworked and underpaid or merely inept, but that's no excuse for the flagrant waste of so much talent and story potential.

Contemporary critics were honest, but not enthusiastic. *Variety* stated, "The horror theme has been revived... in *The Strange Door*. There are good elements of suspense and characterization in this celluloid adaptation of a Robert Louis Stevenson story. As the master fiend, Laughton is well cast. He revels in his lines and leers at his victims almost to the point of overplaying. Karloff competently portrays the loyal servant..." The Brunas brothers and Tom Weaver in their useful but highly opinionated tome, *Universal Horrors*, couple it with *The Black Castle* and deem them, "atmospheric but dramatically anemic period horrors." Scott Allen Nollen, in his biography of Boris Karloff, calls the screenplay "a hackneyed mess" and goes on to say that, "Nothing really happens in *The Strange Door* and most viewers are probably pleased when the final scene drags to a halt." I concur with the "hackneyed mess" part, but the film is certainly watchable enough for all its inadequacies. And I strongly disagree with Nollen's assertion that, "Karloff also affects a tongue-in-cheek style, reflecting the insipidity of the screenplay." He admits that Voltan becomes "truly heroic by the film's end," but cancels this out with, "...the character still appears somewhat flat because of the inadequate writing and direction, and Karloff's apparent lack of interest." Any other actor in this role would have been barely noticed but, far from being uninterested, Boris Karloff makes it matter and makes us care.

Defects aside, *The Strange Door* must have been fun to see at a Saturday double feature with plenty of popcorn and jujubes (or Jordan almonds). Much more fun than watching endless high-speed car chases, ridiculously overpaid bad actors, computer-generated dinosaurs, and other multi-million dollar special effects. The kids today don't know what they missed.

LIKE NOTHING YOU HAVE EVER SEEN!
THE NERVE SHATTERING STORY OF A MAN WHO COMMITTED EVERY OUTRAGE IN THE BOOK ...LIVING A HOLOCAUST OF HORROR BEYOND IMAGINATION!
A SHOCK ENDING THAT YOU DARE NOT REVEAL!
AMERICAN-INTERNATIONAL presents
ROBERT LOUIS STEVENSON'S STUDY IN TERRIFYING EVIL!
HOUSE OF FRIGHT
PAUL MASSIE · DAWN ADDAMS · CHRISTOPHER LEE IN COLOR AND MEGASCOPE
MICHAEL CARRERAS · TERENCE FISHER · A HAMMER FILM PRODUCTION

THE TWO FACES OF DR. JEKYLL
by Tom Johnson

London, 1874. While handicapped children play in his garden, Dr. Henry Jekyll (Paul Massie) discusses his crumbling life with his friend and colleague, Litauer (David Kossoff). A bland, bearded, middle-aged man, Jekyll is the subject of ridicule due to his theory about man's duality. "In every human personality," he tells Litauer, "two forces struggle for supremacy. Man as he is comprises two beings—one whom I call man as he could be... man in his perfection. This 'inner man' is beyond good and evil."

"And the other man?" asks Litauer.

"He, too, is beyond good and evil—man as he would be—man free of the restraints society imposes upon us... subject to his own will."

"A very dangerous man, my friend. This 'higher man' you speak of is the weaker element in us. Our lust and our violence feed the weaker man."

Not only is Jekyll rejected in his professional life, but also at home; his wife Kitty (Dawn Addams) is having an affair with his "friend" Paul Allen (Christopher Lee), a worthless drunkard and gambler. Feeling ignored by her science-obsessed husband, Kitty feels free to enjoy whatever pleasures Paul can provide. In addition to stealing his friend's wife, Paul also constantly "borrows" money from Jekyll who, in effect, is financing his own cuckoldry. "I don't deserve you, Kitty," says Paul. "But I deserve you," she answers. "I deserve nothing better than you."

When Kitty announces that she's going to a dinner party, Jekyll begs her to stay home. When she refuses, Jekyll is overcome by her rejection and—against his better judgment—injects himself with a fluid that will, he thinks, separate his inner beings...

Edward Hyde (Massie), young, clean-shaven, and diabolically handsome, arrives at The Sphinx—a notorious London fleshpot—where he gains the attention of two prostitutes. While dancing with Jenny (Joy Webster), Hyde is stunned... then amused... to see Kitty and Paul. He roughly dismisses his "dancing partner" and introduces "himself" to his wife and his friend. When challenged by the club bouncer (Oliver Reed), Hyde nearly beats the man to death and stops only when Jekyll's personality reemerges. When, as Jekyll, he goes to Kitty for comfort, he is coldly rejected and heartbroken by her account of the "dinner party."

Hyde allies himself with Paul, whom he sees as a passport to further depravity. Back at The Sphinx, Hyde is fascinated by Maria (Norma Marla), who performs an obscene dance with a python. Hyde forces himself upon Maria in her dressing room, and she, accustomed to being courted, becomes infatuated with him. "You do not buy, you do not beg. Is there anywhere... a man who simply takes?"

After "making love" with Maria, Hyde decides to visit Kitty... with similar activities in mind. Although not feeling bound to either Paul or Jekyll, Kitty is repulsed by Hyde and asks him to leave. Furious at his rejection by Kitty in both his personalities, Jekyll/Hyde is lost...

When Paul finds himself deeper in debt than ever, he decides to approach Jekyll again. "These are debts of honor," he tells Kitty. "I can't go bad on them." "Honor? What a typical 'gentleman' you are, Paul. All your honor staked on a card so you have

When Paul (Christopher Lee, right) finds himself deeper in debt than ever, he decides to approach Jekyll (Paul Massie).

none left for any man or woman." He is unexpectedly bailed out by Hyde, who stakes Paul to £5,000 in exchange for a guided tour into perversion. Jekyll now has little desire to exist as himself. "For do I want to return," he writes in his journal, "to a life of frustrated isolation and loveless misery?" With Paul in the lead, Hyde experiences London's lower depths... whorehouses, a brutal bare-knuckle prizefight, opium dens. But these diversions fail to satisfy him; what Hyde really wants is Kitty.

Paul has done the £5,000 in a week. "I suppose I could try Kitty again," he tells Hyde. "Try me instead, my friend... and I'll try Kitty. I'm telling you to obtain your mistress for me. I'm asking for the temporary loan of a proven adulteress." Even Paul is appalled by this suggestion. "How very amusing," Hyde hisses. "Paul Allen, breaker of every law in the moral code—is shocked into morality."

Hyde again approaches Kitty, this time with Paul Allen "in his pocket," and attempts to buy sex with her with Paul's bad gambling debts. "Why not sell," he smirks, "what you have so often given away?"

Rejected once again, Hyde assaults a beggar and heads for yet another house of ill repute. He buys a young girl but is beaten and robbed by her pimp. Hyde awakens, in a mud puddle, as Jekyll.

Kitty and Paul have decided to go away and start a new life... as does Jekyll, who is now horrified by Hyde's grip on him. When he sees Kitty and Paul together in the house, he unconsciously pushes a handicapped child (Janine Faye) to the ground. But... Hyde's hold is too strong—he can now return without the drug.

Perhaps Massie's fine performance was dismissed by many who wrongly assumed he couldn't possibly be as good as his more famous predecessors.

Hyde delivers a "message from Jekyll"—Kitty and Paul are to meet Henry at The Sphinx for a "final reckoning." The couple foolishly think Jekyll plans to buy his way out of the marriage, but Hyde has other plans. He kills Paul with Maria's snake, then rapes Kitty. After she discovers Paul's body, she falls to her death through a skylight.

Maria waits for Hyde in Kitty's room. "Whose room is this?" she asks. "Mine—at last," Hyde replies. After another bout in bed, the insatiable Hyde brushes off Maria's talk of love. As she drifts into sleep he caresses her throat but—overcome by Jekyll—loses control and strangles her, concluding the murder as Henry.

He is confronted by Hyde's image in the laboratory mirror where the monster explains that all of his vile actions were done to force Jekyll to free him. "Unfortunately, my dear Jekyll, I can't destroy you without destroying myself." Hyde reasons that Jekyll will be sought for the murders and will be forced to take refuge as Hyde.

When the police inspector (Francis DeWolff) investigates Kitty's and Paul's murders, he is led to Jekyll's house where he finds Maria's corpse. Meanwhile, Hyde has killed a laborer and sets the laboratory ablaze, making it look as though Jekyll has kidnapped him, then committed suicide. Hyde stumbles from the inferno into the Inspector's arms.

The coroner (Percy Cartwright) pronounces Jekyll a suicide and Hyde a lucky near-victim. As he walks from the hearing with Litauer, Hyde is overcome by Jekyll who emerges as a spent, aged wreck. "I have destroyed him," Jekyll stammers. "And yourself," says Litauer.

of the Horror Film

Not only is Jekyll rejected in his professional life, but also at home; his wife Kitty (Dawn Addams) is having an affair with his "friend" Paul Allen.

> "It is difficult to understand why a script should deliberately
> and consistently part company with the original."
> —*The London Times*, October 10, 1960

After 20 years of mostly forgettable productions, England's Hammer Films found the "big time" by remaking Hollywood's horror classics. *The Curse of Frankenstein* (1957), *Horror of Dracula* (1958), and *The Mummy* (1959) appalled most critics, but audiences were enthralled by Hammer's bold new style. But after a string of successful, if somewhat formulaic horrors, Hammer was looking for something a bit different...

Robert Louis Stevenson's *The Strange Case of Dr. Jekyll and Mr. Hyde* (1886) carries quite a bit of literary weight. Unlike one-shot successes Mary Shelley (*Frankenstein*) and Bram Stoker (*Dracula*), Stevenson's works could stock a library. His tale of a "split personality" with its psychological and moral implications attracted "serious" critics long before they began dissecting Frankenstein and Dracula movies for subtextual meanings.

Thomas R. Sullivan adapted Stevenson's tale for the stage in September 1888—just as Jack the Ripper was writing his own "script" in East London. When Richard Mansfield appeared in the "leads" at the Lyceum, he was so convincing as Hyde that he was briefly a Ripper suspect! As with most adaptations, the original concept was soon lost. Stevenson pictured Hyde as an unpleasant looking, vaguely deformed man of less than average height. Sullivan and Mansfield, courtesy of clever lighting and makeup effects, present Hyde as a snarling monster. Stevenson's story kept Jekyll's secret from the reader until the climax, while the play couldn't wait to show the transformation. The stage production also was more concerned than the novella with Jekyll's sexual frustration. When the story was later adapted for movies, the theatrical version became the model, as with *Dracula* (1931) and *Frankenstein* (1931).

Dr. Jekyll and Mr. Hyde was filmed as early as 1908, but the first "real" movie version starred John Barrymore in 1920. Barrymore's interpretation was as a dome-headed, skeletal-fingered nightmare, best remembered for transforming with a minimum of editing. Fredric March won an Oscar in Rouben Mamoulian's definitive 1931 version, playing Hyde as a bucktoothed Neanderthal, lusting after a prostitute when his wedding plans are put on hold. The 1941 remake had Spencer Tracy in a toned-down makeup and added a Freudian dream sequence for those who didn't quite get Jekyll's sexual frustration.

All three actors, unlike Bela Lugosi and Boris Karloff, were already stars before playing their monsters, giving *Dr. Jekyll and Mr. Hyde* a legitimacy which *Dracula* and *Frankenstein* lacked. Despite the characters' debasement in the fifties through a meeting with Abbott and Costello and the revelation of a son and daughter, Jekyll/Hyde remained a cut above your average monster.

> "A shred of Stevenson encrusted with snake charming,
> gambling, suicide, and rape."
> —*The London Sunday Times*, October 9, 1960

The Two Faces of Dr. Jekyll was Hammer's biggest gamble—and loser—during the late fifties when it seemed as if the company could do no wrong. Consider... The story, familiar even to children, was jettisoned, leaving behind little more than character names. Christopher Lee, England's leading monster, is in the movie but doesn't play the monster. In fact, there is no monster. Although the film contains little visual horror, many of its concepts are morally repellent even today, let alone in 1960. Incredibly, Hammer produced a comedy version of the Stevenson story, *The Ugly Duckling,* earlier that year. Surrounded by better Hammer Horrors, plus Roger Corman's *House of Usher* (1960) and Alfred Hitchcock's *Psycho* (1960), *Two Faces of Dr. Jekyll* was not even embraced by horror fans. And, following in the giant footsteps of Barrymore, March, and Tracy was... Paul Massie!

> "Paul Massie does what he can to save something from a wreck."
> —*The London Sunday Times*, October 9, 1960

The British film industry was going through some radical changes in the late fifties, with a new permissiveness which allowed not only Hammer's horrific fantasies but a realistic bluntness. New young stars, like Laurence Harvey in *Room at the Top* (1959), were emerging, and his amoral Joe Lampton character could have been Hyde's twin. Following the lead of the earlier films might have resulted in Harvey being cast as Jekyll/Hyde, but Hammer chose the less expensive Paul Massie, who was actually quite a catch. Born in Ontario, Canada, in 1933, Massie majored in English and planned to become a teacher, but was sidetracked by music, then the stage. He emigrated to England in 1952 and entered the Central School of Speech and Drama. After a stint in the Royal Artillery, Massie landed his first film role and scored in *Orders to Kill* (1958). His performance as a morally confused World War II assassin won him the British Film Academy's Most Promising Actor Award. Good parts in *Sapphire* (1958) and *Libel* (1959)—in which he played a dual role—placed Massie on the verge of stardom. "I fairly jumped at the opportunity to portray Jekyll and Hyde," he enthused. "The role is an actor's delight and runs the emotional gamut from top to bottom." Unfortunately, *The Two Faces of Dr. Jekyll* effectively ended his career, despite his getting mostly good reviews. Perhaps Massie's fine performance was dismissed by many who wrongly assumed he couldn't possibly be as good as his more famous predecessors.

> "Mr. Christopher Lee has quite a big part as someone
> who has no right to be on the screen at all."
> —*The London Times*, October 10, 1960

Since Jekyll/Hyde is the one classic monster associated with non-horror stars, it's not surprising that Christopher Lee was not offered the role. Lee's status at Hammer during this period was an uncertain one, as he was also passed over in *The Hound of the Baskervilles* (1959) for Peter Cushing in the Sherlock Holmes role, and by Anton Diffring as *The Man Who Could Cheat Death* (1959). However, Lee made the most of the supporting role he was offered, and turned in one of his best performances. Although Lee has been criticized for being "stiff," that is not the case here. He plays Allen as a worthless but charming cad, and is especially effective in several "drunk" scenes that are refreshing in their naturalness. When contrasted to his "stiff" performance in his thankless part in *The Man Who Could Cheat Death*, it's hard to believe that it's the same actor. Despite Massie's interesting performance, Lee easily walks off with the picture.

> "Paul Massie, as the two faced doctor, — loses or gains
> a beard and mustache with the prick of a needle."
> —*The Observer*, October 8, 1960

Initially, Paul Massie had been approached to play only Hyde, which was a break with a tradition dating back to Richard Mansfield. But... who would play Jekyll? Hammer was eventually unwilling to pay two actors; but, considering the foolish make-up device finally used to differentiate the parts, that may have been the way to go. This is what mainly gives *The Two Faces of Dr. Jekyll* its status as a "guilty pleasure"—the brilliance of having a handsome-but-evil Hyde was almost totally negated by the sloppiness of its execution.

Actually, the attractiveness of evil was not a new idea for Hammer, since its amoral Baron Frankenstein (Peter Cushing) and satanic Dracula (Christopher Lee) were clearly intended to be characters whose surface charm disguised their evil intentions. While this is not an especially "deep" concept, it was different and effective, but never more so than in *The Two Faces of Dr. Jekyll*.

After another bout in bed, the insatiable Hyde brushes off Maria's (Norma Marla) talk of love. As she drifts into sleep he caresses her throat but—overcome by Jekyll—loses control and strangles her, concluding the murder as Henry.

> "As it is, Hyde's evil propensities appear to be dwelt on only for the opportunities they offer for X Certificate scenes."
> —*The Daily Telegraph*, October 8, 1960

The Two Faces of Dr. Jekyll has rightly been attacked for both its departure from its source and for its excessive vulgarity, but Hammer went into production with its eyes open. "Our problem," said producer Michael Carreras (*The Kinematograph Weekly*, December 10, 1959), "was that *Dr. Jekyll and Mr. Hyde* has already been filmed four times—and very well filmed, too. Consequently, the public has its own preconceived idea of what to expect. Which is why we got Wolf Mankowitz to write the script. Not only was he a good prestige name, but he came up with a twist which virtually gives us a new story. We're not just making the fifth version of a well-worn screenplay. As it is, we have a sex film rather than a horror picture."

But... if Hammer was guilty of vulgarizing Stevenson's original (and it certainly was!), it was not the first to do so. The 1931 version pushed the limits of screen censorship just as far as Hammer did, and perhaps even farther. It's also unlikely that Stevenson would have recognized much of his impish creature under Fredric March's grotesque makeup. The Spencer Tracy remake was even more obsessed with sex, as Jekyll alternately lusts after the "virginal" Lana Turner and the "sluttish" Ingrid Bergman.

Hyde kills Paul with Maria's snake, then rapes Kitty.

The author is not suggesting that *The Two Faces of Dr. Jekyll* is in any way the equal of these two excellent films (it isn't!). But—if adherence to Stevenson and avoidance of sexual content are the issue, Hammer's version is not the only offender.

> "The twist here is legitimate enough—an ingenious though repellent variation..."
> —*The London Times*, October 10, 1960

Production on *The Two Faces of Dr. Jekyll* began at Bray Studios on November 23, 1959. Company head James Carreras began gloating almost immediately. "The subject, as everybody knows, has been filmed before," he said in *The Daily Cinema* (December 18). "But our script boys have come up with an astonishing new approach and treatment. This new concept is so brilliantly original and yet so simple that a lot of filmmakers will be kicking themselves silly that they never thought of the idea themselves."

The "script boys" were, in fact, Wolf Mankowitz, who, instead of Jimmy Sangster (Hammer's resident Gothic specialist), was chosen for the job. Mankowitz' selection over Sangster, like Paul Massie playing the lead rather than Peter Cushing or Christopher Lee, was another indication that Hammer was changing direction. Mankowitz had recently won an award for the "Best British Stage Musical" (*Make Me an Offer*) and a British Film Academy nomination for Val Guest's *Expresso Bongo*. For the upscale-thinking Michael Carreras, Wolf Mankowitz was just the clever "name" writer he was looking for... but he was, perhaps, a bit too clever.

"The culprit is Mr. Wolf Mankowitz."
—*The London Times*, October 10, 1960

Unfortunately for Mankowitz (and the picture), *The Two Faces of Dr. Jekyll* reads better than it plays. In addition to the absurd "beard business," the public—and the British censor—were not ready for the limits that Mankowitz wished to push. His conception of a walk on the wild side ranges from the mild (a bare-knuckle prize fight) to the mildly disturbing (Hyde smirking through an opium dream). But, the real problem here was sex. The plot is powered by Jekyll's rejection by his wife and his desire to both have sex with her and revenge himself against her and her lover. The picture hits a low note of depravity when Dr. Jekyll (as Hyde) tries to force Allen to procure the unfaithful Kitty like a common prostitute. Although Hyde is having all the sex he can handle with Maria, it fails to satisfy Jekyll's need to even the score. Hyde obliges by murdering Allen, raping Kitty, and causing her suicide. When this still isn't enough, Hyde strangles Maria in Kitty's bed, leaving Jekyll to clean up afterward.

This—and more—was all too much for John Trevelyan, the British censor, who ordered cuts which were sloppily done and painfully obvious. To "cover" these cuts, some misguided soul chose to use optical wipes that, if accompanied by "BIFF!" and "BAM!," would have been at home on the *Batman* TV series of the 1960s. Unfortunately, these devices only draw more attention to the fact that "something's missing." Also, Kitty's rape and Maria's strangulation are so abruptly edited that one can't really be sure what happened! Since these are important plot points, it seems that Mankowitz overestimated Trevelyan's "freedom from convention," a mistake of which Hyde is accused by Kitty.

Although it's unfair to judge a writer's original concept based on what the censor has cut out of it, all we have to go on is what we see on the screen. Despite Mankowitz' good intention to produce something new, his script ultimately failed because it couldn't be done as envisioned.

"You didn't have a single character worth tuppence...
They were a shoddy lot. "
—Terence Fisher, *Films and Filming*

Terence Fisher, since directing *The Curse of Frankenstein*, had done eight horror subjects back-to-back and thoroughly understood what Hammer Horror... and its audience... were all about. Unfortunately, *The Two Faces of Dr. Jekyll* was something a bit different; Michael Carreras was clearly aiming for a more adult, sophisticated audience than was attracted by a *Dracula* or *Frankenstein* picture. Still, Fisher was certainly no stranger to Mankowitz' concept of the attractiveness of evil, since *Horror of Dracula* is practically a dictionary definition. Although something clearly went wrong between the script and the final print, it's difficult to tell who was at fault—Mankowitz, Fisher, the censor, or Hammer. If Hammer was hoping for acceptance at a higher level, the company certainly didn't spend any more time or money on *The Two Faces of Dr. Jekyll* than on a more "lowbrow" movie like *The Mummy*. Some of the shortcuts taken—especially the lack of a "real" transformation scene—are really inexcusable. This was a fault shared with Hammer's *The Curse of the Werewolf* (1960), but Terence

The friendship between Jekyll and Allen is difficult to accept.

Fisher's staging of both almost validates Hammer's unwillingness to spend the extra pound. After injecting the drug (no foaming beakers), the bearded Dr. Jekyll collapses at a table, his head resting on his arms. Photographed from behind, he rises, adjusts his waistcoat, puts on his jacket, and emerges from the laboratory under a street lamp. As he hails a horsecab, the light falls on his handsome, clean-shaven face, split by a maniacal grin. The scene was dictated by Hammer's refusal to do the transformation "properly," and should not be effective. But... somehow it is, possibly because of the audience's surprise at seeing an unconventional handling of a famous movie cliché. Still, this is hardly the stuff of "great cinema."

Discussing "common sense" or "logic" in a horror movie is both senseless and illogical, but... a good horror film should have some sort of internal logic that makes sense within the picture's framework. Although we accept the absurd concept of Jekyll turning into Hyde... and, if we must, losing his beard... some of the smaller moments are harder to swallow. The most annoying of these is the friendship between Jekyll and Paul Allen. It's difficult to see what the reclusive doctor and reckless dandy could ever have in common—even as children! Their "relationship" is an obvious plot device and, while this minor point doesn't destroy the film (after all, it's only a horror movie), it does strike a discordant note. What works perfectly is the later alliance between Hyde and Allen, two kindred degenerates. However, Allen's conversion to righteousness is a bit abrupt and far from believable, despite Christopher Lee's best efforts. "The part of Paul was written for me," he explained in *The Films of Christopher Lee*. "A cad, a sponger, a swindler. The man who lives off women." He added in the pressbook, "I'm

Hyde sets the laboratory ablaze, making it look as though Jekyll has kidnapped him, then committed suicide. Hyde stumbles from the inferno into the Inspector's arms.

bad to the core. I even accept money from my mistress in the film. And a man can't sink much lower than that." Although Hyde would sink to even lower depths, at least he had an excuse.

Perhaps the movie's worst moment is a totally misjudged and poorly executed scene in which Jekyll stands before a mirror that reflects Hyde's image. While this idea may not sound bad, it soon becomes hilarious when the two have a conversation! The sad thing is that the dialogue is fascinating and well-written—and gives our only real glimpse into Hyde's mind. But, due to the inept staging, the scene falls flat. The scene ends with Jekyll, cowering against a wall, speaking in Hyde's voice... the effect is chilling. Why the whole scene wasn't filmed that way is anyone's guess, although the mirror scene was probably forced into the movie for the novelty value of having Jekyll and Hyde in the same shot.

Another forced idea that fails to convince is Allen's death at the "hands" of the python. Although it's barely possible, it seems unlikely that any snake could crush the gigantic Christopher Lee, let alone the relatively small one used in the picture. But, logic aside, Maria has the snake, so Hyde may as well use it! And, against all logic, the scene almost works due to the final shot of Allen's corpse—upside down—with the snake uncoiling from his chest.

It's difficult to judge the impact of the film's sex scenes on the audiences of 1960, but it must have been considerable. As Michael Carreras accurately pointed out, *The Two Faces of Dr. Jekyll* is more of a sex film than a horror film. The sexual activities, both seen and discussed, are extremely well-staged and acted. The most disturbing

Despite the negativity of the reviews, Paul Massie emerged relatively unscathed.

scene has Hyde in bed—Kitty's bed—with Maria after Kitty's rape and suicide. After "making love," Maria foolishly confesses to Hyde that she loves him—a concept he quickly dismisses. "I can't love," says Hyde. "I don't know what love is." Maria, more wisely than she knows, replies, "How sad for you... and maybe for me." As she drifts into sleep, Hyde is overcome by Jekyll and—which one?—strangles her. The scene ends with Jekyll terrified and sobbing.

Cursing on screen was still a rarity in 1960, despite Clark Gable's not giving a damn 21 years earlier. Mankowitz, quite rightly considering the depraved nature of the film, wrote some fairly explicit dialogue ("I told you to go to Hell and take the whore with you!") that was filmed and then dubbed over to appease either Columbia or the censors. This act of pettiness helps to make the picture more ridiculous than it deserved to be when, for example, Paul Allen—gambler, adulterer—utters, "Oh, the heck with it."

The final scene, although marred by some conventional moralizing by "the Coroner," was well written, acted, and directed, ending the movie on a high note. Again, Hammer's close-fisted attitude actually improved the film; instead of the expected rooftop-chase shootout-transformation scene, Hyde quietly metamorphoses (with, naturally, his back to the camera) into an aged, weeping Jekyll.

The Two Faces of Dr. Jekyll was released in the UK through Columbia, and was trade shown on August 20, 1960. The premiere was held at the London Pavilion on October

7, and the film went into general release on the ABC circuit on October 24. Unlike the movies' protagonist, reviewers were not split—almost all of them were appalled: *Time and Tide* (October 15) "It all adds up to an intolerable injustice to the original"; *The Spectator* (October 14) "As silly and nasty as Hammer and Terence Fisher have turned out between them, which is saying something"; *Films and Filming* (December) "This current freewheeling version... isn't noticeably interested in schizophrenia, but only in the plot's attendant sensational aspects of depravity and bestiality"; and *The New Chronicle* (October 7) "Variations are perfectly legitimate if they do not vulgarize the theme on which they are based. Its horrors are penny-dreadful; its psychology is too shallow to engage our pity."

Reviews following the film's American release on August 23, 1961, were equally disparaging: *Variety* (August 24) "There are some blatantly inserted spots of sadism"; *The New York Times* (August 24) "All of the emphasis in this color orgy is upon the depravities of the villainous Mr. Hyde"; and *The New York Herald Tribune* (August 24) "Dr. Jekyll's patented amorality serum is also an effective beard remover." Columbia was unwilling to release the picture in America, even with the cuts, and dumped it—after a year's delay—on American International, who initially retitled it *Jekyll's Inferno*. The movie was eventually paired with *Terror in the Haunted House* under a new title, *House of Fright*, with few references to the source novel.

Despite the negativity of the reviews, Paul Massie emerged relatively unscathed. "Mr. Massie does marvels to transcend this... with a tense, torn performance" (*The New Chronicle*); "Paul Massie manages to contrast the two facets sufficiently to make the transformation about believable" (*The Daily Cinema*, October 7); "Paul Massie's study in dualism is quite passable" (*Films and Filming*); and "Paul Massie keeps the thesping side together and... does a remarkably adept job..." (*Variety*).

In keeping with its subject of duality, *The Two Faces of Dr. Jekyll*, while abounding with ineptitudes, did manage to do several things quite well. The cast is excellent, including Oliver Reed in a small but showy role in his first Hammer film. Typically for Hammer, the sets, costumes, and photography are superior for such a low budget picture. And, for better or worse, the movie introduced a more "adult" approach to horror, even though the emphasis was more on sex than shudders. In a genre with far too few new ideas, and too few production companies willing to take a chance, give Hammer credit for at least trying something different. On the negative side, perhaps the worst thing

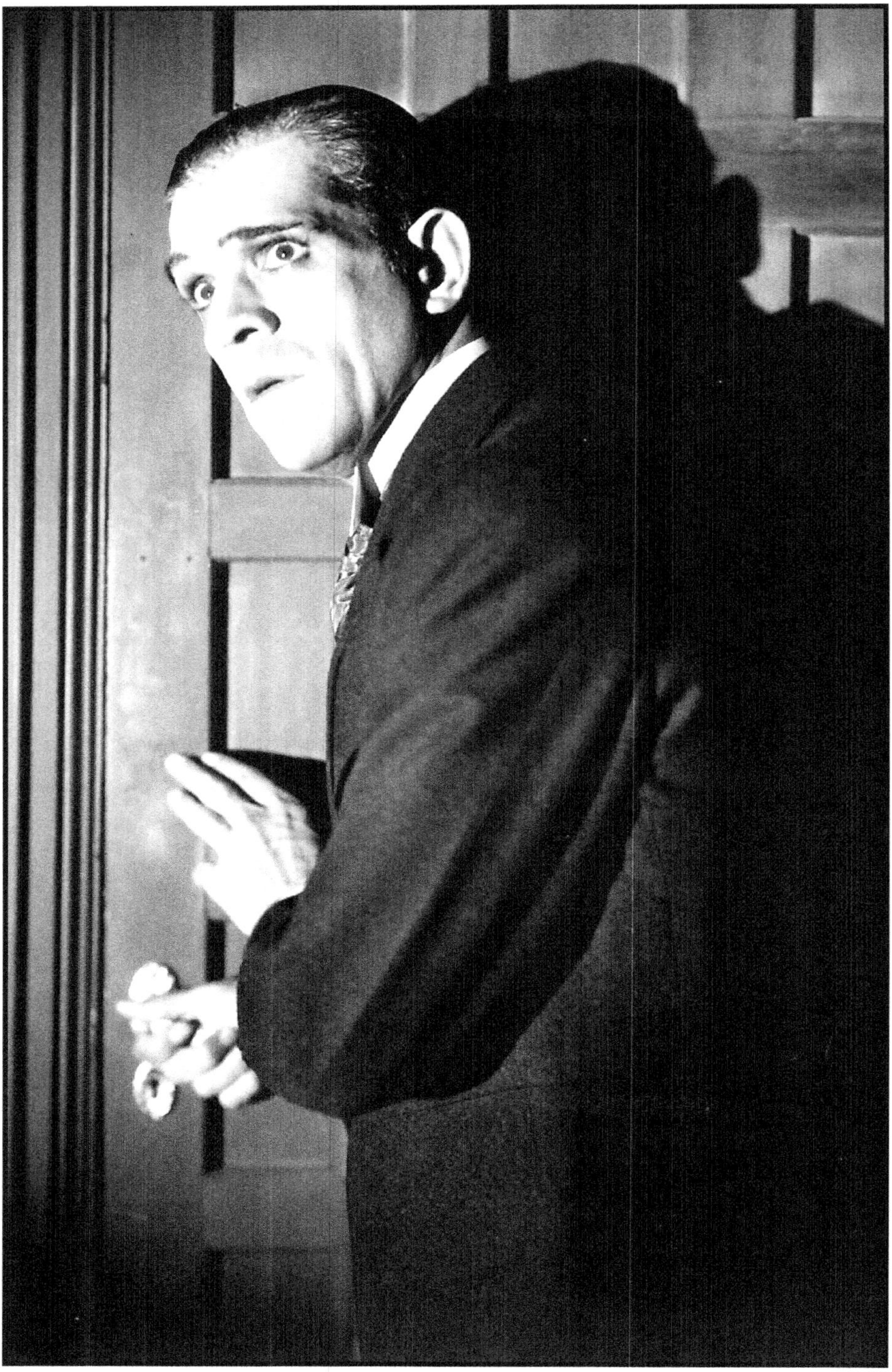

THE UNHOLY NIGHT
by John Soister

One shouldn't leap to the conclusion that guilty pleasures are always the result of either hopeless incompetence (Astor Pictures comes to mind) or miserliness (Monogram, perhaps?). At least a handful of the guiltiest have been ground out by studios noted for their polish and production values. *Sh! The Octopus*, a particular favorite of mine, was an atypical exercise on the lunatic fringe by the brothers Warner, who had made their mark with no-nonsense crime stories and Ruby Keeler musicals. The little picture offered a wry and ballsy variation on the haunted house/colorful mystery killer theme that had packed 'em in since nickelodeon days, but its release was exquisitely untimely (1937 was considered the gateway to the great genre wasteland) and few fans are familiar with it today.

Take *Mark of the Vampire*. Tod Browning's crotchety remake of his lost *London After Midnight* has a splendid performance by Bela Lugosi, scads of atmosphere, and certain scenes featuring Carroll Borland (a little of whom goes a long way) to recommend it. On the flip side, Lionel Barrymore's irritating Professor Zelen, Henry Wadsworth's limpid Fedor, and an absolutely preposterous dramatic framework allow one's mind to drift now and again from MGM's nightmare to thoughts of drinking heavily.

MGM was also responsible for *The Unholy Night*, an early (1929) sound effort featuring an array of the silent screen's big names, and an up-and-coming (and unbilled) Boris Karloff. Based on a rather far-fetched saga of intrigue and tontines (by Ben Hecht, of all people), the *Night* was a long one—at 92 minutes (10 reels), almost half the length of Browning's two vampire epics, mentioned above. Some of the acting herein is excessive (Lionel Barrymore directed; need I say more?), but we mustn't forget that the parameters established by silent film were still very much in evidence everywhere and that old habits were (and remain) hard to break.

As is/was the custom, the pendulum had swung from the tastes and techniques of the previous medium to those of the newer technology. The early talkies, for example, were wont to eschew background music (save for themes trumpeted under main and end titles and such), as if to distinguish themselves further from their silent forebears, for whom sound was continuous melody, flowing forth from orchestra or pipe organ. There's little music in *The Unholy Night*, but by the third time the aging swashbucklers break into their dispirited rendition of *Auld Lang Syne*, you're wishing there had been less. Nor are there many creative sound effects to pick up the slack: An array of screams, Sojin's caterwauling, and the bewildering accents affected by Karloff and Dorothy Sebastian are the only departures from the routine.

Still, the picture offers a wonderful "rich, silly ass" turn by Roland Young (in his first sound feature), one of Ernest Torrence's rare heaves at good guy-dom (he even ends up with Natalie Moorhead), some priceless hoke by Boris, and a decent enough little mystery which could yet have stood a good 20 minutes' pruning.

Like so many of its contemporaries, *The Unholy Night* begins with a prologue:

> The amazing revelations pictured here are compiled from one of the most sensational murder cases on police record. The rare psychosis

Major Mallory (John Miljan) glowers, Dr. Ballou and Lady Violet (Ernest Torrence and Natalie Moorhead) cower, and Sir James (Claude Fleming) stiffens his lip. Photofest

[sic] of the crime and the method of its exposure are stranger than fiction… because they are true!

Uh-huh.

A bobby on patrol declares that "This is the 12th day of the greatest fog London has ever known." A nearby radio elaborates: "Scotland Yard warns everyone not to venture in the streets unless absolutely necessary! Keep your doors locked and your windows bolted!" Such advice is well taken. Within moments of these announcements, a flower girl is abducted, an elderly gentleman is mugged by a lantern-toting bad Samaritan, and a stereotypical Chinaman—replete with skull cap and silk pajamas—is gunned down in cold blood.

This sets the stage for the attack on Lord Montague (Roland Young); his lordship is abruptly strangled from behind, and only the scream of a passerby saves his neck. Revived, he's taken to Scotland Yard, where—this being Britain—the lawmen offer him a brandy and soda as a matter of course. Montague ("Monty" to his friends) is rich, a bit of a lush, and one of only 14 survivors of the brave regiment nearly decimated at Gallipoli in 1915. Sir James Rumsey (Claude Fleming) breaks it to Monty that there are only *10* survivors now, as four have been throttled here and there throughout Lon-

Abdoul Mohammed Bey (Boris Karloff) only has eyes for Efra Cavender (Dorothy Sebastian), but the lady's got her sights set on revenge... and murder.

don that very day! With his lordship's help, Sir James and Inspector Lewis (Clarence Geldart) arrange for the remaining officers ("Tell them to wear their uniforms!") to assemble that night at the Montague mansion.

Later, at the manor house, the police inform Sir James that all of the officers' records are as clean as whistles, but that Lord Montague seems to be living a double life; under the name Spinker, he keeps a flat over in Kensington. An eerie wailing noise is suddenly heard, and Monty attributes it to the resident "Green Ghost," a family forebear who "died of some nasty disease, like spinach." The noise is traced finally to a darkened room, wherein the oversized head of an Oriental man floats above a table. The lights

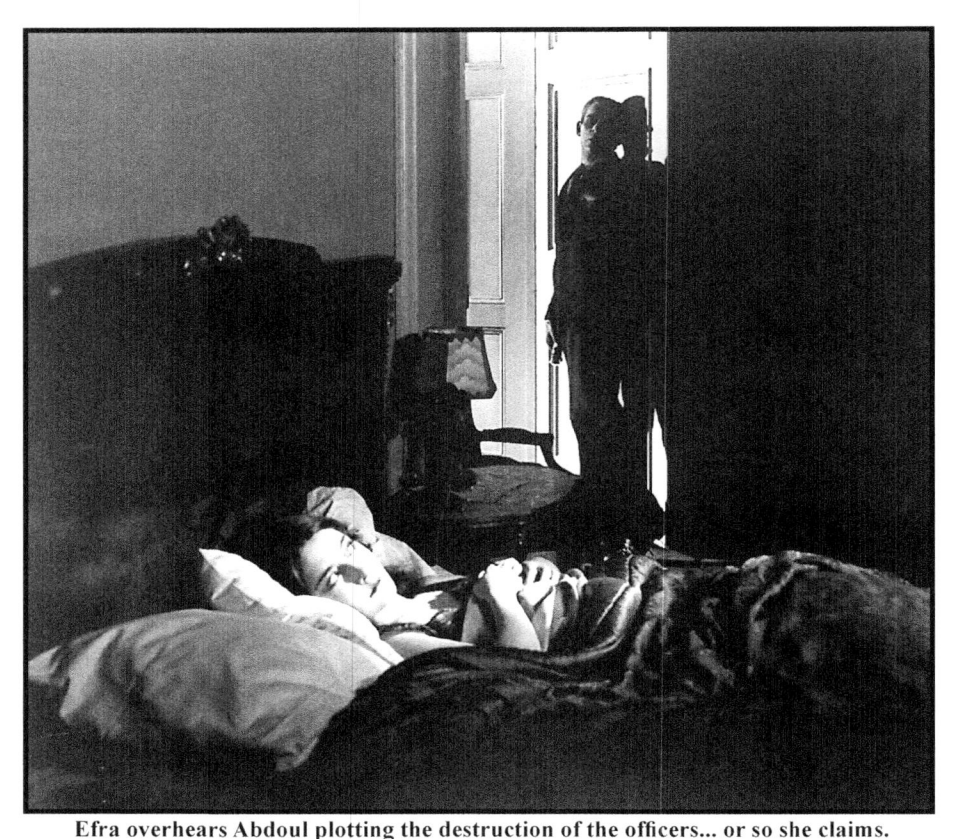

Efra overhears Abdoul plotting the destruction of the officers... or so she claims.

are turned on, a woman (Lady Vi, Monty's sister [Natalie Moorhead]) screams, and her beau, Doctor Ballou (Ernest Torrence), greets Sir James like the old friend he is. The chief inspector hails the medium (Sojin); "How are you, Li Hung? I didn't know you were out of jail.") Li Hung takes that as his cue to leave.

Sir James confers with Dr. Ballou about the matter at hand, but the arrival of some of the invited officers takes the audience's attention away from the discussion. Lieutenant Savor (John Roche), Major Endicott (Lionel Belmore), and Colonel Davidson (Richard Tucker)—the senior man—are the first to enter, and all speak of the still-absent Major Mallory (John Miljan). "Poor old Mallory," moans Endicott. "I saw him three weeks ago, with his shrapnel-scarred face. He looked as if he'd been shell-shocked only the day before."

Other officers join them, and the whole kit and caboodle breaks into a mouthful of *Auld Lang Syne*. In the next room, Lady Vi opines, "They're so happy; to think that they may be doomed like the others." Back in the drawing room, a man in civilian clothes is informed by the butler that "The gentlemen are in the kitchen, sir. Will you join them, Major Mallory?" The scarred officer shakes his head and warms his hands by the fire. From the kitchen, singing merrily (if not terribly well) all the way, comes the body of officers bearing a huge silver bowl brimming with a whiskey punch the men have concocted from a traditional recipe. Monty spots Mallory sitting on the sofa

216   Son of Guilty Pleasures

and he and the men surround their comrade, slapping him jovially on the back; he falls. "Great Heavens," Monty mutters. "Mallory, too!"

Dr. Ballou examines the fallen man and confirms his having been murdered. The soldiers are astounded; the police are annoyed. Things get worse when a veiled and shrieking woman cascades into the room and then collapses. The lady is Efra Cavender (Dorothy Sebastian), daughter of the late Marquis of Cavender, who had dishonored the regiment by switching sides and fighting against his own men after being captured at Gallipoli.

Before all can be digested, in walks Abdoul Mohammed Bey (Karloff), who announces that he has just arrived in England with the Lady Efra and with her late father's will. Pointing to the first, he proceeds to read the second:

> Having for many years nourishing a deep and undying hatred for the officers of my regiment who forced me to leave England unjustly and who subsequently at Gallipoli sentenced me to be shot, I leave, to be divided equally among them, the sum of one million pounds. I do this in the firm conviction that nothing so soon cause discord among friends and destroy character as the sudden inheritance of wealth which I leave them, with my curse and the hope for their utter ruin. Furthermore, I leave to my daughter, Efra, an equal amount—the residue of my estate—and name as her guardians the officers of the regiment. I do this in the sure knowledge that where money fails, nothing so quickly cause discord among men as a beautiful woman.

Harrumphing heroically, the officers swear that nothing on earth will cause them to renounce their friendship or dissolve their spirit of camaraderie. Sir James, however, proceeds to put a damper on things: "Well, gentlemen, I suppose you know what this will means. We now have a motive for the murders." Efra lets no grass grow under her veiled feet and relates (via flashback) how Abdoul—who had *abducted* and not "accompanied" her—had plotted the violent overthrow of what's left of the regiment with one (but she doesn't know which) of the officers!

It's then determined that as the officers had scattered throughout the house to obtain the ingredients for that high-voltage punch, no one has an airtight alibi for Mallory's murder. Tempers begin to flare. Endicott is asked why he had tried to escape by the window earlier. ("Was that a window? I thought it was a door. I was dizzy.") Lieutenant Savor finds it odd that Monty—by far the smallest of the officers—had managed to survive the sort of attack which had successfully done in some of his larger colleagues. Sir James drops his bomb about Spinker, but for naught; his lordship recounts how his alias has provided him with "a safe haven from marriage." In an effort to confound the deadly plot, Monty renounces his share of the claim to Cavender's fiendish testament and calls upon his fellow officers to do the same. To a man, his comrades—none of whom is as lucre-heavy as his lordship—refuse to follow suit. Despite this turn of events, the men conspire to hack their way through another chorus of *Auld Lang Syne*.

Lady Vi has Dr. Ballou give Efra a quick medical once-over—the poor dear has taken to bed—and the officers head upstairs to turn in. Both Major MacDougal (Richard Travers) and Monty hang about outside Efra's room, and the men nearly come to blows

For someone unfamiliar with the twists of *The Unholy Night*, the sudden appearance of the quirkily accented Boris Karloff is a hoot.

(before reconciling) over the mysterious and fascinating woman. "There's a devil in this house, Monty!" swears the major. Ballou takes all this in as he heads back downstairs to give Major Mallory another gander; reassuring himself that the fallen military man is still on the carpet, the doctor indulges in some sneaky business from the window with a person or persons unknown.

At the stroke of midnight (Big Ben appears to be situated just around the corner from the manse), the camera pans around the darkened drawing room, past the fireplace,

Lady Efra gets hers in a beautifully composed shot which doesn't appear in the film. Photofest

to the curtains of the alcove wherein Mallory lay. The curtains flutter, a pair of hands draws them apart, and the major himself walks out! Bearing a strangler's rope, Mallory makes for Colonel Davidson's room; a moment later, noises of a struggle are heard in the hallway.

Morning. Monty is aghast to discover the colonel's body, and the police converge on the room. Sir James and his men move to an adjoining, larger bedroom, where—as the camera pans along at floor level—*six* bodies are seen! And more bad news from below: "Milord," stammers out Monty's old batman, Frye (George Cooper)."He's gone! The dead man! He's walked away!"

A seance with Li Hung (Sojin) sets the tone early in the proceedings. Photofest

Nor is Frye joking. Mallory has flown the coop, leaving only a note, which is thankfully read aloud by Sir James:

> Pray for me. When you read this, I will be with my comrades whom I loved and killed. They suffered, but not as I have. Shell-shocked, cataleptic: drove me mad. This morning, something snapped in my brain. I know now what horrible things I have done. There is no other way out. You will find me at the gate, under the tree.—Arthur Mallory

This sort of thing, of course, makes Dr. Ballou look rather bad and when Mallory *is* found—stabbed through the heart—the physician blusters that the note had been a forgery, the body had been moved, and the stabbing had been done after death! Sir James turns up the heat; Monty is now the last of the regiment, and the million pounds his. However, if something happened to Montague, Lady Vi—whom Ballou fervently wishes to marry—would inherit the tainted fortune! Is there no end to suspicion and accusation?

Sir James: "Mallory had a hand in this, but he was not alone. We have still to find his secret."
Ballou: "I'm afraid he has taken his secret where the living will never trace it."
Sir James: "Then if the living fail us, we must call on the dead to help us."

Big Ben once again chimes at midnight. Li Hung is admitted to the manor house, whereupon he begins to ready his seance gear and to check on the dagger he has secreted up his sleeve.

With Monty, Efra, Vi, and Ballou on the divan, Sir James orders the seance to begin; the lights are extinguished. At the end of the table, the mystic pulls a veil from over his head and peers into the crystal, which now provides the only illumination in the room. (The shot of Sojin's angular face, lit from below, is quite potent.) Faintly, the strains of *Auld Lang Syne* drift through the air. In a long shot, the chairs which flank either side of the rectangular seance table are at once filled with transparent forms of the murdered officers of the regiment! Efra screams, and the lights are turned up instantly. "They were here!" the terrified woman shrieks.

Calm is restored, but the lights are no sooner dropped than the officers are back in formation, pointing accusing fingers at the divan. Efra rises and moves toward the table: "Go away! What have I done to you?!" She is further horrified to see the ghost of Mallory, standing off to the side. Reaching out, she puts her hand *through* the scarred specter. "Get back to your graves!" she screeches at them all. To Mallory: "As long as you live, you do as I tell you… You kill for me! You kill them all for me!"

In the confusion, covered by the darkness, someone grabs the knife from the mystic's hand. The figure stabs Efra and then runs into the hall; through the door, a man is seen to collapse onto the floor. Efra is pronounced dead, Inspector Lewis informs everyone that Mallory has stabbed himself outside the seance room, the officers of the regiment pile out from behind a huge ornamental screen, and Sir James turns to Monty: "Lord Montague, we owe you an explanation."

Abdoul Bey lopes into the room and explains—again, via flashback—how Efra was furious that her father had left half of her money to the regiment, and how, by using her knowledge of "the hypnotic secrets" on the weak-willed, smitten Mallory, she had sought to wreak a terrible revenge. Ballou reveals that his midnight examination of Mallory had shown him alive, but in a cataleptic state: "Before your very eyes, Mallory became an apparent victim, you were all held here under suspicion, and the ghost left free to strike you all down that very night." The doctor had signaled the *police* through the window, and they were awaiting Mallory's murderous attack in Colonel Davidson's room. The rest of the night was spent trying to snap Mallory out of it. "At dawn, he wrote the confession and then tried to do away with himself."

Dr. Ballou continues: "When we read Mallory's note in the library, [Efra] felt her plan had succeeded." It was Efra's scream in the seance room which had finally awakened the major. "In that desperate moment of realization, he grabbed Li Hung's dagger, stabbed the girl and himself, and put a tragic end to our seance." As for how Monty et al saw the "ghosts," Li Hung indicates a set up of lights and mirrors. The drama winding down, Monty is off for an assignation with a Miss Gabby LaVerne ("Frye? Lay out my Spinker suit, will you?"), and the regiment wraps it all up with a reprise of *Auld Lang Syne*.

There's so much fun to be had during *The Unholy Night* that it's best that the weaknesses be dispensed with first. More than anything else, that 92-minute length works against everybody's best interests. While the picture (for the most part) moves at an admirable pace, it occasionally grinds to a halt, as director Barrymore has his middle-aged veterans warble you-know-what yet again. Time is likewise wasted establishing bits and pieces of personality for each of the officers, while having them (save for the

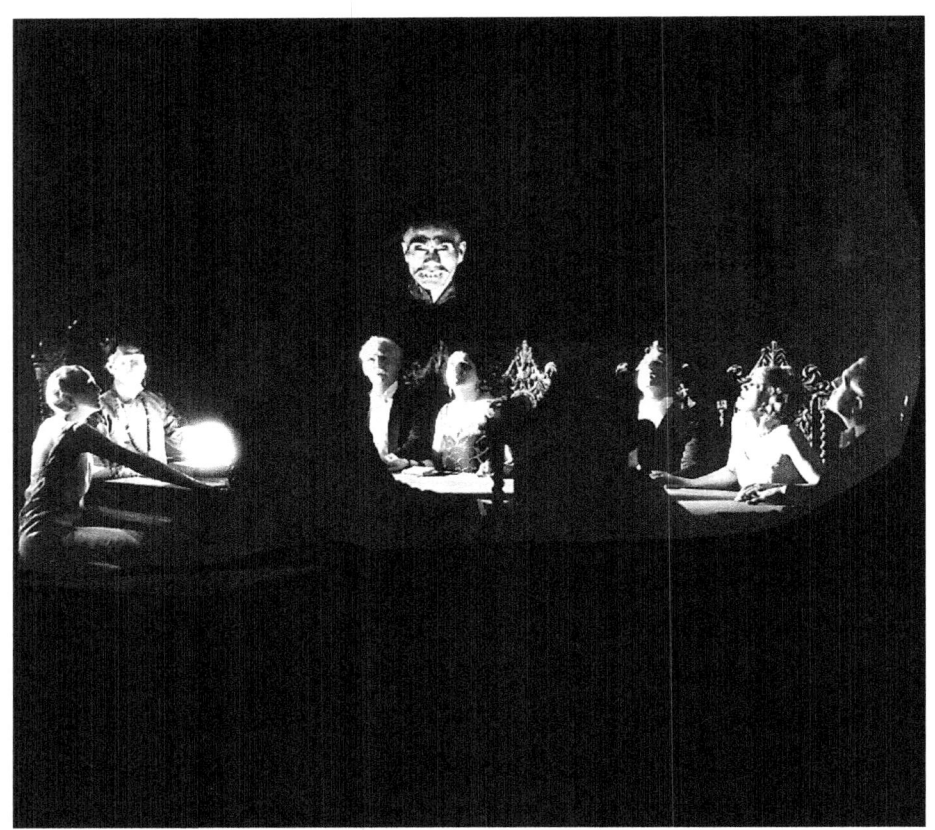

At the end of the table, the mystic pulls a veil from over his head and peers into the crystal, which now provides the only illumination in the room. Photofest

rotund Belmore) appear a company of brunette, mustachioed clones. Roland Young is amusing as all get-out, mouthing Ben Hecht's snappy rejoinders, but the problem lies in that Monty is the *only* witty so-and-so in the picture; virtually everyone else is a comparative stick in the mud. While this sort of thing allows the character of his lordship to shine brightly, it doesn't do a damn thing for the rest of the *dramatis personae*.

With the lady Efra approaching rigor mortis in Abdoul's arms, there's a million pounds stuck in limbo. Still, it's not clear whither goes the *other* million: the cash for which the officers of His Majesty's 4th Rutland had briefly soiled their collective honor. There's little point in renouncing all that loot now that the heavy's been dispatched, but the picture wraps without so much as a nod to the cause of so much murder and mayhem. Perplexing, ludicrous, and not slightly Barrymore-ish is the propensity everyone has to shoot glances sideways, to fume and glower, and to overreact to the extent that one fears for one's heart. Brother Lionel was regarded as "frequently sublime" by John Barrymore, but, as with many of the Great Profile's carefully crafted assessments, the half that's left unspoken is usually the more telling.

Having said all that, let the good times roll.

From the atmospheric credits (an enshrouded skeleton waves its arms under the scrolls, yet over a decent enough chiller-diller theme), through the fog-drenched London appurtenances, to the solidly British expanses of the Montague mansion, *Night* unfolds most enjoyably. Those look-alike Gallipoli survivors may have feet of clay in their well-shined riding boots, but, *Damn!* if you're not glad to discover they're all still kicking at the climax. Young is a standout, not only due to his receiving the lion's share of the script's wit, but because the affable actor—who wrought volumes in the scratch of his head or a tug at his ear—attracts one's eye almost instinctively. Most of his fellow officers wear faces which were familiar to moviegoers of the twenties, but which have dropped from memory with the passage of time. (Genre aficionados need not be prompted to exempt Lionel Belmore from statements such as this.) Contemporary audiences would have suspected something was not quite kosher when Major Mallory was apparently murdered early on; the major was played by John Miljan, who, at the time, was too big a name to waste in so profligate a fashion.

For someone unfamiliar with the twists of *The Unholy Night*, the sudden appearance of the quirkily accented Boris Karloff is a hoot. Although the Briton's Abdoul Mohammed Bey has a couple of substantial scenes and provides some key exposition, his name is conspicuously missing from the opening credits (MGM did *not* think that a good cast was worth repeating). Boris has to be heard to be believed, trying valiantly to sound as close to a lovesick lawyer named Abdoul as his stilted dialogue and lisp would allow. (*Variety* noted the Karloff presence in the credits list of its review, but wasted not a word on him in the review itself.) Dorothy Sebastian does *her* best at approximating Karloff's vocal bravado, but her accent comes and goes once her veil has disappeared.

Apart from this surprise, the appearance of the gap-toothed and emaciated Sojin is another cause for rejoicing. Forty years old when he made his American debut (in *The Thief of Baghdad*, 1924), the little Japanese gargoyle stayed in Hollywood until returning to Tokyo in 1930. With 40-odd features under his belt in a little over five full years, Sojin's popularity was widespread, and the actor was sorely missed by audiences in the States. Back at home, though, he graced many more films until his death in 1954.

Like Karloff, Sojin has two scenes in *The Unholy Night*. His floating noggin in the first of these is appropriately macabre, but this is merely a warm-up for the climax. Following Efra's coming loose at the seams and Mallory's sticking knives in her and in himself, the chung-sam'd mystic proudly points Monty to a wall-length mirror, and—in an absolutely incomprehensible rush of fractured syllables—"explains" how the regimental shades were made to appear at the seance. If this hysterically inept recitation weren't itself enough of a joy, a clarinet-toting(!) George Kuwa reinforces his colleague's testimony by his presence. The screen's first two Charlie Chans *had* appeared together in Paul Leni's *The Chinese Parrot*, which the director had crafted for Carl Laemmle in 1928; with *Parrot* a lost film, though, it is left for *The Unholy Night* to preserve the happy, conspiratorial moment for posterity.

Ernest Torrence is allowed to span the reaches of the film with his integrity and his character's professional competence intact. Mugging shamelessly throughout, Torrence justifies the overuse of his rubber face in his rather loquacious explanations at the picture's end. The actor makes an acceptable (if highly unlikely) hero, and roles like that of Moriarty in Fox's 1932 rendition of *Sherlock Holmes* were usually much more to his (and to his fans') taste. Probably most familiar to non-genre moviegoers as Buster Keaton's bewildered dad in *Steamboat Bill, Jr.*, the Scottish Torrence died in 1933, cutting short his career in sound films.

***The Unholy Night* is just too much of a good thing.**

With few exceptions, critics withheld their beneficence from *The Unholy Night*. *Variety* (10/16/29) opined that:

> It takes nearly two hours [sic] for the Hecht version to cover a lot of aimless conversation, running around, and performances like a bunch of college amateurs, before the whirligig of complications and drivel are all contradicted in a few long-winded speeches by Dr. Ballou and Sir Rumsey of Scotland Yard… It's an all-talker and a 100% lemon.

The New York Times (10/12/29) wasn't much nicer:

> An incoherent and tantalizing talking picture, called "The Unholy Night," is sojourning at The Capitol… But it is very difficult to

John Miljan as Major Mallory: shell-shock victim and avenging angel. Photofest

make head or tail of what the director, Lionel Barrymore, is driving at during some of the sequences.

For what it's worth, *Night* just is too much of a good thing. Lionel Barrymore never takes a few seconds to underscore anything when a minute can be had; skeletons lay buried everywhere; no one is without his or her foibles; glares and grimaces are a dime a dozen, and demonstrably innocent people draw visible sighs of relief when informed that they couldn't have been guilty of something they hadn't done anyhow. Subtlty is nowhere to be found despite the extended running time, and we have far too many superficially similar characters to allow for effective comparisons or contrasts.

But... there's that doozy of a seance scene, Roland Young's infectious personality, Boris Karloff, *and* Kamiyama Sojin. One may argue that the scales don't quite balance, but for lovers of guilty pleasures, any measurable gold at all is as good as the mother lode.

The
VAMPIRE'S
GHOST
Featuring
JOHN ABBOTT
CHARLES GORDON
with
PEGGY STEWART
GRANT WITHERS
ADELE MARA
REPUBLIC PICTURES
LESLEY SELANDER - Director
Screen Play by
JONH K. BUTLER and LEIGH BRACKETT
A REPUBLIC PICTURE

THE VAMPIRE'S GHOST
by John Soister

While my Dad may not have left me much in the way of cash, he was generous to a fault in instilling in me the value of homespun aphorisms. Some 40 years after cutting my teeth on fifties television, however, I'm not quite sure which bits of the wisdom I live by came from my father, and which came from Ward Cleaver or Pappy Maverick. One of the major bits of wisdom I may or may not have received from my Dad was, "Be your own man!" I strive mightily (and on a regular basis) to impress this upon my two sons, Jake and Jeremy, and (with a minor grammatical alteration) upon my daughter, Katelyn. "Do not allow anyone to tell you how to think!" I also counsel them, although I'm still struggling to bring that one in as a pithy soundbite. My Dad probably told me tons of things like that, but—as I'm finding out with my own children—you never pay a lot of attention when you're a kid and that sort of stuff is fresh.

Nevertheless, I can proudly point to at least one example wherein I have followed no one's lead save my own: I seem to be virtually alone in this world in my enjoyment of Republic's first monster movie, *The Vampire's Ghost*.

For most film fans, Republic's chief claim to fame was its output of great serials. From *Darkest Africa* (1936) to *Panther Girl of the Congo* almost 30 years later, the studio constantly demonstrated to all concerned that their chapterplays offered the best special effects (kudos to the amazing Lydecker brothers), the greatest stuntmen (far more important to the flow of the two-reel episodes than any ferschulugginer leading men), the broadest spectrum of colorful (and original) heroes and villains, and the most creative employment of plywood in the industry. Head honcho Herbert Yates saw to it that B Westerns were also an in-house mainstay. Utilizing sets that actually *gained* perceived authenticity as they grew more dilapidated, cheap (if not totally free) acreage for location shooting, old clothes, and lots of dust, the regular flow of Republic horse operas spawned generations of fans every bit as dedicated as the serial buffs.

While these two prominent feathers-in-the-cap kept the younger set enthralled, the little studio occasionally tried to rope in older and/or more demanding audiences, for whom blazing six-guns held little appeal and whose attention span could see them safely beyond the running time of the average serial chapter. It is to be deplored that Judy Canova's talents, along with the hillbilly mystique of the Weaver Brothers and Elviry, served as the springboard to this new sophistication. Still, amid a spate of non-countrified musical comedies, wartime dramas, and low-budget period pictures, Yates' staff did turn out a handful of mysteries and mellers with varied results. Only three filmed adventures of "Mr. District Attorney" were needed to dig the cinematic grave for *that* popular radio hero, and—more depressingly—an incipiently successful series of Ellery Queen features was cut down prematurely by the inexplicable casting of comic Eddie Quillan as the sleuth in the second offering, *The Mandarin Mystery* (1936).

The year before the Quillan debacle, Republic had launched its first horror film, *The Crime of Dr. Crespi*, which offered an on-his-way-down Erich von Stroheim yet another crack at lechery, sadism, and revenge. Thankfully, Dr. Crespi's crime was not one of inflicting boredom: The film featured some full-blooded vignettes, boasted impressive camerawork, and fit in quite nicely with myriad other horrors then making the

"THE VAMPIRE'S GHOST"

JOHN CHARLES
ABBOTT · GORDON

PEGGY STEWART
GRANT WITHERS
ADELE MARA

rounds from the majors. In fact, Universal stalwarts Edward Van Sloan and Dwight Frye—paired together for the third time—helped lend the studio's premier chiller effort a touch of legitimacy. Republic, however, couldn't take any bows over *Crespi*; the fledgling studio had merely acquired the completed picture (and others) from Liberty Pictures (and others), with which Monogram and Mascot (and others) had merged to form Republic Pictures in 1935. (Monogram's W. Ray Johnston and Trem Carr would become disenchanted with the new organization almost immediately, and would withdraw Monogram's assets and identity—with an eye to reopening their own studio in less than a year.)

Serial monstrosities notwithstanding, it wouldn't be until 1944 that the Yates organization would try its hand again at the genre we all know and love. Having snatched the rights to an up-and-coming runaway hit of a science fiction novel (*Donovan's Brain*) from its impatient and arrogant author (Curt Siodmak) for less than $2,000, Republic dusted off its top horror man—von Stroheim—and paired him with Yates' pretty but vapid girlfriend—Vera Hruba Ralston—in 1944's monster-less *The Lady and the Monster*. (Providing the brain upon which the meaningful glances, overdone lighting schedules, and hurled chairs turned was all-around leading man, Richard Arlen, who had had experience with both ladies *and* monsters in Paramount's 1933 classic, *Island of Lost Souls*.) The picture made money, while demonstrating that Yates was more adept at acquiring hot properties than he was at choosing paramours or leading ladies. Criticism of *The Lady and the Monster* ran the gamut from faint praise to Curt Sidomak's opinion, quoted by Tom Weaver: "It was a piece of shit."

Later in '44, alone among countless schoolmarms, frontier women, and ranchers' tomboyish daughters, *The Girl Who Dared* toyed with the supernatural—and paid for it. Unfortunately, not many picturegoers paid for it, and the film—a pseudo ghost story-cum-radiation poisoning-mystery with tenuous ties to piracy—vanished without so much as promising an increased dividend to the stockholders. Apart from a couple of sickly "ghost" comedies, a tepid adaptation of a radio play on telepathy, and the three mid-forties' "monster extravaganzas" (*The Vampire's Ghost, The Catman of Paris*, and *Valley of the Zombies*), Republic produced only one other feature of interest to genre fans; it was, in many ways, its best effort: *The Woman Who Came Back*. If those assorted vampire and werewolf variations could be chalked up to Universal's influence, the strength and presence of *Woman* was doubtless due to Val Lewton's school of psychological chills.

Constructed around a number of the Russian producer's trademark techniques—creative lighting, the power of suggestion, the heart-stopping "bus" shots—Walter Colmes' tale of witchcraft and possession unfolds with a succession of remarkable experiences before collapsing in a heap of rational explanations and a disappointing denouement. Still, for the body of the film, Nancy Kelly and Otto Kruger help the audience suspend its disbelief to an extent to which Lewton would have been proud. A departure from Republic's usual *modus operandi*—wits are much more in evidence than fists during the unspooling—*The Woman Who Came Back* remains among the most intelligent and thought-provoking pictures produced by the action studio.

Not so *The Vampire's Ghost*.

For that epic, Leigh Brackett adapted her own original story (with John Butler's assistance), resulting in yet another tale of the familiar Undead, albeit with the novel setting of the African jungle. Of course, location shooting à la Republic usually meant the familiar recesses of Bronson Caverns, but the creative arrangement of a couple of acres of potted ferns managed to lean more toward the feeling of oppressive menace than did the redressed Western shacks or the expansive backlot street sets.

Via voice-over, vampire Webb Fallon (John Abbott) drones on about the weariness brought on by immortality and the strange allure that Africa holds for him, while Bud Thackery's camera meanders along the amazingly smooth streets of an African village in a (more or less) p.o.v. maneuver. Fallon's hand—note that unusual ring—pushes open the door to a little house, and it's all over for the comely native lass cowering inside.

The killing, it seems, is not the first the village of Bakunda has seen, and an impromptu gathering of nonnative residents leads to a brainstorming session on what the hell to do. Among those present is Father Gilchrist (Grant Withers), who wears a pith helmet, a high-water cassock, and a hefty cross that you just *know* is going to see some action; he's the local missionary and symbolizes the true faith (i.e., the white man's religion). Thomas Vance (Emmett Vogan), a trader/merchant who is also father to gawky heroine Julie (Peggy Stewart), represents the more mature, methodical approach to life. Rugged hero/love interest Roy Hendrick (played by Buster Crabbe clone, Charles Gordon, as if he suffered alternately from lockjaw, the vapors, and constipation) is charming, if impetuous and basically useless—just like every other juvenile hero in films of this sort. Presumably, he's still a virgin.

Anyhow, none of these basic white bread types has a clue as to what's going on, so Roy decides to pay a visit to saloonkeeper, Webb Fallon, whose proximity to the seamier side of village life might furnish some useful information. At the saloon, we note that vampires are not only creatures of the devil, but are also phenomenally adept

Leigh Brackett adapted her own original story, resulting in yet another tale of the familiar Undead, albeit with the novel setting of the African jungle.

gamblers; burly Jim Barrat (burly Roy Barcroft) loses his ready cash and his share in his boat (*The Bakunda Queen*) to Fallon's unerring knack with dice. Losing his patience as well, the erstwhile skipper storms out amid a stream of invective, only to return moments later with a couple of feisty pals. A fight breaks out (Barrat loses *that*, too), during which the noble Roy (who has attempted to aid Fallon in the lopsided struggle) is sapped. Out of it, he misses Fallon's bringing the rampaging loser to a screeching halt with a wild-eyed hypnotic stare.

Nightfall finds Roy, Father Gilchrist, and the Vances playing host to Fallon at the Vances' house. There's just no way that *this* vampire never drinks wine, nor eats pot roast, but a strange thing does happen over coffee. When pressed as to why he's in Jerkwater, Africa, Fallon waxes philosophic about compulsion and the like, intimating that his fate is somehow tied to the Dark Continent. The saloonkeeper goes on at length—his comrades either nodding sagaciously or staring uncomprehendingly—and manservant Simon Peter (by the look of things, the *only* local convert of the stolid Father Gilchrist) chances to glance into the mirror on the wall...

(Universal, which had introduced the concept of vampirism to the world of sound movies, had proven itself remarkably lax when it came to keeping straight the various mythic details. Bram Stoker's *Dracula*, the court of last appeal when it came to such

Setting up shop in geographical digs more proper to Tarzan, Jungle Jim, or any of those White Goddesses nursed by gorillas or something has *got* to be peculiar for a vampire.

things, had maintained that the Count [and, presumably, other like creatures] cast no reflection in mirrors. Tod Browning's *Dracula* gave the notion life when Edward Van Sloan failed to catch sight of Bela Lugosi in a cigarette box mirror. [Inasmuch as his character had been saddled with a pair of Coke-bottle lenses by the wardrobe department, the wonder is that Van Sloan could even see the *cigarette box*.] The 1931 original tossed integrity to the wind, though, when the little mirror failed to take in Dracula's *clothes*, as well. Of such silliness, apathy is born. In *House of Frankenstein*, John Carradine's thirsty Count returned from whatever infernal reaches he had been haunting when a stake was withdrawn from the ribcage of his skeleton, and he lugged his soup and fish along with him. The end of the film [and ditto with sequel, *House of Dracula*] saw those duds melt away—with his epidermis—in the morning sun, leaving only the noble bone structure with which his most recent misadventure had begun. Nor did Baron Latos' remarkably resilient wardrobe take *its* turn in the glass, either. Hey, in the mid-forties, Universal's Dracula was the undisputed King of the Undead. Did you expect him to buy off the rack?

Columbia's Dracula clone—Armand Tesla in 1944's *Return of the Vampire*—at least had a sense of fair play. When a small mirror was held up to his sleeping form, only his head failed to make the cut; the rest of his white tie and tails—supported by

of the Horror Film 231

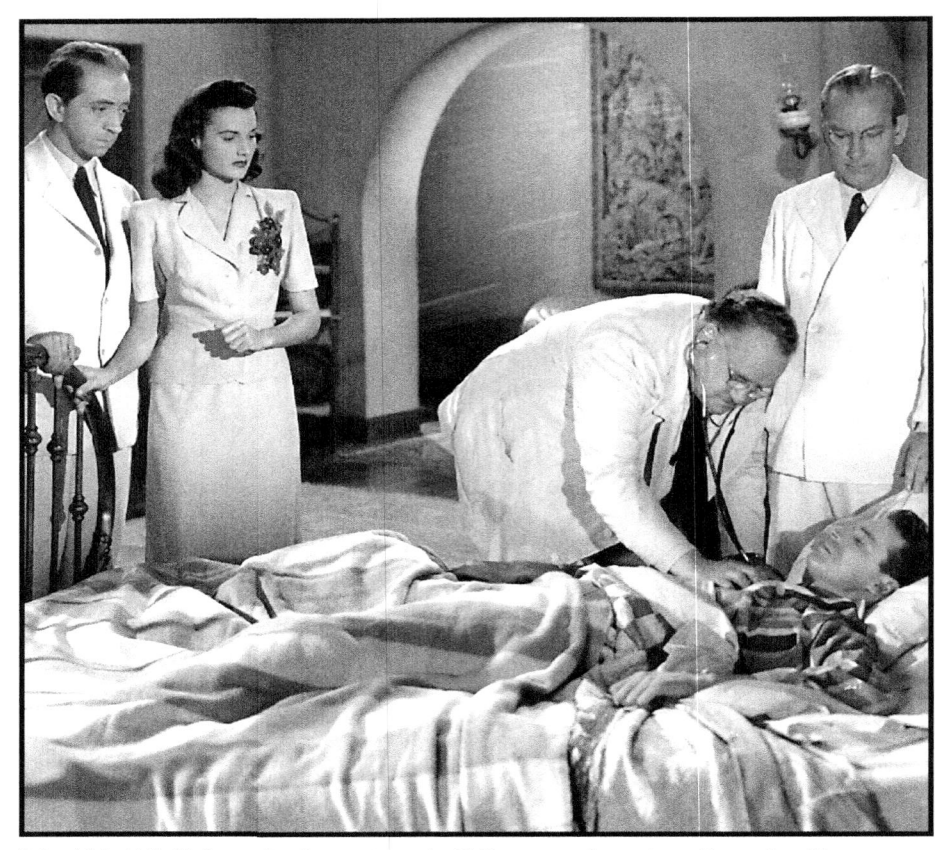

John Abbott (left) does what he can to make Fallon more than a two-dimensional bogeyman, but isn't given much help from the screenplay.

a wire form rather than by the manly Lugosi chest—was as plain as the, er... nose on Bela's face in the mirror sequence in *Abbott and Costello Meet Frankenstein*. Here, then, amid the nickel-and-dime ambiance of *The Vampire's Ghost*, we find only the second example of Hollywood's playing the game according to Hoyle.)

So... per the miracle of (rather shaky) matte work, Simon Peter gapes at the reflection of a free-floating teacup and a baggy but disembodied suit. Fallon follows the servant's gaze and shatters the mirror with a particularly potent glare; no one seems terribly fazed by any of this.

Showing some pluck, Roy is off to quiz the natives in nearby Mohongo the next morning. Accompanied by Simon Peter, a handful of locals, and Webb Fallon (who beats Gary Oldman to the punch by some 50 years by sporting sunglasses and traipsing about in the noonday sun), Roy hasn't been among the ferns for two minutes when he inadvertently springs a booby trap. A bullet is sent crashing into one of the native carriers—Taba—but only after it apparently passes right *through* Fallon. That evening, Simon Peter and the bandaged Taba hold a powwow, agree that the bug-eyed white man is a vampire, and prepare to do him in with a spear which they first immerse in some molten silver they've somehow come up with.

Before they can put their plan into action, though, they are attacked by a group of frenzied, straight-shooting natives; Taba is gunned down. (It may be that the various voodoo accouterments—found here and there throughout the picture—are territorial markers. As they are never adequately explained, and as voodoo doesn't play an *integral* part in the story, this may merely be an unprovoked attack, added gratuitously for dramatic purposes [similar to the scads of thinly motivated Indian attacks which fleshed out Republic's B Westerns].) Taking advantage of the brouhaha, Simon Peter lets fly the silver assegai. Fallon goes down; so does Simon Peter, who catches a bullet from the bad guys.

When the smoke clears, Roy is placed under the wounded vampire's hypnotic spell. Fallon relates how, during the reign of good Queen Bess, he had accidentally caused a woman's death, had fled England, and had metamorphosed into the undying creature whom Roy will now serve. Bidding Roy to carry him to the mountaintop, Fallon also instructs the mesmerized hero to bring along the small wooden box, filled with earth from Fallon's grave back in Britain. The vampire slowly regains his strength under the light of the rising full moon, while Roy, who has been hypnotically enjoined from uttering a word about what he's been told, returns to Bakunda with what's left of his party.

Back in town, Roy's dispiritedness prompts everyone (including Julie) to think him ill. While he sits around helplessly, Fallon decides that *he* cannot continue to wander through eternity without some female companionship and targets the angular Julie, rather than the more pleasantly curved and sexier Lisa (Adele Mara), who dances in his saloon. (Up to this point, Lisa has done little more than stroll once or twice across the screen, but it's no surprise to regular picturegoers that her plight is but another case of a working woman falling for her boss. Well, if not actually *falling* for him, at least being cognizant enough of him to resent his attentions to another.)

Lisa vengefully conspires with Barrat, who is going to pit his card skills against Fallon's, while wagering whatever he's come up with since his spectacular losses earlier. The saloonkeeper cuts to a King, but Lisa brazenly cuts to the Ace, which she and the former skipper had marked on the sly. The two victorious cheats foolishly leave the marked card where Fallon can examine it, and the outraged vampire follows the two into the desolate streets where, amid a splendid interplay of shadows and reaction shots, he does away with both.

While all this is going on, the natives (and their drums) have been restless. They have positively identified the Englishman as a vampire, and Father Gilchrist is moved to perform an act of faith. Maneuvering the incapacitated Roy into church, the missionary leads him in prayer; the words of entreaty uttered in God's house undo the vampire's spell, and Roy is again filled with piss and vinegar. Fallon hasn't exactly been napping, however. Hypnotizing Julie, he leads her off into the jungle, intending to vampirize her at a certain haunt of the damned that very night. The good guys are quick to follow, as Roy has the native drums beat a constant tattoo, keeping him (and Vance, Father Gilchrist, and Simon Peter—with his silver spear) apprised of Fallon's progress and direction.

A series of cuts establishes the chase, and the onset of dusk finds Fallon and his bride-to-be at the pagan "Temple of Death"—a barren thatched hut, housing a four-armed idol of the Kali variety. For the first time in the picture, Fallon is allowed to act

Lisa (Adele Mara) has done little more than stroll once or twice across the screen, but it's no surprise that her plight is but another case of a working woman falling for her boss.

vampirically, and he leans toward Julie's throat. Against the flickering firelight, the shadow of Father Gilchrist's cross backs the startled bloodsucker away from his prey, and Roy hurls the plated spear with the unerring accuracy of a movie hero. Falling behind the altar, the impaled Fallon vainly tries once again to enslave Roy. Simon Peter puts the torch to the Temple of Death, and the heavy idol falls, pinning Fallon to the ground; the relentless flames promise eternal rest for the weary vampire.

Not a great deal has been written about *The Vampire's Ghost*; it is, after all, a *very* inconsequential little movie. The few critiques which do exist spend most of their brief remarks excoriating the movie for its departures from type. This line of argument is valid enough, I guess; it certainly is the common thread running through just about every published mention of the film. Heck, I would be less than honest if I claimed that *Ghost* was anything other than a *mediocre*, very inconsequential little film. It just happens that my particular karma is to be heedless of the caveats of others.

In his enjoyable *Poverty Row Horrors*, Tom Weaver grouses a bit that "...in *The Vampire's Ghost*, writers Butler and Brackett get almost every aspect of the vampire mythos wrong, voodoo plays a role in the film, and it's set, jarringly, in Africa..." As usual, Tom's comments are right on the money, but he doesn't cut the film that extra little slack it needs to defend itself. John Butler's and Leigh Brackett's attempt at infusing some novelty into the traditional theme via the jungle setting has got to count for something. If nothing else, the tramping among the vegetation offers a welcome respite from the increasingly hackneyed reaches of backlot Tyrolean sets.

Chaney's *Son of Dracula* (1943), in fact, had set the Vampire King (all that "Alucard" nonsense and "son" misdirection apart) smack dab in the middle of the Old South, solely to give those old themes and locations a rest. (Well, maybe not solely; it's a near certainty that wartime restrictions on set construction, utilization of existing assets, conflicting shooting schedules, and Chaney's limitations—could you imagine *him* lurking about in Transylvania?—may have had a hand in the creative mounting.) While the character himself may not have suffered from the radical change in climate, Universal's Dracula would never again bear the mantle of sole supernatural heavy in any subsequent picture.

From those hoary broken battlements, via England and the American South, to some indeterminate patch of Africa is quite a move, though. Setting up shop in geographical digs more proper to Tarzan, Jungle Jim, or any of those White Goddesses nursed by gorillas or something has *got* to be peculiar for a vampire. At the very least, the novel situation raises more questions than the screenplay can safely answer. That Fallon feels an almost spiritual attachment to the Dark Continent is carefully established; just *why* this is so is never adequately explained. Causing a young woman's death may have been more than probable cause for leaving town in a hurry, but... Africa? And since Fallon met his own death in England (that soil in the little chest is from his native grave), why would he junket to parts unknown *after* he was in a position not to care a whit about the consequences of his action?

With all the various voodoo doodads hanging about hither and yon, one would suppose that the zombie (although technically indigenous to the Caribbean) or some such would be a more familiar other-worldly "type" to the superstitious natives. Why Taba and Simon Peter (and, given the constant tintinnabulation of the drums, *most* of the tribal members in the vicinity) are so well versed in up-to-date vampire-destroying technologies is perplexing. Neither native turns to his respective religion to help him out (again, the voodoo mentions in the film are merely window dressing), but both agree that a silver assegai is the ticket. If Fallon is (presumably) the *only* bloodsucker within drum range, how did everyone get so knowledgeable about vampires all of a sudden? Is there a library somewhere? Or had there been *other* vampires—fought and destroyed by native canniness and a handy cache of silver—whose existence was unknown to the white settlers in the area?

As for the vampire mythos, some variations on the Universal guidelines have already been mentioned. Later films perpetuated nuances that the little Republic picture introduced; in *Kiss of the Vampire*, for example, the clannish undead swarm about during the day, pausing only occasionally (but dramatically) to check the cloud cover. (Other of the abundant lot of Hammer vampire films do a great deal more harm to the integrity of the mythos than the innocuous *The Vampire's Ghost*. Stoker had cautioned that vampires could not cross running water, referring to streams, rivers, seas, and the like, as these both represented and embodied the pure forces of life in nature. The wildly uncomfortable *Dracula A.D. 1972* corrupts this understanding to include the pressurized flow of water in a showerbath, surely not what Stoker had intended. Taking this bastardization to its logical end, there could be no more facile or assured way of slaying vampires than with a fire hose—or a water pistol!)

More disturbing with regard to the rulebook of vampiric behavior (but still a minor grievance) is Fallon's apparent ability to ingest foodstuffs like any mortal. One of the few areas that the novel's Van Helsing *doesn't* touch on (in the grating speech pattern

Stoker inflicted upon him in his longwinded expository passages) is Dracula's digestive system, but the portrait that the peculiar old professor paints is of the vampire as *leech*, gorging itself on blood, and only on blood. (Contemporary novelist Fred Saberhagen, in his requisite Dracula series, has the Count—known in his New World environs as Matthew Maule—occasionally pause to spit up [surreptitiously, of course] any items of food or drink which he has been forced to swallow, usually in the interests of preserving his true identity. It's a grand [and logical] touch.)

Something could be made of the fact that none of Fallon's prey seem to emerge as members of the undead themselves. Webb has been in the area for a while (all those natives drumming, all that cheap booze flowing), but there is no indication of other vampires (either colleagues *or* victims). Perhaps the strain flowing in the veins of Webb Fallon—itself the result of a "curse" rather than of the bite of another—is not passed on via the extended canines. Other types of vampirism—apart from the "traditional" one found in films like *The Vampire's Ghost*—are discussed and depicted in several movies of later decades; among them, *Captain Kronos, Vampire Hunter* (1972), in which the parasites suck their victim's *youth*, are impervious to Christian iconology (going so far as to simulate the shape of a cross in order to sucker in some chuckleheaded villagers), and can only be destroyed by steel. Go figure.

Grant Withers' starring days were over by the time he signed to do *The Vampire's Ghost*, but he had been Alex Raymond's Jungle Jim in Universal's popular 1937 serial, and so was no stranger to low-budget greenery. As Father Gilchrist, though, he seems ill at ease and downright exhausted in most of his few scenes. Regarding this as the actor's effort to build characterization would be the charitable thing to do; viewing the performance as a calculated exercise in expending only so much energy on a rather poorly delineated part in a nothing little B is probably more like it.

Emmett Vogan shuttled back and forth between Monogram and Republic, generally playing bankers who got shot or storekeepers who got shot before Johnny Mack Brown or Ken Maynard straightened things out. When not being gunned down in Dodge, Abilene, or Broken Elbow, Vogan appeared in several serials, including *The Purple Monster Strikes* (1945, with Roy Barcroft) and *The Crimson Ghost* (1946, with future Lone Ranger, Clayton Moore; both from Republic). He was usually shot in his serials, too.

Peggy Stewart was likewise a B Western fixture, spending most of her career under contract to Republic. An appearance in something different would have been a novelty for Stewart (all five of her serials had Western themes), but inasmuch as the film at hand borrows heavily from standard horse opera procedure, her walking on through it was really a nonevent. Charles Gordon made only a handful of films (of which *The Vampire's Ghost* is the best known) before returning to a radio career; the anonymity of the microphone lent itself more to disguising his simpliste performances than did the cold lens of the movie camera.

While Roy Barcroft's turn as Jim Barrat is brief, the veteran heavy's career was anything but. Born Howard Ravenscroft in 1902, the husky actor—easily among the most popular personalities in the Western or serial genres—chalked up well over a hundred appearances wherein he helped the chief villain (if not played by Barcroft himself) make life as miserable as possible for anyone on the side of the angels. He grumbled his way through Universal's *The Night Key* (1937) and brought up the rear for

The pagan "Temple of Death"—a barren thatched hut, housing a four-armed idol of the Kali variety.

Bela Lugosi in 1939's *The Phantom Creeps*. Other genre films abetted by the Barcroft touch were the clever and sophisticated *Rosemary's Baby* (1968), and the imbecilic and spectacularly crude *Billy the Kid vs. Dracula*, two years earlier. As was fitting, Barcroft's last two films were Westerns: *The Reivers* (1969) and *Monte Walsh* (1970). This last was released posthumously as Roy Barcroft, loved by his colleagues and by the legions of fans who hissed at his every move, died in 1969.

John Abbott, of course, is probably the *last* person one would think of in the role of Webb Fallon. Watching the slight actor with the Bette Davis eyes duke it out with Roy Barcroft, Tom Steele, et al. would probably lead to a chuckle or two, unless one were reminded of *another* facet of that etched-in-granite vampire mythos; namely, that the undead possess great strength, even when not six-foot hunks with chiseled abs. Abbott does what he can to make Fallon more than a two-dimensional bogeyman, but isn't given much help from the screenplay. Had there been greater mention of that intriguing Elizabethan England connection, or more on the mysterious hold which Africa has on the vampire, he might have had a chance. As it stands, the Brackett/Butler bloodsucker is a tight-lipped cipher in more ways than one.

With all the various voodoo doodads hanging about hither and yon, one would suppose that the zombie would be a more familiar other-worldly "type" to the superstitious natives.

I met John Abbott on Broadway some years back. He was appearing in a play (the name of which I've forgotten), and I literally bumped into him while on my way to see Arthur Kopit's *Indians*. Very graciously pausing to sign an autograph, the affable actor was alternately pleased to be recognized and remembered, and mildly disconcerted that most of my memories of him were from his parts in things like *The Saint in London*, *They Got Me Covered*, and... *The Vampire's Ghost*. The body of Abbott's screen work is quite extensive, covering over three and a half decades and more than 70 features; unlike most of his *The Vampire's Ghost* co-stars, the gaunt actor seldom showed up in Westerns and *never* graced a chapterplay.

Lesley Selander's direction in *The Vampire's Ghost* pretty much reflects the style and limited bag of tricks he displayed in the countless oaters he churned out left and right for Republic. The stalking scene, mentioned above, is exceptional only in comparison with the rest of the picture; deepening the shadows or prolonging the suspense of the pursuit would have called for more awareness of nuance than any of Selander's gunfights or horseback chases ever required. *Ghost* was only one of several non-Westerns the genial house technician left behind, but a couple of rare forays into another studio—the equally budget-conscious Monogram—allowed Selander the opportunity to helm both the

238   Son of Guilty Pleasures

last official Charlie Chan picture (Roland Winters' *Sky Dragon*, 1949), and what was undeniably one of Monogram's most expensive features ever: *Flight to Mars*. I don't think it would be fair to attribute the demise of the Chan series to Selander's leaden touch, or to ask him to accept total blame for the plodding pace of the 1951 Cinecolor space opera, but neither film offers more than the most rudimentary display of creative camera placement or composition.

If *The Vampire's Ghost* is (in Phil Hardy's words) "a real shoestring shocker"—and it is—it is also an unusual little thriller for daring not to go with the flow of the increasingly stale vampiric formula. (Leigh Brackett would enjoy much more renown for her work with Howard Hawks than for stuff like this, but stuff like this—which played a significant role in the writer's career—helped hone her creative edge. Miss Brackett died in 1978, without seeing the fruits of her labor in George Lucas's mega-hit *The Empire Strikes Back*.) Its innovations in casting, locale, and interpretation may have been dictated by budgetary concerns rather than by panache, but many of the (then) offbeat aspects of the vampire's wherewithal have been vindicated by elaborate and expensive treatments in more recent, more "prestigious" productions.

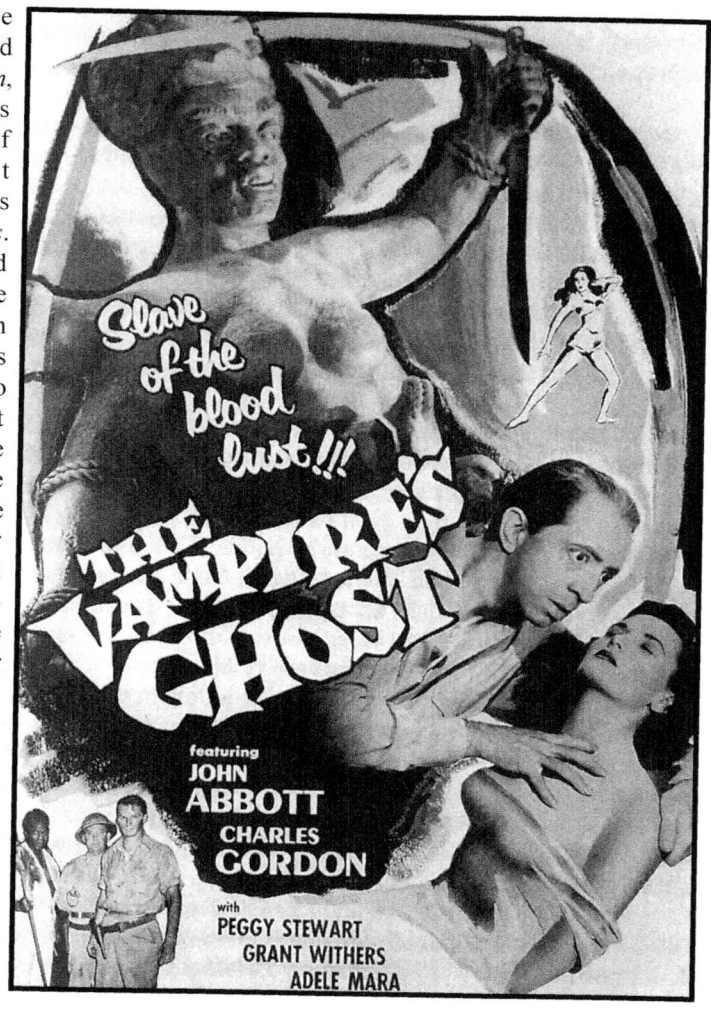

CREDITS

The Brain That Wouldn't Die
CREDITS: Director: Joseph Green; Producer: Rex Carlton; Associate Producer: Mort Landberg; Screenplay: Joseph Green; Original Story: Rex Carlton and Joseph Green; Additional Dialogue: Doris Brent; Director of Photography: Stephen Hajnal; Camera Operator: John S. Priestley; Art Director: Paul Fanning; Supervising Film Editor: Leonard Anderson; Film Editor: Marc Anderson; Special Effects: Byron Baer; Make-up: George Fiala; Theme Music "The Web": Abe Baker and Tony Restaino (by permission of Laurel Records); Production Manager: Alfred H. Lessner; Sound: Robert E. Lessner and Emil Kolisch; Assistant Director: Tony La Marca; Assistants to the Producer: James Gealis and Linda Brent; Property Man: Walter Pluff, Jr.; Gaffer: Vincent Delaney; Grip: John Haupt, Jr.; Script Supervision: Eva Blair; Running Time: 81 minutes; Released by American International Pictures, 1962

CAST: Herb Evers (Dr. Bill Cortner); Virginia Leith (Jan Compton); Leslie Daniel (Kurt); Adele Lamont (Doris Powell); Bonnie Shari (Stripper); Paula Maurice (B-Girl); Marlyn Hanold; Bruce Brighton (Dr. Cortner); Arny Freeman; Fred Martin; Lola Mason (Donna Williams); Doris Brent (Nurse); Bruce Kerr (Announcer); Audrey Devereau (Jeannie); Eddie Carmel (Monster)

Creature with the Atom Brain
CREDITS: Producer: Sam Katzman; Director: Edward L. Cahn; Screenplay: Curt Siodmak; Cinematography: Fred Jackman, Jr.; Editor: Aaron Stell; Art Director: Paul Palmentola; Set Decorator: Sidney Clifford; Special Effects: Jack Erickson; Music Director: Mischa Bakaleinikoff; Assistant Director: Eddie Saeta; Sound: Josh Westmoreland; Unit Manager: Leon Chooluck; Black and white; 69 minutes; a Clover Production released by Columbia Pictures, June 1955

CAST: Richard Denning (Dr. Chet Walker); Angela Stevens (Joyce Walker); S. John Launer (Captain Dave Harris); Michael Granger (Frank Buchanan); Gregory Gay (Professor Steigg); Linda Bennett (Penny Walker); Tristram Coffin (DA McGraw); Pierre Watkin (Mayor Bremer); Don C. Harvey (Lester Banning); Paul Hoffman (Dunn); Edward Coch (Jason Franchot); Nelson Leigh (Dr. Kenneth Norton); Lane Chandler (General Saunders); Harry Lauter (Reporter); Larry Blake (Reporter); Karl Davis (Creature); Charles Horvath (Creature)

Frankenstein Conquers the World
CREDITS: Screenplay: Kaoru Mabuchi; Written from a Synopsis by Jerry Sohl; Based on a Story by Reuben Bercovitch; Director of Special Effects: Eiji Tsuburaya; Directors of Special Effects Photography: Teisho Arikawa and Motonari Tomioka; Art Director: Takeo Kita; Make-Up: Riki Konna; Cinematographer: Hajime Koizumi; Music: Akira Ifukube; Film Editor: Ryohei Fujii; Optical Photography: Tukio Manoda; Executive Producers: Reuben Bercovitch and Henry G. Saperstein; Director: Ishiro Honda; produced by Toho Co., Ltd. and Henry G. Saperstein Enterprises, Inc. and released in Japan in August 1965 with a running time of 91 minutes; released in the U.S. by

American International Pictures and UPA Productions of America in June 1966 with a running time of 87 minutes; Released in Italy as *Frankenstein alla conquista della Terra* (*Frankenstein Conquers the World*); released in Germany as *Frankenstein Der Schrecken mit dem Affengesicht* ("Frankenstein the Terror with the Ape Face"); referred to in various publications as *Frankenstein Meets the Giant Devil Fish, Frankenstein vs. Baragon, Frankenstein vs. the Giant Devil Fish,* and *Frankenstein vs. the Subterranean Monster*

CAST: Nick Adams (Dr. James Bowen); Tadao Takashima (Dr. Kenichiro Kawaji); Kumi Mizuno (Dr. Sueko Togami); Susumu Fujita (Osaka Police Official A); Yoshibumi Tajima (Submarine Commander); Takashi Shimura (Hiroshima Army Doctor); Jun Tazaki (Okayama Police Chief Hideo Nishi); Yoshio Tsuchiya (Lieutenant Kawai, Submarine First Officer); Hisaya Ito (Police Official B); Kenji Sahara (Okayama Police Officer Tadokoro/Crewman in Submarine); Koji Furuhata ("Frankenstein"); Haruo Nakajima (Baragon)

Frankenstein Daughter
CREDITS: Director: Richard Cunha; Producer: Marc Frederic; Screenplay: H.E. Barrie; Director of Photography: Meredith Nicholson; Film Editor: Everett Dodd; Music: Nicholas Carras; Make-up: Harry Thomas; Art Direction: Sham Unlimited; An Astor Pictures Release; Running time: 85 minutes

CAST: John Ashley (Johnny Bruder); Sandra Knight (Trudy Morton); Donald Murphy (Oliver Frank); Felix Locher (Carter Morton); Wolfe Barzell (Elsu); Sally Todd (Suzy Lawlor); Harry Wilson (Monster); George Barrows (Monster on fire)

The Giant Gila Monster
CREDITS: Director: Ray Kellogg; Executive Producer: Gordon McLendon; Producer: Ken Curtis; Screenplay: Jay Simms; Original Story: Ray Kellogg; Director of Photography: Wilfrid M. Cline; Camera Operators: George Gordon Nogle, Henry A. Kokojan; Camera Assistants: William John Ranaldi, Harry L. Gianneschi; Music: Jack Marshall; Special Songs: Don Sullivan; Music Associate: Audray Granville; Production Manager: Ben Chapman; Special Photographic Effects: Ralph Hammeras, A.S.C., Wee Risser; Art Designer: Louis Caldwell; Set Decorator: Louise Caldwell; Sound: Earl Snyder; Sound Effects: Milton Citron, James Richard; Assistant Director: Edward Haldeman; Script Supervisor: Audrey Blasdel; Make-up: Corinne Daniel. Outdoor Scenes filmed at Cielo; Running Time: 74 minutes; A Hollywood Pictures Corporation Production, released by McLendon Radio Pictures, 1959.

CAST: Don Sullivan (Chace Winstead); Lisa Simone (Lisa); Fred Graham (Sheriff); Shug Fisher (Harris); Bob Thompson (Mr. Wheeler); Ken Knox (Steamroller Smith); Janice Stone (Missy); Jerry Cortwright (Bob); Beverly Thurman (Gay); Don Flournoy (Gordy); Clarke Browne (Chuck); Pat Simmons (Sherry); Pat Reeves (Rick); Ann Sonka (Whila); Cecil Hunt (Compton); Tammie Russell (Mrs. Blackwell); Grady Vaughn (Pat Wheeler); Yolanda Salas (Liz Humphries); Howard Ware (Eb Humphries); Stormy Meadows (Agatha Humphries); Desmond Doogh (Hitchhiker); with Gay McLendon and Jan McLendon

Horror Island

CREDITS: Producer: Ben Pivar; Director: George Waggner; Associate Producer: Jack Bernhard; Assistant Director: Seward Webb; Screenplay: Maurice Tombragel, Victor McLeod; From the original story *Terror of the South Seas* by Alex Gottlieb; Cinematography: Elwood "Woody" Bredell; Camera Operator: Walter Strenge; Editor: Otto Ludwig; Art Director: Jack Otterson; Associate Art Director: Ralph M. DeLacy; Set Decorations: Russell A. Gausman; Sound Supervisor: Bernard B. Brown; Sound Technician: Jess Moulin; Musical Director: Hans J. Salter; Gowns: Vera West; Running Time: 60 minutes; Released by Universal, 1941; Budget; $93,000; Filmed at Universal City, California

CAST: Dick Foran (William Martin); Peggy Moran (Wendy Creighton); Fuzzy Knight (Stuff Oliver); Leo Carrillo (Tobias Clump ["The Skipper"]); John Eldredge (Cousin George Martin); Lewis Howard (Thurman Coldwater); Hobart Cavanaugh (Professor Jasper Quinley); Walter Catlett (Sergeant McGoon); Iris Adrian (Arleen Grady); Ralf Harolde (Rod "Killer" Grady); Foy Van Dolsen (The Phantom/Panama Pete); Emmett Vogan (The Stranger); Walter Tetley (Delivery Boy); Eddy Chandler (Docks Cop); Stuntmen...Eddie Parker; Dale Van Sickel; John Burton

Hunchback of Notre Dame

CREDITS: Director: Jean Delannoy; Producers: Robert and Raymond Hakim; Production Manager: Ludmilla Goulian; Screenplay: Jean Aurenche and Jacques Prevert, based on the Novel by Victor Hugo; Cinematography: Michel Kelber; Camera Operator: Ivanoff; Editor: Henri Taverna; Sound: Jacques Carrere; Music: Georges Auric; Production Design: Rene Renoux; Choreography: Leonide Massine

CAST: Gina Lollobrigida (Esmeralda); Anthony Quinn (Quasimodo); Jean Danet (Phoebus); Alain Cuny (Claude Frollo); Phillipe Clay (Clopin Trouillefou); Danielle Dumont (Fleur de Lys); Robert Hirsch (Gringoire); Roger Blin (Mathias Hungadi); Marianne Oswald (La Falourdel); Jean Tissier (Louis XI)

Invasion U.S.A.

CREDITS: Director: Alfred E. Green; Producer: Robert Smith and Alfred Zugsmith; Screenplay: Robert Smith and Franz Spencer; Director of Photography: John L. Russell; Editor: W. Donn Hayes; Production Design: James W. Sullivan; Music: Albert Glasser; Cinematography: John L. Russell; Running time: 74 minutes; Columbia; 1952

CAST: Gerald Mohr (Vince Potter); Peggy Castle (Carla); Dan O'Herlihy (Mr. Ohman); Robert Brice (George Sylvester); Erik Blythe (Ed Mulfory); Wade Crosby (Congressman); Tom Kennedy (Tim); Phyllis Coates (Mrs. Mulfory); Aram Katcher (Fifth Columnist Leader); Knox Manning (TV Newsman); Noel Neill (Airline Ticket Agent)

Juggernaut

CREDITS: Director: Henry Edwards; Producer: Julius Hagen; Screenplay: Cyril Campion and H. Fowler Mear; Adaptation and Dialogue: Heinrich Fraenkel; Based on a Novel by Alice Campbell; Photography: Sidney Blythe and William Luff; Editor: Michael Chorlton; Art Director: James Carter; Musical Direction: W.L. Trytel; Production Company: J.H. Productions; Trade Show Date: September 8, 1936; Made at the Twickenham Film Studios; Premiere: London; October 1936; BBFC Certificate: "A"; Released in America by Grand National: April 1937; Reissue Title: *The Demon Doctor*; Running time: 64 or 70 minutes.

CAST: Boris Karloff (Dr. Sartorius); Joan Wyndham (Eve Rowe); Arthur Margetson (Roger Clifford); Mona Goya (Lady Yvonne Clifford); Antony Ireland (Captain Arthur Halliday); Morton Setten (Sir Charles Clifford); Mina Boucicault (Mary Clifford); Gibb McLaughlin (Jacques); J. H. Roberts (Chalmers); Victor Rietti (Doctor Bousquet). (Every cast list I've seen uses the pressbook spellings of Anthony, Selten, and Nina rather than Antony, Setten, and Mina, as they appear in the titles. I decided to use the names from the titles.)

The Omega Man

CREDITS: A Walter Seltzer Production; Director: Boris Sagal; Producer: Walter Seltzer; Screenplay: John William and Joyce H. Corrington, Based on the Novel *I Am Legend* by Richard Matheson; Director of Photography: Russell Metty, A.S.C.; Art Directors: Arthur Loel & Walter M. Simonds; Set Decorator: William L. Koehl; Assistant Director: Donald Roberts; Film Editor: William Ziegler; Unit Production Manager: Frank Baur; Music: Ron Grainer; Action Coordinator: Joe Canutt; Sound: Bob Martin; Costumers: Margo Buxley & Bucky Roug; Make-up: Gordon Bau; Supervising Hair Stylist: Jean Burt Reilly; Production Assistant: Shirley Cohen; Titles: Pacific Title; Technicolor; Filmed in Panavision; 98 minutes; 1971

CAST: Charlton Heston (Neville); Anthony Zerbe (Matthias); Rosalind Cash (Lisa); Paul Koslo (Dutch); Eric Laneuville (Richie); Lincoln Kilpatrick (Zachary); Jill Diralo (Little Girl); Anna Aires (Woman in Cemetery Crypt); Brian Tochi (Tommy); Family members (Devereen Bookwalter; John Dierkes; Monika Henried; Linda Redfearn; Forrest Wood)

Privatte Parts

CREDITS: Producer: Gene Corman; Director: Paul Bartel; Original Screenplay: Philip Kearney and Les Rendelstein; Director of Photography: Andrew Davis; Music: Hugo Friedhofer; Film Editor: Morton Tubor; Production Manager: Donald Heitzer; Assistant Director: Arne Schmidt; Production Design: John Retsek; Sound: Jeff Weder; Costume Designer: Liz Manny; Assistant Producer: John B. Bennett; Running time: 86 minutes; Released by MGM, 1972

CAST: Ayn Ruymen (Cheryl Stratton); Lucile Benson (Aunt Martha Atwood); John Ventantonio (George Atwood); Laurie Main (Reverend Moon); Stanley Livingston (Jeff); Charles Woolf (Jeff's Dad); Ann Gibbs (Judy); Len Travis (Mike); Dorothy Neumann (Mrs. Quigley); Gene Simms (First Policeman); John Lupton (Second Policeman); Patrick Strong (Artie)

Robot Monster

CREDITS: Director-Producer: Phil Tucker; Executive Producer: Al Zimbalist; Associate Producer: Alan Winston; Photography: Jack Greenhalgh; Special Effects: Jack Rabin and David Commons; Original Screenplay: Wyott Ordung; Editor: Merrill White; Associate Editor: Bruce Schoengarth; Music: Elmer Bernstein; Makeup: Stan Campbell; Property Master: John Orlando; Wardrobe: Henry West; Production Supervisor: Clarence Eurist; Sound Director: Lyle E. Willey; Production Associate: Irving Lerner; Assistant Director: Robert Barnes; Script Supervisor: Teddy Schilz; Assistant to Producer: Herbert Luft; Stereo (3-D) Director: Gordon Anvil; Stereo Technician: Ben Colman; Automatic Billion Bubble Machine: N.A. Fisher Chemical Products. Running time: 62 minutes. A Three Dimensional Pictures production released by Astor Pictures, June 1953

Cast: George Nader (Roy); Gregory Moffett (Johnny); Claudia Barrett (Alice); John Mylong (Professor); Pamela Paulson (Carla); Selena Royle (Martha); George Barrows (Ro-Man); John Brown (Voice of Great One and Ro-Man)

Sssssss

CREDITS: Producer: Dan Striepeke; Executive Producers: Richard D. Zunuck and David Brown; Director: Bernard L. Kowalski; Screenplay: Hal Dresner from a Story by Dan Striepeke; Director of Photography: Gerald Perry Finnerman; Art Director: John T. McCormack; Music: Pat Williams; Set Decorator: Claire P. Brown; Sound: Waldon O. Watson and Melvin Metcalfe; Editor: Robert Watts; Unit Production Manager: Doc Merman; First Assistant Director: Gordon Webb; Second Assistant Director: Charles Dismukes; Creative Make-up: John Chambers and Nick Marcellino; Associate Producer: Robert Butner; Graphic Montage: John Neuhart; Cosmetics by Cinematique; Title and Optical Effects: Elkin/Universal; Technical Advisor: Ray Folsom; Animals furnished by Hermosa Reptile and Wild Animal Farm, Inc.; A Zanuck/Brown Production released July 1973 by Universal Pictures in color by Technicolor; Running time: 99 minutes; Rating: PG; Released to video by MCA Universal Home Video in 1997

CAST: Strother Martin (Doctor Carl Stoner); Dirk Benedict (David Blake); Heather Menzies (Kristina Stoner); Richard B. Shull (Doctor Ken Daniels); Tim O'Connor (Kogen); Jack Ging (Sheriff Dale Hardison); Kathleen King (Kitty); Reb Brown (Steve Randall); Ted Grossman (Deputy Morgan Bok); Charles Seel (Old Man); Ray Ballard (Waggest Tourist); Brendan Burns (Jock Number 1); Rick Beckner (Jock Number 2); James Drum (Hawker Number 1); Ed McCready (Hawker Number 2); Frank Kowalski (Hawker Number 3); Ralph Montgomery (Hawker Number 4); Michael Masters (Hawker Number 5); Charlie Fox (Arvin Ley Doux); Felix Silla (Seal Boy); Noble Craig (Tim, the Snake Man); Bobbi Kiger (Kootch Dancer); J. R. Clark (Station Attendant); Chip Potter (Postal Clerk)

The She Creature

CREDITS: Director: Edward L. Cahn; Screenplay: Lou Rusoff, Based on an original Idea by Jerry Zigmond; Photography: Frederick E. West; Music: Ronald Stein; Art Direction: Don Ament; Producer: Alex Gordon; Editor: Ronald Sinclair; Assistant Director: Bart Carre; Associate Producer: Israel M. Berman; Set Decorator: Harry Reif; Released by American International, 1956; Running time: 77 minutes

CAST: Marla English (Andrea); Tom Conway (Timothy Chappel); Chester Morris (Dr. Carlo Lombardi); Ron Randell (Lt. Ed James); Frieda Inescort (Mrs. Chappel); Cathy Downs (Dorothy Chappel); El Brendel (Olaf, the Butler); Paul Blaisdell (the She-Creature); Frank Jenks (Detective); Lance Fuller (Ted Erickson); Paul Dubov (Johnny); Bill Hudson (Bob); Flo Bert (Marta); Jeanne Evans (Mrs. Brown); Kenneth MacDonald (Doctor); Edward Earle (Professor Anderson)

The Strange Door

CREDITS: Director: Joseph Pevney; Producer: Ted Richmond; Screenplay: Jerry Sackheim; From the Story *The Sire de Maletroit's Door* by Robert Louis Stevenson; Assistant Director: Jesse Hibbs; Director of Photography: Irving Glassberg; Editor: Edward Curtiss; Art Directors: Bernard Herzbrun and Eric Orbom; Musical Director: Joseph Gershenson; Special Effects: David S. Horsley; Set Decoration: Russell A. Gausman and Julia Heron; Sound Recording: Leslie J. Carey and Glenn E. Anderson; Make-up: Bud Westmore; Costumes: Rosemary Odell; Released: Universal-International Pictures; Running time: 81 minutes; 1951

CAST: Charles Laughton (Sire Alan de Maletroit); Boris Karloff (Voltan); Sally Forrest (Blanche de Maletroit); Richard Stapley (Denis de Beaulieu); Michael Pate (Talon); Paul Cavanagh (Edmond de Maletroit); Alan Napier (Count Grassin); William Cottrell (Corbeau); Morgan Farley (Rinville); Charles Horvath (Turec); Edwin Harker (Moret)

The Two Faces of Dr. Jekyll

CREDITS: Producer: Michael Carreras; Assosciate Producer: Anthony Nelson-Keys; Director: Terence Fisher; Screenplay: Wolf Mankowitz from Robert Louis Stevenson's *The Strange Case of Dr. Jekyll and Mr. Hyde*; Photography: Jack Asher; Music: Monty Norman & David Heneker; Art Director: Bernard Robinson; Make-up: Roy Ashton; Supervising Editor: James Needs; Released in the U.S. May 3, 1961 by American International; Running time: 88 minute; *The Two Faces of Dr. Jekyll* [aka *House of Fright, Jekyll's Inferno, Dr. Jekyll and Mr. Hyde*]

CAST: Paul Massie (Dr. Jekyll/Mr. Hyde); Christopher Lee (Paul Allen); Dawn Addams (Kitty Jekyll,); David Kossoff (Litauer); Janine Faye (Jane); Francis DeWolff (Inspector); Norma Marla (Maria); Magda Miller (Sphinx Girl); Oliver Reed (Young Tough); William Kendall (Clubman); Pauline Shepherd (Girl in Gin Shop); Helen Goss (Nannie); Dennis Shaw (Hanger-on); Felix Felton (Gambler); Percy Cartwright (Coroner)

The Unholy Night

CREDITS: Director: Lionel Barrymore; Story: Ben Hecht; Screenplay: Edwin Justus Mayer; Adaptation: Dorothy Farnum; Recording Engineer: Paul Neal, Douglas Shearer; Art Director: Cedric Gibbons; Photography: Ira Morgan; Film Editor: Grant Whytock; Gowns: Adrian; MGM; September 14, 1929; 92 minutes

CAST: *(In Lord Montague's Home)* Ernest Torrence (Doctor Ballou); Roland Young (Lord Montague); Dorothy Sebastian (Efra Cavender); Lady Violet (Natalie Moorhead); Sydney Jarvis (Jordan, the Butler); Polly Moran (Polly, the Maid); George Cooper (Frye, the Orderly); Sojin (Li Hung, the Mystic); and Boris Karloff (Abdoul Mohammed Bey [unbilled]); *(In Scotland Yard)* Claude Fleming (Sir James Rumsey); Clarence Geldart (Inspector Lewis);*(In the Doomed Regiment)* John Miljan (Major Mallory); Richard Tucker (Colonel Davidson); John Loder (Captain Dorchester); Philip Strange (Lieutenant Williams); John Roche (Lieutenant Savor); Lionel Belmore (Major Endicott); Gerald Barry (Captain Bradley); Richard Travers (Major MacDougal)

The Vampire's Ghost
CREDITS: Executive Producer: Armand Schaefer; Director: Lesley Selander; Associate Producer: Rudolph E. Abel; Original Story: Leigh Brackett; Screenplay: John K. Butler and Leigh Brackett; Photography: Bud Thackery and Robert Pittack; Art Director: Russell Kimball; Set Decoration: Earl Wooden; Film Editor: Tony Martinelli; Sound: Dick Taylor; Musical Director: Richard Cherwin; Dance Director: Jerry Jarrette; Republic Pictures Corporation, Released 5/21/45; Running time: 59 minutes

CAST: John Abbott (Webb Fallon); Grant Withers (Father Gilchrist); Peggy Stewart (Julie Vance); Charles Gordon (Roy); Emmett Vogan (Vance); Roy Barcroft (Jim Barrat); Adele Mara (Lisa); Martin Wilkins (Simon Peter); Frank Jacquet (The Doctor); Jimmy Aubrey (a Tramp); Zack Williams (Taba); George Carleton (the Commissioner); Fred Howard (the Inspector); Floyd Shackelford (a Native); Pedro Rigas (the Waiter); Tom Steele, Charles Sullivan (Sailors); Jim Thorpe (a Gambler); Constantine Romanoff (a Bystander)

INDEX

Abbott, John 229, 232, 236-237
Adams, Nick 43, 45, 52
Adamson, Al 24-25
Addams, Dawn 199, 202
Adrian, Iris 83
Allen, Karen 161
Arkoff, Sam 173-174
Arlen, Richard 228
Arnold, Edward 176-177
Ashley, John 57, 60
Auric, Georges 98
Baer, Buddy 63
Bakaleinikoff, Mischa 38
Barcroft, Roy 230, 236-237
Barrett, Claudia 148-149, 152
Barrie, H.E. 60
Barrows, George 62, 149, 151-152
Barrymore, John 59, 203
Barrymore, Lionel 213, 223, 225
Bartel, Paul 137, 143, 145
Barzell, Wolfe 58-59, 62
Beck, John 42
Beery, Wallace 61
Belmore, Lionel 216
Benedict, Dirk 164
Bennett, Linda 35
Benson, Lucile 139
Bergman, Ingrid 206
Bernstein, Elmer 157
Bissell, Whit 58
Blaisdell, Paul 173-182, 184, 186-187
Blancy, Harry 11
Blau, Fred 166
Borland, Carroll 213
Brackett, Leigh 229-230, 234, 237-238
Brain that Wouldn't Die, The 11-27
Bredell, Elwood 80, 85, 177, 185
Brice, Robert 103, 106
Brown, David 164
Brown, Reb 165
Browning, Tod 148, 213, 231
Bruce, Lenny 158
Burton, John 80
Burton, Tim 137

Butler, John 229, 234, 237
Cahn, Edward L. 29, 31, 33-35, 38, 174, 176-179, 181, 185-186
Canova, Judy 227
Carlton, Rex 11, 18, 23-26
Carmel, Eddie 23
Carr, Trem 228
Carradine, John 24, 176, 230
Carreras, James 206
Carreras, Michael 205, 207-208
Carrillo, Leo 78, 80-81, 86
Cartwright, Percy 202
Cash, Rosalind 128
Castle, Peggy 103, 106, 109
Catlett, Walter 83
Cavanagh, Paul 193
Cavanaugh, Hobart 81
Chambers, John 164, 166, 169
Chandler, Eddy 78
Chaney, Jr., Lon 169, 234
Chaney, Lon 91, 96
Cline, Wilfrid 74
Coffin, Tristram 31, 33, 37
Colmes, Walter 229
Commons, David 155
Connery, Sean 127
Conway, Tom 177, 179, 183, 185
Cooper, George 220
Corman, Gene 137, 145
Corman, Roger 102, 137, 153, 173, 175, 181, 186, 203
Cottrell, William 191
Craig, Ed 17
Craig, Noble 164
Creature with the Atom Brain 29-39
Crosby, Wade 103
Cunha, Richard 61-63
Cushing, Peter 58, 204-206
Daniel, Leslie 12, 22
Dante, Joe 163
Davis, Karl 32, 37
de Laurentiis, Dino 159
Dellanoy, Jean 98
Denning, Richard 29, 35, 38

DeWolff, Francis 202
Dietrich Marlene 78
Diffring, Anton 204
Domergue, Faith 164
Dresner, Hal 164
Edwards, Henry 122
Eldredge, John 81
English, Marla 174, 176, 179-180, 183-184, 185-186
Erickson, Jack 38
Evers, Herb (Jason) 12, 21
Fanning, Art 17
Farley, Morgan 191
Fiala, George 23
Fisher, Shug 66, 74
Fisher, Terence 207-208, 210
Fleming, Claude 216
Foran, Dick 78-79, 83, 86-87
Ford, Harrison, 161
Forrest, Sally 191, 195
Frankenstein Conquers the World 41-55
Frankenstein's Daughter 57-63
Frederic, Marc 62
Frye, Dwight 59, 107, 228
Fuller, Lance 185-186
Furuhata, Koji 46, 53-54
Gausman, Russell A. 85
Gay, Gregory 30, 37
Geldart, Clarence 216
Giant Gila Monster, The 65-75
Gibbs, Ann 138
Gil, Rosemarie 161
Ging, Jack 165
Glasser, Albert 108
Gordon, Alex 173-174, 176-177, 179, 183, 185
Gordon, Charles 229, 236
Gottlieb, Alex 77
Gough, Michael 58
Goya, Mona 111-113, 116, 119, 122
Graham, Fred 66, 68, 73
Grainer, Ron 133
Granger, Michael 30, 37
Green, Alfred, F. 103, 106
Green, Joseph 11, 14, 16-21, 23-27
Guest, Val 207

Hajnal, Stephen 15
Hakim, Raymond 91
Hakim, Robert 91
Hammeras, Ralph 68
Harolde, Ralf 83
Harvey, Laurence 204
Hecht, Ben 213, 223
Herrmann, Bernard 158
Heston, Charlton 127-128, 130, 132-135
Hitchcock, Alfred 183, 203
Hoffman, Paul 38
Honda, Ishiro 52-53
Horror Island 77-89
House of Fright (see *Two Faces of Dr. Jekyll, The*)
Howard, Lewis 82
Hunchback of Notre Dame, The 91-99
Hunt, Cecil 67
Ifukube, Akira 48
Inescort, Frieda 185
Invasion U.S.A. 101-109, 155
Jackman, Fred 31
Jacobs, Red 173
Janssen, David 52
Jenks, Frank 187
Johnson, Jason 159
Johnson, Tor 59
Johnston, W. Ray 228
Juggernaut 111-123
Karloff, Boris 60-61, 111-112, 114-119, 121-123, 162, 166, 170, 189-190, 191-197, 203, 213-218, 223-225
Katcher, Aram 107
Kato, Haruya 47
Katzman, Sam 29, 35
Kellogg, Ray 68, 73
Kelly, Nancy 229
Kemmer, Ed 63
Kendrick, Florina 161
Kennedy, Tom 107
King, Kathleen 165
Knight, Fuzzy 78-79, 87
Knight, Sandra 57-58, 60-61
Knowles, Patric 86
Knox, Ken 69
Kossoff, David 199

Koster, Henry 81
Kowalski, Bernard 165, 186
Kruger, Otto 229
Kurosawa, Akira 53
Kuwa, George 224
Laemmle, Carl 224
Lamont, Adele 12
Lang, Fritz 183
Laughton, Charles 91, 98, 189-190, 192-195, 197
Launer, S. John 30, 36
Leakey, Phil 61
Lee, Christopher 127, 199-200, 202-208
Leith, Virginia 11-12, 15, 19-21, 25
Leni, Paul 224
Lewis, Herschell Gordon 18
Lewton, Val 148, 183, 193, 229
Livingston, Stanley 142-144
Locher, Felix 57, 59-60-61
Lollobrigida, Gina 91-92, 94-98
Lopez, Jennifer 161
Lorre, Peter 176, 182, 185
Lugosi, Bela 59, 203, 213, 231-232
Lynch, David 137
Main, Laurie 143
Mamoulian, Rouben 203
Mankowitz, Wolf 205-207, 209
Mann, Peter 46
Mara, Adele 233-234
Marcellino, Nick 164, 169
March, Fredric 203, 206
Margetson, Arthur 112, 116
Marla, Norma 199, 205
Marshall, Jack 74, 75
Martin, Strother 162, 167-168, 170
Massie, Paul 199-201, 203-204, 206, 209-211
Matheson, Richard 127, 129-130, 132
McCalla, Irish 63
McLaughlin, Gibb 114-115, 119
McLeod, Victor 77
Menzies, Heather 162-163, 167, 169
Miljan, John 217
Mitchum, Robert 74
Mizuno, Kumi 45, 52-53
Moffett, Gregory 149

Mohr, Gerald 103, 106, 109
Moorhead, Natalie 214, 216
Moran, Peggy 81-84
Morris, Chester 176-177, 179, 182, 186
Mulfory, Ed 103
Mulhall, Jack 177
Murphy, Donald 57-61
Mylong, John 150, 157
Nader, George 148, 150
Nakajima, Haruo 48
Nakao, Sumio 45
Napier, Alan 189, 192
Nicholson, Jack 57, 60, 183
Nicholson, Jim 173, 176, 178
O'Brien, Willis 42
O'Conner, Tim 165
O'Herlihy, Dan 103, 106
Omega Man, The 125-135
Ordung, Wyott 153
Otterson, Jack 85
Parker, Ed 80
Pate, Michael 191
Paulson, Pamela 149
Peck, J. Eddie 161
Petrillo, Sammy 13
Pevney, Joseph 189, 193
Pierce, Jack 61
Polanski, Roman 129
Price, Vincent 129
Private Parts 137-145
Quillan, Eddie 227
Quinn, Anthony 91, 93-99
Rabin, Jack 108, 155
Ralston, Vera Hruba 228
Randell, Ron 177, 179, 182-183, 185
Rathbone, Basil 73
Raymond, Alex 236
Reed, Oliver 199, 211
Risser, Wee 68
Roberts, J.H. 119
Robot Monster 62, 147-159
Robson, Mark 183
Roche, John 216
Romero, George 129
Royle, Selena 149, 157
Rusoff, Lou 174, 179, 185-186

Ruymen, Ayn 138, 144
Sackheim, Jerry 197
Salter, Hans J. 78
Sanders, George 183
Sangster, Jimmy 206
Saperstein, Henry G. 51
Schallert, William 107
Schoelen, Jill 171
Schoengarth, Bruce 158
Scorsese, Martin 158
Sebastian, Dorothy 214, 217, 223
Sekizawa, Shinichi 42
Selander, Lesley 237-238
Setten, Morton 114, 116
Shapiro, Ken 159
She-Creature, The 173-187
Shimura, Takashi 44, 53
Shull, Richard B. 165-166
Simms, Jay 65
Simone, Lisa 66, 73-74
Siodmak, Curt 29, 31, 35, 39, 228-229
Skinner, Frank 48
Smith, Robert 108
Sojin, Kamiyama 214, 223-225
Spencer, Franz 108
Spielberg, Steven 161
Sssssss 161-171
Stanhope, Paul 61-62
Stapley, Richard 191, 195-196
Steele, Tom 237
Steiger, Rod 166
Stein, Ronald 179, 182
Stell, Aaron 35
Steon, Janice 69
Stevens, Angela 29, 35-36
Stewart, Peggy 229, 236
Strange Door, The 189-197
Strange, Glenn 61
Striepeke, Dan 171
Strock, Herbert L. 63
Sullivan, Don 66, 68, 73-74
Takashima, Tado 45, 53
Thackery, Bud 229
Thomas, Harry 60-62
Thompson, Bob 66, 73
Todd, Sally 58-60, 62

Tombragel, Maurice 77
Torrence, Ernest 214, 216, 224
Tourneur, Jacques 183
Tracy, Spencer 206
Travers, Richard 220
Travis, Len 138
Trevelyan, John 207
Tropp, Martin 53
Tucker, Phil 147-148, 150, 158-159
Tucker, Richard 217
Turner, Lana 206
Two Faces of Dr. Jekyll, The 199-211
Unholy Night, The 213-225
Vampire's Ghost, The 227-239
Van Dolsen, Foy 83-84
Van Sickel, Dale 80
Van Sloan, Edward 228, 230
Ventantonio, John 140
Victor, Katherine 159
Vogan, Emmett 229, 236
Voight, Jon 161
von Stroheim, Erich 228
Wadsworth, Henry 213
Waggner, George 83-85
Walters, Luana 177
Watkin, Pierre 37
Wayne, John 78
Webb, Clifton 190
Webster, Joy 199
Welles, Orson 119
West, Frederick 181-182
White, Merrill 158
Wilder, W. Lee 147
Williams, Pat 167
Wilson, Harry 61-62
Winters, Roland 238
Withers, Grant 229, 236
Wood, Ed 61, 63, 151
Wyndham, Joan 111-112, 114, 116, 120
Yates, Herbert 227-228
Young, Roland 214-215, 223, 225
Zanuck, Richard D. 164
Zerbe, Anthony 132
Zigmond, Jerry 173
Zimbalist, Al 158
Zugsmith, Alfred 108

AUTHORS

Bruce Dettman is a San Francisco-based writer whose film related articles have appeared in *Filmfax, The Monster Times, Fangoria,* and *Good Old Days*. He also co-authored the book *The Horror Factory* and lectures on horror cinema. He is a contributor to *Midnight Marquee Actors Series: Lon Chaney, Jr.*

Jim Doherty is a recording engineer and a film music fanatic, with an obsessive interest in composer Bernard Herrmann. His vast collection of obscure Herrmann music was tapped by the producers of the Academy Award-nominated documentary, *Music for the Movies: Bernard Herrmann*. Jim has written for *Midnight Marquee* and *Soundtrack*. He was once named "Author of the Year" by the American Literary Guild. But then he woke up. Jim lives in Chicago with too little space for his various collections, and too little time to implement most of his esoteric schemes. He is petted and humored by his unbelievable sympathetic wife Janet, who shares his belief in the mystical healing powers of bad movies after a stressful day at work.

Dennis Fischer is the author of the book *Horror Film Directors* (McFarland, 1991) and is currently working on a follow-up on Science Fiction Directors. He and his wife, along with their two children, live in California. His oldest son Jared, like his father, does not feel guilty watching any film, no matter how wretched it might be.

Jeff Hillegass has had work published in *Cinemacabre, Little Shoppe of Horrors,* and *Gruesome Twosome*. Despite an aversion to professional sports, he works as an editor for NFL Films, but justifies it with the fact that the company's early films served as an inspiration for director Sam Peckinpah's slow-motion bloodbaths in *The Wild Bunch*. Jeff lives in New Jersey with his wife Kathryn, his cat Aston, and his dog Griffin. The dog would have been named Martin, after James Bond's Aston Martin DB5 in *Goldfinger*, but Kathryn nixed the idea.

David J. Hogan is the author of *Who's Who of the Horrors and Other Fantasy Films, Dark Romance: Sexuality in the Horror Film,* and *Your Movie Guide to Drama Video Tapes and Discs*. He contributes to *Cinefantastique, Moviegoer, Filmfax,* and *Outre*. Hogan lives with his wife Kim and three children in a rambling house filled with books, music, and movies.

John "J.J." Johnson has authored *Cheap Tricks and Class Acts: Special Effects, Makeup and Stunts from the Fantastic Fifties* and co-authored *Fantastic Cinema Subject Guide*. He is also a feature writer for *Collecting Hollywood* and contributing writer for *Movie Collector's World, Filmfax, Classic Images,* and Jon Warren's *Movie Poster Price Guide*. He is currently writing an epic Western novel. John lives in Keizer, Oregon.

Tom Johnson, well known Hammer fan, has co-authored *Peter Cushing, the Gentle Man of Horror* and *Hammer Film: An Exhaustive Filmography* both from McFarland. He has also contributed to many film magazines including *Midnight Marquee, Filmfax,* and *Monsters from the Vault*.

Steve Kronenberg practices law in Florida and is also a major horror film memorabilia collector with an impressive poster collection displayed prominently in his law office.

Randy Palmer became a monster movie fan at age five with a theatrical viewing of *The Fly*; began writing professionally in 1971 for *Famous Monsters*, eventually became an editor at Warren Publishing; also a writer for *Fangoria, Gorezone, Cinefantastique, Imagi-Movies*, Britain's Hammer-oriented *Halls of Horror*, and other publications of the cinemagination. He also writes video game reviews and articles for *PC Entertainment, Sega Guide* (incorporated into *Game Players* mag), and is a writer-editor for one of the earliest video game publications, *Videogaming Illustrated* (later changed to *Video & Computer Gaming Illustrated*). His book on make-up artist Paul Blaisdell is now available from McFarland. Randy passed away after the first printing of this book.

John E. Parnum, inspired by his chapter on *Ssssss* is back at work on his history of snakes in horror, fantasy, and science fiction films for McFarland. Coinciding with *The Slithering Cinema*, he is writing a book on double features (*Gruesome Twosomes*) for Midnight Marquee Press, as well as contributing to their forthcoming books on Alfred Hitchcock and Vincent Price.

John would like to acknowledge his wife Edie for some last minute refinements, and once again thank his daughter Laura for taking the time to edit this chapter, providing helpful suggestions, and knowing when to temper some of his naughty prose. John passed away last year and is missed greatly.

Bryan Senn, a psychometrist at a Seattle-area hospital, is the author of *Golden Horrors: A Critical Filmography of 46 Works of Terror Cinema, 1931-1939* (McFarland, 1996) and co-author of *Fantastic Cinema Subject Guide* (McFarland, 1992). He lives in Kent, Washington with his wife Gina and son Dominic. He has just completed *Drums of Terror: Voodoo in the Cinema* for Midnight Marquee Press which will be available July of 1998.

David H. Smith works for a great metropolitan newspaper in South Florida, and just recently celebrated a crystal wedding anniversary with his indulgent wife Lynn; their young son Colin enables him to justify watching English-dubbed movies starring men in rubber suits again and again. David plans to become a fixture on the Midnight Marquee Press author roster, has contributed to several genre magazines and fanzines, hopes to someday complete his Skywald magazine collection, and thinks the mellotron is the most awesome musical instrument ever developed.

David wishes to thank Damon Foster, Stuart Galbraith IV, Ed Godziszewski, and Ronnie Burton (and *G-Fan* magazine) for extensive research assistance, and Kip Doto for the chance to see 'em as they should be seen (Viva Naschy!). Also, an especial hope for health and happiness to actress Michelle Bauer in appreciation of her "Gargantuan" endorsement (which sadly met the editor's ax) and for her personal encouragement.

Don G. Smith is an associate professor in history and philosophy of education at Eastern Illinois University. He is the author of *Lon Chaney, Jr.* from McFarland and is working on a book on the films of Edgar Allan Poe.

John Soister, a sixties fanzine editor (one-shot *House of Horrors*), co-editor (*Photon,* briefly), and all-around LoC curmudgeon, has contributed to the *Midnight Marquee Actors Series.* He teaches high school modern and classical languages and is currently working on a book on Universal Pictures for McFarland. John lives in Orwigsburg, PA with his wife Nancy and children: Jake, Katelyn, and Jeremy.

Gary J. Svehla created his first publishing venture at the ripe old age of 13, *Gore Creatures.* Thirty-five years later he is still publishing the magazine, now called *Midnight Marquee,* as well as overseeing Midnight Marquee Press, a full time job for the two person team of Gary and Susan. Gary still teaches high school English. He has contributed to *Monsterland, Amazing Cinema, Movie Club, Monsters from the Vault, Bits & Pieces,* and *Monster Times* as well as many of the titles published by Midnight Marquee Press.

Nathalie Yafet is an actress and singer who lives in New Jersey with her incredibly patient pianist, programmer husband, Steven. She has also been know to harass and be harassed by the inimitable Tom Weaver for her strong views of the career of Boris Karloff.

Nathalie would like to thank her parents for not disposing of her monster magazines, Steven for his continual support, Uncle Forry for his early inspiration, Greg Mank for urging me to write again, and to Gary and Susan for giving me this opportunity.

*If you enjoyed this book
visit our website
at www.midmar.com
or call for a free catalog
410-665-1198
Midnight Marquee Press, Inc.
9721 Britinay Lane
Baltimore, MD 21234*

Printed in Great Britain
by Amazon